advanced praise

As a woman in long-term recovery that manages a Syringe Services Program, it's refreshing to see a novel that shines light on the work we do. *Bridgetown* honors harm reduction and is beyond entertaining—it's educational and unapologetically empowering.

> Jen Cutting, C.A.R.C., C.R.P.A. — YouTuber,
> Founder, Supplies For Life

Jordan Barnes has written a compelling novel that entertains while teaching the valuable lessons about harm reduction and the opioid epidemic. Well worth the read.

> Peter Canning, Author, Killing Season: A
> Paramedic's Dispatches from the Front
> Lines of the Opioid Epidemic

Jordan Barnes' first work of fiction is equally as magnificent as his memoir. Harm reduction and syringe exchanges are life-saving interventions, but rarely found in literature. *Bridgetown* illuminates tragedy, hope, and the human condition through a groundbreaking lens: the lens of a syringe exchange during an overdose crisis. With vivid characters and a painfully realistic plot, this book brings the message of harm reduction into the hearts and souls of its readers.

> Morgan Godvin, Editor at JSTOR Daily,
> Activist, Writer, and State Drug Policy
> Commissioner

As a person who spent years in active addiction, I was blown away by the struggle, hope, and knowledge woven into Barnes's riveting novel. Barnes's ability to capture the emotional turmoil of those in active addiction is unparalleled. A must-read for anyone affected by addiction in any capacity.

Kyle Ruggeri, C.A.R.C. — Founder/CEO,
Soberdogs Recovery

Jordan Barnes presents a realistic and devastating portrayal of the world of harm reduction and syringe exchanges in a way that allows readers to empathize and understand what it is like to support people when they really need it the most. He adds a human element to substance use that is often criminalized or stigmatized in most communities even today, which reminds us of the trauma that occurs to so many. It can lead us down paths we never intended or imagined, and to the true power of hope and empowerment when the "Harley Hammonds" of the world find a way to give a voice to those who have yet to find their own. All those who provide services and support to vulnerable populations should remember this important message about treating people as human beings and avoiding retraumatization. Thank you Jordan Barnes for reminding us and others about the importance of that work.

Dr. Shelly L. Bartow, Executive Director,
Delaware Opportunities Inc. & Longtime
Supporter or Harm Reduction

BRIDGE TOWN

BRIDGE

A HARM REDUCTION NOVEL

TOWN

JORDAN P. BARNES

Copyright © 2021 Jordan P. Barnes
"Nightlandia" Cover Photo © 2020 Alex Wittwer
ISBN-13: 978-1-7347166-6-5 (Paperback)
ISBN-13: 978-1-7347166-5-8 (Hardcover)
ISBN-13: 978-1-7347166-7-2 (eBook)
Library of Congress Control Number: 2021948180

Island Time Press, LLC.
Kailua, HI 96734

This is a work of fiction. Unless otherwise indicated, all names, characters,
businesses, organizations, working relationships, places, events and incidents in this
book are either the product of the author's imagination or used in a fictitious
manner. Any resemblance to actual persons living or dead, events or locales is purely
coincidental.

Cover Design and Book Layout by Jordan P. Barnes www.JordanPBarnes.com
Cover Photo "Nightlandia" by Alex Wittwer www.AWittwer.22slides.com
Edited by Jessey Mills www.JesseyMills.com
Audiobook Narrated by Savannah Gilmore

dedication

For Haven Wheelock, MPH.
Your work matters, more than you'll ever know.

by the same author

ONE HIT AWAY: A MEMOIR OF RECOVERY

AVAILABLE ANYWHERE BOOKS ARE SOLD

- WINNER, 2020'S "BEST BOOK OF THE YEAR" AWARD, INDIES TODAY
- WINNER, BOOK READERS APPRECIATION GROUP MEDALLION
- WINNER, NONFICTION COVER DESIGN AWARD, THE BOOK DESIGNER
- FINALIST, 15TH ANNUAL N.I.E.A. (NATIONAL INDIE EXCELLENCE AWARDS) BOOK AWARDS — ADDICTION & RECOVERY CATEGORY
- FINALIST, 2021 INDEPENDENT AUTHOR NETWORK BOOK OF THE YEAR AWARDS — SPIRITUAL/INSPIRATIONAL CATEGORY

RIP CITY: A PORTLAND SOB STORY

AVAILABLE EXCLUSIVELY IN THE AMAZON VELLA STORE

RULES TO DIE BY: A HEROIN ADDICT'S TAKE ON LIFE IN LONG-TERM RECOVERY

AVAILABLE FOR **FREE** AT

JORDANPBARNES.COM/RULESTODIEBY

"There comes a point where we need to stop just pulling people out of the river. We need to go upstream and find out why they're falling in."

Desmond Tutu (Oct. 7, 1931-Dec. 6, 2021)

contents

principles of harm reduction

www.HarmReduction.org

Harm reduction is a set of practical strategies and ideas aimed at reducing negative consequences associated with drug use. Harm reduction is also a movement for social justice built on a belief in, and respect for, the rights of people who use drugs. Harm reduction incorporates a spectrum of strategies that includes safer use, managed use, abstinence, meeting people who use drugs "where they're at," and addressing conditions of use along with the use itself. Because harm reduction demands that interventions and policies designed to serve people who use drugs reflect specific individual and community needs, there is no universal definition of or formula for implementing harm reduction.

However, National Harm Reduction Coalition considers the following principles central to harm reduction practice:

1. Accepts, for better or worse, that licit and illicit drug use is part of our world and chooses to work to minimize its harmful effects rather than simply ignore or condemn them.
2. Understands drug use as a complex, multi-faceted phenomenon that encompasses a continuum of behaviors from severe use to total abstinence, and

acknowledges that some ways of using drugs are clearly safer than others.

3. Establishes quality of individual and community life and well-being—not necessarily cessation of all drug use—as the criteria for successful interventions and policies.

4. Calls for the non-judgmental, non-coercive provision of services and resources to people who use drugs and the communities in which they live in order to assist them in reducing attendant harm.

5. Ensures that people who use drugs and those with a history of drug use routinely have a real voice in the creation of programs and policies designed to serve them.

6. Affirms people who use drugs (PWUD) themselves as the primary agents of reducing the harms of their drug use and seeks to empower PWUD to share information and support each other in strategies which meet their actual conditions of use.

7. Recognizes that the realities of poverty, class, racism, social isolation, past trauma, sex-based discrimination, and other social inequalities affect both people's vulnerability to and capacity for effectively dealing with drug-related harm.

8. Does not attempt to minimize or ignore the real and tragic harm and danger that can be associated with illicit drug use.

Learn more at www.HarmReduction.org

author's note

This book is an informational resource intended to educate the public on the critical role that harm reduction advocates play in our community, specifically relating to public health and substance use disorder. It is not intended as a substitute for the medical advice of physicians. The reader should consult a physician in matters relating to their health and particularly with respect to any symptoms that may require diagnosis or medical attention, such as opioid use disorder or substance use disorder.

It's important to note that as a former injection drug user, elements in this story were drawn from my personal remembrance of how harm reduction services supported me. I consider myself fortunate to have friends who currently work in the field who have assisted, corrected, directed and taught me much about the inner workings of the movement. They have walked me through much of the data, descriptors, language, logic, reasoning and science behind many of the practices and protocols referenced in this book, and for that I am incredibly grateful. I am certain this book would not exist without them, but please remember that as the author, any and all errors are my own.

Harm reduction principles, concepts, ideas and services described in this book are very much alive and real, and this does not encompass all of the efforts and implementations out there. New means, methods and strategies are constantly being rolled out by forward-thinking minds. Laws are being challenged or defended, and policies are being drafted and passed. Brilliant minds are assessing today's climate and lobbying for a safer future for people who use drugs.

An important distinction to make is that while many people use drugs, drug use alone is not an indicator of substance use disorder. However, people with *and* without SUD can all benefit from harm reduction efforts. With that said, if you or someone you know is struggling with substance use disorder and you don't know where to turn, take solace in the fact that there are countless humans out there who are or who have dedicated their efforts and existence toward improving the health and wellbeing of people who use drugs.

Lastly, because this book contains scenes detailing drug use, overdoses and death, please proceed with caution if you're in a fragile state of mind or new to recovery. If you need help, either with quitting drugs or learning how to use them safer, know that resources are available to you and that you are never alone.

www.AA.org
www.Al-Anon.org
www.HarmReduction.org
www.NA.org
www.NaloxoneForAll.org
www.Nar-Anon.org
National Suicide Prevention Lifeline:
1-800-273-8255
www.NeverUseAlone.com

"Nightlandia"
Alex Wittwer

BRIDGE TOWN

one
pocket check

"You know the drill, motherfucker—*spit it out!*" The man checked his footing on the wet sidewalk and staggered toward the dope dealer he was robbing. As he closed the gap, a familiar face came charging down the sidewalk, waving her hands in the air as if she had the power to stop him.

The woman approached from behind the dealer and stopped halfway between the two men. Standing off to the side, she glanced at the dealer before shifting her amber eyes back to the man. She raised her palms in part to calm him down, but also to buy herself time as she fought to remember his name. Although he was a client of hers, it had been months since they'd last crossed paths and she drew a blank while staring into the cavity of his stained, hooded sweatshirt.

Opting for a new approach, Harley released her breath and dropped her hands to her thighs. "Please. Let's lower the syringe so we can talk about this."

"Talk?" The client wiped a slick of spit off his lips then rubbed it on his chest. "What's there to talk about? This has nothing to do with you."

Harley squared her shoulders and pointed up the sidewalk. "Now that's where you're wrong. This has everything to do with me. Bridgeworks is right around the corner, *remember*?"

"You think I don't know that?" the client asked, tugging on

1

the cuff of his sweater to reveal a blood-filled syringe. The top of his track-marked hand bore a crude and unfinished rose tattoo, likely a stick-n-poke from prison paid for with bartered commissary items. "I may not deserve it," he said, his eyes running down the length of his sleeve, "but even I catch a lucky break now and then." He licked his lips and held the needle inches away from the dealer's neck. "This is your last shot, motherfucker. Either spit out the dope or I'll pump this blood in your jugular and we can both die from AIDS."

The dealer raised his chin in defiance. "You won't get away with this."

Harley noticed a tremble in the client's hand but believed it was more from withdrawal than fear. It was nearly nine a.m. and she knew that if he was still chasing his morning fix, he was liable to be beyond desperate.

The client hiked his pants up with one hand and glanced at Harley. "You need to get out of here before this gets ugly. You don't want to witness what I'm prepared to do."

Harley scoffed at the notion and closed her eyes. Her entire adult life had revolved around standing tall in the whirlwind of harm reduction, yet despite a lifelong commitment to non-violence, she wanted to tackle him and hated how her small size betrayed her. To witness any blood-borne disease becoming weaponized—especially so close to her needle exchange—was unforgivable in more ways than one.

She opened her eyes and made herself watch. She started with the dealer, who maintained a calmness despite being towered over. To block the sun's glare, she raised her hand to her brow but still couldn't place his face, which wasn't unusual considering the recent wave of crackdowns by the Portland Police Bureau. It was common knowledge that after any surge in arrests, a backwash of new street dealers would pour into the city to wage war over valuable clientele and territory.

Her focus was broken as the dealer's jet-black eyes glanced up the sidewalk and landed on two men in expensive suits walking their way. Instinctively, Harley took a small step forward, giving them enough breathing room to pass by. She resisted the urge to attract their attention, knowing full well the men would likely not know how to help even if they wanted to. Jabbing a wisp of lilac hair behind her ear, she watched the suits pass from the corner of her eye and let them fall out of focus.

She slowed her breathing as a bus roared by, and a wall of icy air tore through her like a cleansing breath. As the three of them stood there, she thought about the past few weeks around Bridge-works and how they had been efficiently uneventful. Perhaps deep down, a part of her missed the occasional chaos because it offered an opportunity to bring order to the table, but there were limits to her presence being validated. In her line of work, there could never be exceptions for violence.

Harley smothered a surge of panic and turned to face the dealer. "I don't know who you are or where you came from, but no one deals anything within three blocks of my exchange. Ever." Before he could respond she turned to the client wielding the syringe and stared down its barrel. "You already know where I stand. End it now."

"If you say so." He placed his thumb on the plunger as if cocking the hammer on a revolver. "You heard the lady. Three . . . Two . . ."

Without a word, the dealer clasped his mouth and spat a wad of slimy balloons into his palm.

The client snatched the drugs and popped them into his mouth without wiping off the saliva. "Now turn out your pockets."

"You're even stupider than you look, *puta*. How would I have any money if I haven't sold any shit today?"

The client raised the needle to the dealer's eye. "You think I'm—"

With a loud whack, Harley's palm chopped down his arm and she thrust herself in front of the dealer, facing the client.

"You got what you came for, right? Or is it never enough?!"

Without looking behind her, she reached for the dealer's chest and pushed him away. "Go! Get out of here!"

She stretched her cashmere cardigan around her torso and heard shuffling behind her as the dealer strutted up the sidewalk.

The client looked over her shoulder and leaned into her. "You act like I was going to—"

"Just stop," Harley spat, her stare burrowing deeper into his hardened eyes. "You couldn't just follow him for a block or two? You had to pull this shit off right here?"

His cold eyes searched hers. "And risk letting someone else get to him first? Why would I—"

"Because it's not all about you!" She ran her nimble fingers through her hair, looked around to see if they were being watched and thought of several ways this incident could blow up in her face. "Listen to me—some things are bigger than us, and there's a reason we ask people not to deal within three blocks of Bridge-works." Harley spun in place to make sure the dealer wasn't circling back. "And since when does someone violating our request make it okay for you to rob them?"

He fumbled through his pocket, pulled out a small orange cap, disarmed the needle and made the syringe disappear. "You make it seem like such a big deal when no one even saw what happened. Besides, we both know it was all a bluff. The blood is coagulated and as far as I know, I don't have HIV. Now if you don't mind, I'll be on my way."

She grabbed the cuff of his sweater. "I don't think you know how lucky you are. Imagine if you caught him on a bad day and he fought back. What if you got hurt? What if I had another stabbing on my block? Imagine what would happen if cops locked down the street again and no one could get to our exchange."

With a fix in sight, the client appeared notably less sick. "You know what? You're right," he said. "I fucked up. I promise it won't happen again."

"Good, now get the hell out of here before your dealer friend circles back."

The client nodded and turned to walk away.

"Oh, and one more thing," Harley called out as he sauntered away. "It wouldn't hurt to stop by sometime soon to get tested. It only takes a few minutes and there's no reason for you not to know what you're working with."

As Harley walked down the sidewalk, she became lost in a number of emotions. Those who zoomed by in cars saw her as a woman in need of both self-care and a long vacation, or any vacation, really. What they couldn't see in passing was that it was not a foreign look on her, and while attractive, her face was often hardened with concern. But while the pressure was constant, the weight was rarely seen in her bright eyes, eyes that others trusted and looked to as a safety net.

Once she reached the end of the block, Harley rounded the corner and released her pent-up pressure with a forceful laugh.

"Something funny?" a distant voice yelled out.

Harley looked up, squinted and sensed a tinge of relief as her feet kicked into gear. Halfway down the block was Gabby, standing tall by the bike rack in front of the Bridgeworks syringe access program. She turned her attention back to her bike and fought to wiggle a U-Lock around the frame.

"It's a strange sight seeing you here so early," Harley called out. She passed a row of windows tinted with frosted privacy film and stopped just shy of the entrance.

"Hopefully not as strange as what's waiting for us." With her keys, Gabby pointed at a partially filled trash bag leaning against the door.

Harley approached the bag and gave it a nudge with her shoe. Somewhat satisfied, she undid the knot and held her breath while she peered into the opening. Her caution was warranted since people who less than cared for their existence had targeted the exchange countless times over the years. The crimes commonly took place under the cover of darkness where cowardice flourished, often making Harley the first to discover and attend to everything from graffiti to broken glass to smeared feces or worse. With relief, she closed the bag and heaved it over her shoulder. "We're good. It's just another monthly care package from Sadie's brother. I'll stash it in my office until she drops in next."

"You sure? I thought we didn't accept donations for individuals. You don't think it sets a bad precedent?"

"No, not at all," Harley said, adjusting the bag over her shoulder. "The logic behind not accepting deliveries for a specific client is that we can't violate someone's privacy by confirming or exposing their relationship to us. But in this instance, it just so happens that a kind soul donated some food and clothes, and I know the perfect person who could put these items to good use. Think of it like a random sponsorship."

Harley winked at Gabby and stuck her key in the door. The deadbolt clicked and though distracted, the sound triggered a learned behavior to pause at the entrance and leave all of her personal problems outside. Moments later, Harley placed the bag next to her feet and squatted to collect some letters scattered on the floor. As she stood up, her thin fingers rifled through them and arranged the stack based on priority.

"You really don't know why I'm early?" Gabby asked, locking the door behind her. "Let me guess, you forgot already."

As Gabby stepped over the trash bag and into the lobby, a faint smell of one too many beers hung in her wake. Harley thought of saying something but instead ran through a mental list of any special occasions she may have forgotten. It didn't take long for her to give up. "I don't know what I'm forgetting, but whatever it is, I'd say you're dressed for the occasion."

"You think?" Gabby twirled, showing off her apricot jumpsuit and creating a mess of curly black hair. She immediately reached for a wall and waited for her vision to stop spinning. "They say you only get one first impression, right?" She parted her hair and wiped the sleep from her bleary eyes.

"I don't know how you do it," Harley admitted. She pulled at her own clothes, which were professional in nature, but appeared rushed and thrown together as though she had a bad habit of waking up late.

"It's just second nature, but I like your style too. It shows an outward confidence that says you don't care what others think, tampered with a kind of vulnerability that works to keep you approachable. It's a good look." As Gabby spoke, she rubbed her forehead in an effort to ease her migraine.

"Let me guess. Another long one?" While Harley masked her concern well, she was grateful not to have walked in Gabby's shoes for some time.

"I think so . . . from what I can remember." Gabby dug through her purse and fished out a roll of chapstick. "You know what? Why don't you come out with me sometime? We used to have such a blast."

Harley bit her tongue. They both knew she would be lying if she said no.

"And everyone needs a means to vent, right? I know a few dives where we can get drinks for free, and then I can finally connect you with this cute bartender who's right up your alley."

"I appreciate the offer, but I'm in no rush to date again. At least not with the amount of hours I'm putting in here. It wouldn't be fair to him." Harley smiled then scratched the back of her head. "But on the bright side, who would have guessed learning how to love myself again and playing Monopoly alone could be so rewarding?"

Gabby capped her chapstick and tossed it into her purse. "You can still have a good time with someone without dating them."

While Harley smirked, she attempted to recall the last time she had found herself verifiably drunk. This was owed to how long it had been since her last bender and not because she had blacked out and suffered short-term memory loss.

"I will say this though, I think I'm starting to understand why you quit going out years ago. I could really use the extra hour of sleep right now," Gabby said. "One would think I'd learn that it never ends well when I open a bar tab."

"Ah, I remember my late twenties," Harley mused.

Gabby laughed. "I would hope so. You're only thirty-two."

"Thanks for reminding me," Harley said jokingly. She tapped her lips and tried to picture who else was on the schedule. Years ago, she had sought approval from her boss to allow employees to negotiate their work schedules with each other. April had agreed, as long as Harley assured her she'd enforce the buddy system in the exchange room. "Okay, now it's killing me. What the hell are we celebrating?"

Gabby crossed her arms and leaned against the wall. "Oh, you really did forget. I can ruin the surprise, or you can find out in about five minutes."

"I can wait. Who knows, maybe it'll cheer me up."

"Something got you down?"

"Yeah, but if you don't mind, let me get some coffee in me before I bring you up to speed," Harley said, starting for her office. "Oh, and I know I've said this before, but as much as I love seeing your pretty smile, you do know you can take a day off from time to time, don't you?"

Harley lugged the bag into her office and flipped on her coffee maker. Within seconds, the potent aroma of *Hair Bender*—her favorite blend from Stumptown Coffee Roasters—invaded the furthest corners of the room. She understood that while life was full of compromises, it was also far too short for bad coffee.

While waiting for the carafe to fill, Harley thought about how she admired Gabby as a colleague. She'd promoted Gabby from intern to paid staff member a few years ago and had never looked back, even on days where she showed up after a long night. Gabby was reliable and approachable, which were strong qualities demanded of someone in her position and traits that Harley sought to reinforce. But as much as Harley loved Gabby for who she was, there was always room to grow, and Gabby's tendencies to be a stickler and take things personally often blew up in her face. Harley knew better than anyone else that the job was draining enough as it was, and while she agreed everyone needed the means to vent, there were far healthier ways to deal with the stresses of work than painting the town red night after night.

The coffee maker beeped and Harley reached for her cup, a gift from a former intern that was rinsed but never washed. As she filled it to the brim, she admired the sublimated image on the side that read "Keep Portland Weird," a motto the city had embraced long enough for it to become a self-fulfilling prophecy. She studied her oily reflection on the surface, then hunched over and slurped enough to where she felt comfortable transporting her drink.

When she spun around to take her first steps toward her desk, she remembered a secret her childhood friend had taught her— when walking with a hot beverage, the trick to prevent burning her hand was to keep her eyes fixated on her destination. In college, she had learned the subconscious tended to over-compensate. In real life, she discovered the only way around it was to beat it at its own game.

A sharp knock interrupted her focus and a splash of coffee dribbled down her hand.

"I'll get it," Gabby called out.

Harley cursed under her breath and shook the coffee off of her fingers as Gabby passed by her open door. Excited chatter emanated from the lobby which motivated Harley to investigate. Leaving her mug behind, she followed Gabby's footsteps and entered the lobby.

Gabby locked the door behind a young man and slowly spun around. "You two remember each other, right?" She winked at Harley.

"Don't be silly, Gabs. Of course we do. Good morning, Mateo. I bet you're excited to start your first day," Harley said, hoping it wasn't obvious she had completely spaced about their new intern.

"Oh, absolutely. I've been excited all week." He fixed the collar on his purple polo and adjusted his hair which was neatly tied back in a low bun. His keen eyes reflected a certain intelligence and awareness of his surroundings.

"Perfect. We love having foreign exchange students here, and I'm willing to bet we can learn just as much from you as you can from us." Harley glanced at the clock. "It looks like we have some time before we start. Why don't we all have a quick huddle in my office before it's go-time?"

As the trio moved into Harley's office, she pulled back a chair at her desk and offered it to Mateo. "Please, have a seat and help yourself to coffee if you'd like."

Mateo declined and sat down while Gabby leaned against the frosted windows and waited for Harley to circle her desk.

"I know you mentioned you're excited to start," Harley said. "You're not nervous, are you?"

Mateo placed his hands on his lap and shook his head. "No, not really. Why? Do I look it?"

"Not especially. I only ask because it's not uncommon for interns to be nervous on their first day."

"Really? Why's that?"

"I think for a variety of reasons and all of them are valid. Some interns pressure themselves to strive for perfection while others fear needlestick injuries and contracting diseases. That's probably one of the more common fears, but in my mind it's a healthy fear because it helps us all to respect the slew of procedures designed to mitigate those risks. We've also seen a number of interns who have this idea in their heads that working with our clients is inherently dangerous, which—from my experience—couldn't be further from the truth."

"I second that," Gabby said, "and would add that most of those fears come from society telling us not to trust people who use drugs because they're all dangerous."

Mateo twisted in his chair to face her. "But that's not true."

"Not if you ask me, but it's still a misconception we fight day after day." Gabby paused and wrung her hands. "Trust me. It won't take long before you see how beautiful this exchange can really be."

Harley nodded, hoping Mateo would stick it out long enough to see that for himself. "But you should also know that as important as our syringe access program is, we also aim to offer any leg up that could benefit someone struggling with substance use disorder. These services include our Narcan distribution program, testing for diseases and drug checking, along with providing outside referrals to detox and rehab programs."

"You know, I remember reading about the testing," Mateo said, leaning forward, "but not the other programs. Am I right to assume my job is to help with the syringe exchange so you can focus on the more important services, like making referrals?"

"I wouldn't put it like that," Harley said. "It's all important work and many of our clients aren't interested in the other services, so let's not underestimate how important the supply side of our operation is. For example, what would you say if I told you that last year we handed out well over a million needles."

"I would say that sounds like a lot to give out and take in."

Harley smiled. "It is, and we typically reclaim around ninety-five percent of what we distribute. I know that leaves about fifty-thousand syringes unaccounted for, but it works out when you realize how many go to people passing through town or get confiscated as evidence during arrests."

"There's also the issue of used needles being considered as paraphernalia and as an arrestable offense," Gabby added. "Obviously this disincentivizes some people from bringing them back to us so our biohazard disposal service can incinerate them."

Mateo started doing the math on his fingers. "I'm listening, just trying to work out the numbers."

"It's almost three thousand a day. Give or take," Harley said. "Which may sound like a lot but trust me, it's not enough. We know this because part of our contract with the county requires us to poll our clients and submit reports to the health department. I can tell you with absolute certainty that despite our efforts, too many people frequently reuse and share their gear."

Mateo went silent for a moment.

"I know it's a lot to take in, but the point is that we're a work in progress." Harley inhaled a deep breath and withdrew a file from her desk. "Let me just check and make sure we have everything we need before you start orientation," she said, flipping through the papers. "Okay, I have your waivers and attendance sheet from your HIPAA training and blood-borne pathogens classes." She closed the file and peered over her desk. "And you're wearing closed-toed shoes. Looks like you're ready to rock."

"I'm looking forward to my first day," Mateo said, rubbing his palms together. "Do you remember yours?"

Harley recalled a faint memory and grinned. "I do. Like it was yesterday."

"Sounds like a life-changing experience?"

"I would probably describe it as life-saving more than anything else."

"Really?" Mateo asked, grabbing his armrests. "Can I ask why?"

Harley glanced at Gabby.

"What?" Mateo asked. "Did I say something wrong?"

"No, not at all. I just get this question a lot and from where I sit, I want the focus to be on the people we serve rather than on my journey."

Mateo's face softened. "I'm sorry. I didn't mean to make you uncomfortable."

"Oh, no, it's not that. I mean, you didn't, but even if you had I've learned it's okay to be uncomfortable, especially with things that define who we are." Harley slumped back into her chair. "I found this field in a roundabout way after my older brother passed away from an overdose right before his twenty-first birthday."

Mateo interlocked his fingers and looked down for a moment. "I'm so sorry to hear that."

"Thank you. As you can imagine, it turned my world upside down. But the one thing I will say is that I believe his passing ultimately saved me, in more ways than one." For a moment Harley considered going deeper but a quick glance at the time changed her mind. "More on that later. Right now you have a lot to get through today, but if you remind me to revisit this later, I'll give it the attention it deserves."

"Of course."

"Perfect. So let's go ahead and have you start off by shadowing Gabby, unless you have any questions?"

Mateo rubbed his chin before shaking his head. "Not off the top of my head since the training packet was pretty thorough. It was like a masterclass on client confidentiality, active listening, protecting my mental health and setting boundaries."

"That's what we like to hear, especially when all of those are essential to keeping this space, yourself and one another safe." Harley took a sip of coffee and wiped her lips. "Assuming we haven't scared you away, are you ready to get to work?"

two

great pit of carkoon

"Long time no see." Harley propped the door open with her heel and greeted a string of clients as they filtered inside. A mass of bodies clamored around the small space, followed by the presence of a sharp and pungent odor. The smell was not strange to Bridgeworks and occasionally prompted a debate among clients over whether the aromas were more abrasive in the sticky summer or wet winter months. But it mattered little if the source could be pinpointed—no one was ever asked to wait their turn outside.

Hugging the wall, the single-filed line in the lobby snaked out the door and extended a number of car lengths down the sidewalk. In many ways, the familiar faces were a sign of the times, tracking in either a sense of relief that calmed Harley's nerves or a spark of anxiety anytime a client stopped coming around.

Harley weaved through the lobby and managed to make it back to her office in record time. With Bridgeworks only being open to the public from ten to two, she often arrived early and stayed late to knock out her duties, which allowed her to remain as available as possible when clients needed her most. During the day, her office door was propped open unless she was counseling a client or in case someone needed a friend. It was a practice passed down to her that sought to see people never as distractions but as opportunities to make an impact.

One of the first things she did after being promoted to supervisor was to reposition her desk to face outward. The arrangement took some getting used to, but after a client had remarked that it was "pretty fucking Feng Shui," she quit second-guessing herself and let the energy flow. Though it defied ergonomics, she slid her computer monitor to the far side of her desk instead of keeping it front and center. It was more important to maintain a direct line of sight with her people than to endure the slightest tinge of neck strain each day. This small act, Harley believed, was one of the reasons people felt comfortable confiding in her, which helped her help them. Connecting with others and being present was a skill that sometimes required sacrifice, but she believed in the payoff. Plus there was no better vantage point in sight, and as Harley got to work, she watched clients from her desk and wondered who would be the first to take a moment of her time.

There was no space for chairs in the lobby where clients often managed themselves and each other by forming an orderly line against the wall. The only time things got out of hand was when it rained. When it did—which happened more often than not—the huddled masses would pack in and keep tabs on one another like trading pits at the stock exchange.

Inside the exchange room, Gabby was manning the Bio Bin while Mateo assisted and took notes. The cramped room was no larger than a master bedroom, but it felt even smaller because three of the four walls were lined with bone-colored melamine cabinets. Harley was also to blame for decking out the floors with beautiful, bleachable linoleum after she had the nasty carpet yanked out with a vengeance.

Against the fourth wall loomed the infamous Bio Bin—something of an altar known to draw in all walks of life from the furthest corners of the city. It was a custom-made syringe counting table that reeked of medical-grade sterilization wipes and set Harley back the cost of materials plus a case of beer to have a friend with carpentry skills construct it. While he was at it, he also skinned the square table with thin-gauge stainless steel and added a six-inch square opening in the center designed to feed used needles into a sharps disposal container below. A raised lip around the perimeter helped to keep needles from flying everywhere and though this ridged border was an afterthought, all had since agreed it was absolutely necessary.

The only items allowed to legally pass the point of no return were syringes, but if clients wanted to pitch other drug paraphernalia into the bin, staff tended to conveniently turn a blind eye. It was Harley's response after realizing the trash bag in the lobby kept growing legs. It was discovered an entrepreneurial spirit was making off with the trash to rinse traces of drug residue out of used cookers. In a last-ditch effort to clear her conscience, Harley removed the temptation altogether after multiple failed attempts to change the behavior.

The Bio Bin earned many nicknames over the years, but by and far Gabby's favorite was when someone compared it to the Great Pit of Carkoon, home to Sarlacc and the beast's endless rows of sharp teeth. When she first caught the reference and pictured Luke, Han and Chewie fighting their way out of the abyss, she pedaled home, dusted off her Return of the Jedi DVD and never looked at the Bio Bin the same way again.

A client stepped up to the Bio Bin and swung his backpack to the front of his chest.

"What's going on, Gabs?" Asher caught his breath, unzipped the front pocket and turned to the new guy. "And hey you."

"Hi, I'm Mateo." He reached out to shake the client's hand but was greeted with a fist bump instead.

Asher was old enough to smoke but not old enough to drink legally, and he would never admit it was a constant struggle for him to blend in. He would likely deny he was often cautioned to "go home" by his peers, and the same went for their suggestion that he wasn't built for the streets, despite his stocky frame that should empower him to fend for himself. This tough love made his hard life harder, which seemed to be a shared experience for those who couldn't catch up with the pack.

He withdrew a handful of needles and counted them out as

he dropped one after another in a ritualistic sacrifice to Sarlacc. "Sixteen . . . seventeen . . . and . . . . . . eighteen. That's all I got for today."

"Fulls, right?" Gabby asked.

"Yes, please."

She turned to Mateo. "Can you grab one of those bags and add eighteen of the one cc syringes, please?"

Mateo nodded and counted out the syringes. He dropped them into a paper bag loaded with metal cookers, twist ties and a number of other supplies.

"Any chance I can get some extra cookers too?"

"That all depends on what we have," Gabby said, turning to Mateo. She pointed to a cabinet door under the counter behind him. "They should be down there. And sorry Ash, I thought I had it, but what's your code again?"

He thought for a second. "ASVA-M-1102."

"Perfect." Gabby noted it on her clipboard and set her pen on the counter.

Mateo reached in and withdrew a gallon-sized plastic bag stuffed with small metal cookers that were not much larger than bottle caps. He scooped out a handful and dropped them into the bag.

"Nice." Asher flashed an awkward smile and vanished out of sight.

Gabby leaned toward Mateo. "Not that you would know this, but that's probably more than he needs. It's okay to be generous, but it's all a delicate balance between giving clients what they want and maintaining stock of what everyone needs so we don't run out, especially when it comes to the essentials."

Mateo listened carefully but his concentration was broken by the sound of high heels clicking on the linoleum. He turned to face a distinguished woman dressed in an elegant pantsuit, closing the door behind her. When she spun around, her prim face was hidden behind an impenetrable pair of Jackie Onassis sunglasses.

"Good morning, Gabriella," the woman said before turning

to Mateo. "And good morning, sir. I don't believe we've met. Can I ask, are you a client or employee?"

Mateo's back went stiff. "Neither, ma'am. I'm an intern."

"Very nice. I didn't catch your name."

"I'm Mateo."

"Nice to meet you. I take it you've been briefed on client confidentiality and all that jazz?"

He nodded and gave her a thumbs up, just to be safe.

"Lovely." The woman turned to Gabby. "In that case, my usual please."

"You got it." Gabby turned to Mateo. "Please make Ms. Martin a health kit with ten halves and extra prep pads."

He immediately set to work and handed her a bag that disappeared into her full grain leather satchel.

"Thank you so much. Until next time." Ms. Martin spun on her heels and slipped into the lobby, leaving the door open behind her.

"Never in a million years would I have guessed—"

"It's not for her. It's for her son," Gabby whispered, raising a hand to hold the next client at bay and out of earshot. "She's what we call a 'secondary exchange client' and she comes in every week without fail."

"Wait. If that's all for her son, isn't that considered enabling?"

"The way I see it she's only enabling her son to be safer," Gabby said, then wiped her lips. "Trust me, it can't be easy on her. But my guess is she's trying to protect him and help him stay out of legal trouble. He is the son of a city prosecutor after all, but that never leaves this room, understand?"

Mateo pretended to zip his lips as Gabby waved in the next client.

The following client came forward and held a bundle of syringes over the Bio Bin. "TELA-M-0294. I've got fifty fulls here."

"Is that so?" Gabby asked, eyeing the bunch of syringes after jotting down his code.

"Fine." His finger tore off the rubber band and he began counting them out. "Two . . . four . . . six . . . eight . . ."

"We don't like it, but the policy is a one-for-one swap out. Depending on how busy we are, we ask people to count out anything less than a hundred syringes. Anything more, it's okay to estimate, within reason."

"Twelve . . . fourteen . . ."

"Can't you weigh them?" Mateo asked.

"Not really, because we see a lot of syringes full of coagulated blood, and intentional bloodletting isn't something anyone wants to encourage."

"Twenty . . . twenty-two . . . twenty-four . . ."

"Makes sense," Mateo said, watching the needles shower down into the black hole. "Though I would've thought you'd give people as many syringes as they wanted." He scrunched his face.

"Don't even get me started on the one-to-one policy," Gabby said, shaking her head but not moving past the thought. "Okay, but only because you're new. So here's the deal: if someone comes to us empty-handed, they can get ten needles a day. Otherwise it's an even swap because of our contract with the county, despite a mountain of research that proves a free access model is more effective at slowing the spread of diseases. Why they won't let us follow the science is beyond me, but we're aiming to get there, which is why we tend to call Bridgeworks a syringe access program, even though most people know us as a syringe exchange." She ran her fingers through her hair. "Great. Now I'm all riled up. Fucking politics."

Mateo glanced at her oddly. "Politics?"

"No, *fucking* politics." She held up her hands and took a deep breath. "Harley has been fighting this misinformed policy forever, but everything is messy and tied into the operational budget."

"Thirty-four . . . thirty-six . . . thirty-eight." The client's hand was empty. "Sorry, I could have sworn I had counted fifty."

She cocked an eyebrow. "No reason to be sorry. We're all human. Would you like fulls or halves?"

. . .

The morning rush went on seamlessly for a few hours and from her desk, Harley watched the steady stream of clients waiting to exchange their dirty needles for fresh supplies. At times a new face would meander inside and get schooled by existing clients. It was rare that someone didn't know the process and though not complicated, newcomers were bound to be shown the ropes if they stepped out of line.

"Excuse me. Coming through."

Harley looked up to spot a fidgety young client weaving his way to the front of the line. The guitar case strapped to his back swung from side to side like a broken pendulum.

"Again, I don't mean to cut, but I'm in a real rush. So if no one minds, I'll just—"

"Hey, bud!" An older man lifted his forearm to block the swinging guitar from hitting him. "You can back the fuck up with your bullshit. Who the hell are you actin' like you got somewhere to be and we don't."

The kid steadied his guitar case and raised a finger to his lips. "Please keep it down. I'm in a rush to meet my dealer. He's right around the . . ." The kid looked over to see if Harley was still watching him. "Look, I'll be ten seconds, tops, and I'll make it up to you."

"Make it up, my ass." His furrowed brow shrouded gentle eyes that hid a deeper wisdom. "I'll tell you what: as long as you promise to pay it forward, you can go right ahead. But move with a purpose, okay? Just because I don't have anywhere to be doesn't mean I can't wait to get there."

The kid thanked him with praying hands, then reached behind his back to steady his guitar as he slipped into the exchange room. He smeared sweat off his neck and rattled off his client code.

Mateo glanced up. "Can I ask what's up with the code names?"

Gabby opened her mouth to answer, but Clay beat her to it. "It helps them track data, which is important for funding, right?" She crossed her arms and nodded as Clay kept the train moving.

He was spindly and sporadic, always on the go and seemingly never at ease. The calloused pads on his fingertips were stained brown from tobacco he had bummed or scavenged from ashtrays. Dropping to his knees, he tore open his guitar case, pulled out an acoustic Martin and steadied it against the wall. The second he withdrew his hand, the guitar started to slide over.

Mateo lunged forward and saved the day. "May I?" he asked, picking it up.

Clay reached out but had a change of heart and withdrew his hand. "Go for it, but be careful, okay? She might not look like much, but she's all I've got."

"She's in good hands," Mateo said confidently. He plucked a few strings and began tuning the guitar by ear.

"That don't sound like ten seconds to me," the man at the entrance to the exchange room called out.

Clay waved him off and turned his attention back to the hard-shell case. He flung open the storage compartment, grabbed a handful of needles and tossed them into the Bio Bin. "Ten, please."

To Gabby's dismay, the relaxing flamenco strumming stopped. "Halves or fulls?" Mateo asked.

"Fulls."

Gabby could hear the anxiousness in his voice. "By the way, why is it that every time I see you, you're in a rush?"

"Because I'm so broke I don't even have time to spend."

Gabby feigned a laugh. "Don't quit your day job."

"Now that's a good one." Clay packed it up and complimented Mateo's technique on his way out. As he slipped past Harley's open door, he felt her stinging eyes tracking his every move.

"Anyone in the market for an iPhone?" he whispered. "It's not stolen."

"Clay!" Harley yelled. "Knock it off."

"Sorry, I didn't think you could hear me."

"That's not the point. You know the rules."

Harley attempted to get back to work but decided to trust her gut. She intended to see Clay out, but he was long gone by the time she reached the lobby.

"Don't he know the police can track you nowadays through them phones?" the older client asked.

Harley smiled, pivoted around him and poked her head into the exchange room. "Hey Gabs, you got a second?"

Gabby turned to Mateo. "Are you good if I step out for a moment?"

Mateo nodded and waved in the next client.

Gabby stepped into Harley's office and motioned at the door.

"You can close it for now." Harley plopped into her chair and placed both palms on her desk. She considered how to bring Gabby up to speed without setting her off, knowing her explosiveness was easily triggered. Clearing her throat, she said, "Do you happen to know the name of the client with a rose tattoo on his hand?"

Gabby thought for a moment. "I want to say yes, but I'm not seeing his name in my mind. Does he show his face around here often?"

"From time to time."

"Maybe we'll see him around soon?"

"I doubt it. He robbed a dealer this morning, right around the corner."

"So that's what's been under your skin all morning?"

Harley put her hands on her head. "It's definitely up there."

"And did anyone see?"

"Besides me? I don't think so."

"Well, that's good for us but not for him. So I take it he's cut off?"

"No. Not yet."

Gabby buried her face in her hands. "Please don't tell me you're going to let this shit fly."

"That's not how I see it. I don't think pulling our services from someone should be used as a form of punishment. I already confronted him about what happened. I don't see him doing it again."

"And why not?" Gabby asked, looking up. "He's already proved he has no restraint, so how can you be so certain the next time will be any different?"

"Because I asked him not to."

"And you believe him?"

Harley crossed her arms. "Why shouldn't I?"

"Because he knows the rules: no buying, selling or being an ass within three blocks of B-SAP."

"Trust me, I know," Harley said, then thought for a moment. "And now he knows I know he knows, which . . . if I'm still making sense, is reason to believe he won't do it again."

Gabby rubbed her eyes and tensed up. "But think of the fallout if we ever got shut down."

"It would devastate our community, but it's not like I would stand by and let it happen."

"What if they have another run-in and it's not so pretty next time? Or what if the dealer posts up outside our entrance waiting to ambush the guy?"

Harley thought back to a number of fights she had broken up over the years. Most stopped at words, but some of them went the distance and there were a few she'd like to forget. All of them could have been avoided in a perfect world, but she knew the world was far from perfect. "I'm not trying to discredit you, but you know I've always struggled with hypotheticals. This also isn't the first or last time a dealer is going to have it out for a client."

"I'm confused. What's your plan if the dealer comes back?"

"I don't think he will because part of me feels like getting robbed from time to time is part of the job description. Although I will say the dealer was young and might want to save his reputation, so others don't see him as a pushover."

"Perfect. So who's the dealer?"

Harley wiped her face. "No clue. I haven't seen him around before."

Gabby headed for the door and rested her hand on the doorknob. "Do you mind if I take five, circle the block and make sure no one's looking for trouble?"

"Only if you promise me you'll be safe." Harley flicked her pen onto her desk, watched it roll in an arc and cursed as it fell to the floor.

"Hold up," Harley called as she darted out of the exchange and into the noon sun. She jogged down the uneven sidewalk and hurried after Gabby, who had stopped in her tracks to spark a cigarette. "Care if I join you?"

Gabby took the lead but paused a step later. She sucked down a drag and blew a burst of smoke over her shoulder. "I know I'm good at training, but I'm not sure Mateo's prepared to be left alone on his first day."

Harley glanced back at the exchange and wondered if Gabby was serious. "He's not alone. Lurch is in there with him."

"Good call. I love Lurch. Something about him being a quiet storm has always struck me as so settling."

They hooked the first corner and scanned the street for any suspicious activity.

"I'm sorry if I was out of line back there. I just don't want people mistaking your kindness for weakness," Gabby said. She took another deep drag and blew the smoke away from Harley. "I know it's your style to give people the benefit of the doubt, but I say if someone is going to rob another person with a needle, why not make an example of him and warn others not to walk all over us?"

"No one's walking over anyone, but again, the only harsh response I have would be to cut him off, which does more harm than good."

24

They rounded the next corner and walked in silence for half a block.

Gabby was the first to break stride as she snubbed out her cigarette on the sidewalk. "What I don't get is why let anyone jeopardize what we've built? At what point does being nurturing become a detriment, and where does seeing the best in everyone blind us to reality? Where do we draw the line?"

Harley understood where Gabby was coming from but still felt driven to lead her in the right direction. She thought over a number of responses and chose her words carefully. "You will never see me punish anyone for making a mistake or for having a lapse in judgment. It's only when someone refuses to learn from their mistakes that we ultimately have a problem . . . and even then I'll do what it takes to work with them because everyone is teachable."

They rounded the last corner and Gabby halted. She reached out, hooked Harley's arm and dug in her heels. "Oh, fuck. I think our friend is back."

Harley froze for a second and pulled her arm away. She imagined how she would approach this situation the next time it occurred, but she wasn't expecting it to happen again so soon.

A Subaru Legacy sat idle on the road about a hundred feet away from the entrance to Bridgeworks. Harley knew the vehicle well after she and another staff member recently confronted the driver about stalking the exchange. The woman peeled out in a fury, almost side-swiping her coworker and taking him along for a ride.

"Should we call the cops?"

Harley cringed at the idea. "Maybe not yet, because I've been in this position before and the cops won't solve the problem. I say we talk to her and see what she wants."

"Do you think finding out what she wants is worth getting hurt?"

"No, but as I've said, I've been in similar positions before. I don't know who or what she's after, but whatever she wants, I'm willing to bet she's more desperate than dangerous. Either way, there's only one way to find out. Just follow my lead and let me do the talking."

The two women approached the car from behind. Harley walked around to the driver's door and distracted the driver by tapping on the window. Startled, the woman flew forward in her seat. Her keys were hanging in the ignition, but by the time she started her car, Gabby had pressed her thighs against the front bumper, blocking the woman's escape. The woman laid on her horn, but Gabby pointed toward her ears, pretending she couldn't hear.

"Get out of the frickin' way!" the driver yelled through her windshield.

Gabby dropped her palms onto the hood in case she was about to go for a ride.

Harley tapped on the driver's window again. "Please calm down. I only want to talk."

"I have nothing to say to you." Drops of spit covered the inside of her window as the woman began panicking.

"I think you do, and now's your chance. There's no reason to be stalking our exchange all day."

The woman tossed her sunglasses on the dashboard and cracked open the window. "Are you serious?" she exclaimed, her chin trembling. "How about why the hell are you supplying needles and drug paraphernalia to my daughter?"

"I'm not sure who your daughter is, but yes, part of my job does involve—"

"Your *job*?"

"Yes, and it's clean medical supplies, not paraphernalia," Harley said simply. "I feel like that's an important distinction and I'm happy to talk to you about—"

"Just stop," the woman begged. She covered her mouth with her palms, seemingly at a loss for words until her words burst through her fingers. "My baby is running around this city with her dirtbag boyfriend, injecting heroin and meth into her body all day and night. She's going to die, and no one in their right mind seems to care."

"That's not true. Not only do we care, but there's a ton of support for anyone tha—"

"And I'm not '*stalking*' your exchange. I'm trying to save my daughter."

Harley glanced at the ground. "I apologize for my poor choice of words. Look, I understand where you're coming from and I want to help you, but my concern is that this isn't how you—"

"Oh, how would you know? Do you have a daughter hellbent on killing herself?"

Harley paused. "No, but I—"

"Then just stop." The woman put her car into park and opened the door. Harley took a step back while Gabby rounded the hood of the car. "Someone should shut you down before you hurt anyone else and I swear to God if no one else will, I'll do it myself. I'll do it for the sake of my daughter."

"I really don't think you understand what we do here. We're not here to hurt anyone. We're here to provide support to anyone who needs it at a time in their life where so many feel alone."

"What makes you think my daughter needs your support when she can turn to me? I raised her and she knows right from wrong. Troubled or not, deep down, she's still a good person."

"Of course she is," Harley said, motioning for Gabby to stay back. "Just because—"

"My daughter is not a bad person," she exclaimed, her words melting into moans. Slipping a shaky hand into her pocket, she removed a small picture of a young woman on her way to prom. "Where is my baby?"

As soon as Harley recognized the face in the photo, she looked away.

The woman froze. "What's wrong? You claim to support her and yet you can't even look at her?"

The portrait trembled in her hand, and Harley didn't know what to make of it. She couldn't confirm nor deny knowing anyone who used their services and knew it wasn't her place to decide if or when someone needed to be found. The mother was obviously concerned for her daughter, but she could also be a potential source of her own daughter's trauma. Either way, it wasn't a call Harley was prepared to make on behalf of anyone.

"Do you have a missing person flyer?" Harley asked. "I have a bulletin board in the lobby, so we can post it there."

"You think a *flyer* is going to save her life?" The woman creased the photo and forced it back into her pocket. She threw her car door open and crumbled back inside. "You know what else kills me? It's not so much that you're refusing to help me find her. It's how you can stand right there—close enough to feel my pain —and can't even think to ask what her name is."

three
rogue wave

"Talk to me," Gabby said as she tailed Harley into her office and closed the door.

Harley circled her desk and stood by her chair, but rather than taking a seat she began tidying her workspace.

"Don't shut down on me."

"I'm not," Harley said, struggling to see clearly. She looked around for something to occupy her hands or mind and settled on an inventory list. "I'm just upset, but we shouldn't let this distract us from our work today."

"There's plenty of time to get our work done. Are you okay?"

Harley flipped the paper in her hands as the numbers blurred. "You know how it is. No matter how many times something like this happens, it still sucks." She dabbed her eyes dry with the back of her hands. "I know that woman is hurting and understand her emotions are running high, but hopefully she returns after she's calmed down a bit so she can see for herself that we're not the enemy."

Gabby went quiet and gave Harley space to process everything when a faint barking from outside broke the silence.

Harley peered at the ceiling. "And of course I forgot about Lurch."

"I'll relieve him. Are you okay to be on your own for a bit?"

Harley pulled her chair back and settled into it. "I'll be fine."

Gabby slipped out of the office and went into the exchange room to find Mateo standing next to a tall, darkly bearded and not particularly handsome fellow. From his chipped nail polish to his crudely penciled-in eyeliner, the man's outfit showcased a deep affinity for the blackest of blacks and beyond.

"*Hey you guys!*" she said, imitating Sloth from *The Goonies*. "Thanks for holding down the fort."

Lurch sucked his cheeks in and gave his health kit a shake to acknowledge that he had what he came for. He reached down with a hand draped in silver rings and odd stones, then hoisted a heavy rucksack onto his back. It was his silent way of saying goodbye.

Gabby jotted his code down from memory and waved him off. "Catch you on the flip side, Lurch."

He moped his way to the lobby and never looked back.

"I like Lurch," Gabby said. "And I *ruv* Count."

"Who's that?" Mateo asked.

"Lurch's dog, and hopefully our official mascot some day. Okay, so where were we?"

Mateo shrugged. "I don't know where you disappeared to, but I've been here the whole time."

"I doubt Harley hired you for your sense of humor, but I've been wrong before." Gabby laughed and looked around the room. "By the way, you mentioned you're finishing up your bachelors at Portland State University. I take it you're living in campus housing?"

Mateo nodded. "I'm staying in the Montgomery dormitory right up the road."

"Good choice. Nice and quiet. And what brought you to Portland?"

"Portland sounded like a fun city and so far it hasn't disappointed. It's not too big or small, but the main selling point was that I imagined a year or two in a progressive town would give me ideas about ways I can better serve my community once I return home."

"I think that makes a lot of sense. It never hurts to expand your horizons. So what are you studying?"

"Sociology, with a minor in Communications."

"Very cool. They're both useful majors which will come in handy here since harm reduction and social justice feed off one another," she said, interlocking her hands.

"I think that's what appealed to me the most."

"Me too, because it's all intertwined. It's also why we practice an evidence-based, client-centered approach to reduce the social harms associated with substance use disorders."

Mateo followed along as a female client entered the exchange room.

Gabby turned around and grabbed her clipboard. "I have to say the best part about this field is that we can fight for whatever we don't have, which probably explains why Harley has a special place in so many hearts." She turned to face the client at the Bio Bin. "Am I right? Or am I right?"

The client slowly shook his head. "Sorry, Gabs. I wasn't paying attention."

"It's all good. The point is that Harley is forward-thinking and always pushing for policy reform," Gabby said, leaning back against the wall. "You know, I also remember my first day like it was yesterday. I was standing right where you are, an intern as well, eager to raise hell and make a change for the better. And because I see some of myself in you, I'm going to tell you something someone told me that left a big impact: your work matters, more than you'll ever know."

The client smiled. "That hit me in the feels, Gabs."

"That's because it's true." Gabby turned back to Mateo. "You're going to meet a lot of people here, and most of them will never forget you as long as you treat them the way you would want to be treated. Do that, and the difference you can make in someone's journey is *unlimited*." She waved her arm around. "It's what this all boils down to, but keep in mind it's important never to do more harm than good. You can have nothing but good intentions, and trust me, that's not enough."

Mateo handed the client her new needles and waved in the next one.

The client stepped to the side but not toward the exit. "Do you mind if I stay? I want to hear the rest."

Gabby smiled. "That's fine by me, but it's up to him." She pointed to the next client in line. "*Privacy laws.*"

The client walked into the exchange room and pulled out a stack of syringes from a bag. "I don't give a shit. I'm just here to swap these out."

Gabby laughed. "So Mateo, here's what I need from you. First, try to be sensitive to the needs of others without assuming their needs. We're not here to judge, pick sides or project our values onto others. Our clients get enough of that everywhere they go, so there's no room for it here."

"Amen to that," the female client whispered.

"Which means your job," Gabby continued, "is to stay empathetic and composed, all while developing a trauma-informed lens."

Mateo cocked his head.

"Thirty-three fulls, please." The male client started counting out his needles, dropping them into the Bio Bin.

Gabby found that she was distracted and slowed down. "It's a perspective which recognizes most people you meet are fighting or have fought a battle of some sort. By accepting this existence of trauma, you're less likely to be a source of re-traumatization."

"I'm not sure I follow," Mateo said.

"Think of it like this: if you ever work with a sexual assault survivor, one way to protect their emotional safety is to avoid asking them to relive their assault."

"You can say that again," the female client said.

"And the same goes for using language or labels on someone without their permission, like calling a client a 'junkie'."

"Even if someone self-identifies as one?" Mateo asked, rolling up a paper bag full of supplies and then handing it to the male client, who dipped out of the room.

"People can call themselves whatever they want," Gabby said, "but if you pick up on it and someone overhears you, they may not know the person you're talking about, which is a bad look."

Mateo thought for a moment. "Do you think I said anything today that did more harm than good?"

"Not to me you didn't," the female client said.

Gabby stepped forward. "And nothing I heard, but I also wasn't in here with you and Lurch."

Mateo peeked into the lobby. "We didn't talk much, which was probably best because I think he would've killed me if I said the wrong thing."

Gabby cocked an eyebrow. "What makes you assume he's violent?"

Mateo's laughter trailed off.

"You don't owe me an answer. Just think about it."

While the two looked blankly at each other, the female client slipped out of the room.

Gabby peeked into the lobby for a moment. "It looks like we have a lull in the line so let's run through some of the ways I like to stay busy. First, note that while none of this is complicated, you always want to be mindful of your surroundings and be intentional with your movements, especially when distributing, collecting or disposing syringes. Since you're new I'll have you spend most of your downtime labeling and packaging supplies like these." Gabby grabbed a small clear bag filled with tiny cotton balls. "You can't imagine how much time we spend making these."

"What are they for?" Mateo asked.

She studied the familiar package. "These are dental cottons and act as last-chance filters. People drop them into their cookers then suck up the fluid through them. They're meant to filter out any cut in a shot by removing any impurities left floating in the fluid." She flicked the bag. "I'm not sure if you're competitive, but my record is about two hundred of these stuffed in an hour. How familiar are you with blood-borne infectious diseases?"

Mateo grimaced. "A little."

"That's not quite good enough. Excuse me for a sec." Gabby stepped out of the exchange room and into the lobby. She opened the door to the testing room and grabbed some pamphlets from a brochure stand. "Please make it a point to read these," she said, walking back into the room, "and let me or Harley know if you have any questions. We don't go through the motions here, so you need to understand what you're giving out. As they say, knowledge is power."

Mateo looked at the pamphlets. "And we test clients for all these diseases, right?"

"Yeah, the staff does."

"Not the interns?"

"No, because there's a lot more to it than the testing. In fact, the actual testing for HIV, Hep C and syphilis isn't the hard part." She paused for a moment. "It's giving people their results that can take a toll."

"Makes sense. I guess I wouldn't want to be the bearer of bad news."

"None of us do, but it's a critical component of harm reduction. But you know what's interesting? Most clients get tested not for their own sake, but to know what they have so they can protect their friends."

Mateo paused. "Really?"

"That's what they tell us, which to me says a lot. But it makes sense when you think about it, and I see it as the driving factor behind what we do. Remember, we exist to give people the tools and knowledge to not only protect themselves but their community."

Mateo placed his hands on his hips and took it all in.

"Anyway, that's pretty much it. The only other thing we ask is for you to report any incidents to staff. Oh, and before I forget, we also need to get you up to speed on how to respond to an overdose."

"Back in Spain I volunteered at a health clinic where they

taught me how to inject Narcan."

"I remember seeing that in your application—the part about volunteering." Gabby reached into her purse and pulled out a single-use Narcan intranasal spray packet. "I wonder if they had these? They're simpler to use than the intramuscular injectables."

Mateo leaned forward. "Where can I get some for myself?"

"In a perfect world, from us, but the nasal sprays are about ten times the price of the injectables, so take a guess which ones we stock. Also, we tend to stock naloxone, which is just the generic version of Narcan. But go ahead and take this. I have a few more stashed here and there."

Mateo took the nasal spray sealed in a foil packet and spun it in his fingers.

"And just so you know, that's only loaded with a single dose, so don't prime or do a test spray before using it. I wish I had more to spare, but we can always get you some vials of the injectables as a backup."

"*Vials*?" Mateo stopped inspecting the packet and looked up. "How many do you think I need if each vial contains ten doses?"

"Oh, you had the multi-dose vials in Spain? Those were the old days, and we've since moved to handing out single-dose vials to prevent cross-contamination. We don't want someone sticking a needle into a vial more than once and possibly infecting a friend."

Mateo scratched the back of his neck. "You know, I never thought of it like that, but that's a good point."

"Like I said, we're constantly evolving and learning as we go." Gabby reached out and patted him on the shoulder.

"Sadie, must you always come in right as we're wrapping things up?" Gabby asked, clicking her pen as the last straggler of the day entered the exchange room.

"I'm confused. You don't enjoy ending your day on a high note?"

Sadie's blue eyes widened with wonder and glistened as she bounced on her tiptoes. She was in her mid-twenties and from more places than anyone in their right mind could imagine. She often mentioned growing up in Miami, though every now and then she was from Aurora. Depending on the weather, she may have hailed from Glendale, Austin, Modesto or oddly enough, Shanghai. Anyone who took her at her word soon discovered that her mind moved a mile a minute.

For those who could follow along, Sadie was borderline riveting. Not only did she know everyone, but she always seemed to know someone from somewhere. Her luck was unimaginable, and how she often found herself at the right place at the right time was downright unbelievable.

"Looks like we got new blood," Sadie said, drawing out the last word.

Mateo reached out to shake her hand. "Hi, I'm Mateo."

She pointed at his hand and waved him off. "Thanks, but no thanks. That's how you get germs. And you're new. Where'd you come from?"

Mateo rescinded his offer. "Madrid."

"Madrid? *Madrid?*" Sadie tapped her chin. "Have I been to Madrid?"

"It's in Spain," he said, hoping to jog her memory.

"Oh, si, si. Now *that* was a fun trip. I was there a few years ago on a study abroad trip. It was around Christmas, and me and some classmates had broken off from the pack and slid into an alley. I stuck my head into my backpack to sniff a rail and I heard these booming canons, like in *The Hunger Games.* I looked up and saw a hoard of Spaniards charging our way, so we had no choice but to join. I've never moved so fast in my life. *Viva la Spain!*" Sadie said, shuffling her feet. "Talk about a rush."

"I bet," Gabby said. She glanced at the clock. "Okay gal, we need to ándale and close up shop. What's your code again?"

"Oh, I didn't stop in for supplies. I was in the neighborhood and figured I could use a sharps container to clean up my camp a little. Any chance I can grab one?"

"What's mine is yours, assuming we have some in stock." Gabby reached into a cupboard and grabbed a small red container. "Also, before I forget, please check in with Harley before you take off. I think your brother dropped off another care package for you this morning."

Sadie snorted and snatched the container. "Muchas gracias," she said, then held the container above her head while poorly impersonating a flamenco dancer.

Mateo watched in confusion while she stomped her feet toward the exit. When he was convinced she was out of earshot, he turned to Gabby and asked, "Do you think she thinks I'm stupid?"

"What makes you say that?"

"Pamplona's nowhere close to Madrid. It's a few hundred miles away, and las fiestas de San Fermín is in July, not December."

Gabby nodded. "I wouldn't overthink Sadie's wandering mind."

"I don't like liars."

"Well . . . I wouldn't say she's lying."

"And I don't like being lied to."

Gabby flashed a bitter smile. "Of course you don't. No one does, but that's not how I see it, and neither should you. Remember, not every client you'll meet is going to exist in the same reality as you. You shouldn't hold that against them, especially if they mean no harm."

Mateo thought for a moment and laughed it off.

"Exactly. If you keep your sense of humor, I'm willing to bet you'll last longer than most."

"Alright, I'm out of here unless you need anything from me. I think Mateo is off to a great start and . . ." Gabby paused at the door. "Hey, is something wrong?"

Harley sat frozen at her desk, lost in her computer monitor. "Before you go, I think you need to look at this." She scrolled back up to the top of the email and angled her screen to face Gabby. "Do you remember Heather from the last Harm Reduction Conference in Anaheim?"

Gabby twisted a tuft of hair at the base of her scalp.

"She led the panel about the looming fentanyl threat with Dr. Baker and—"

"Oh, right."

"Well, it looks like it's happening."

Gabby scanned the email and covered her mouth.

"I know. I don't want to believe it either," Harley said, her arms slapping the sides of her chair.

"Four *hundred* percent? How?"

Harley stared at her door. "Time will tell, but if it's like she predicted, the problem is that while fentanyl is a cheap and profitable way to increase the potency of a batch, it's notoriously difficult to work with, especially for amateurs. This makes variability a real concern, especially since we estimate something like eighty percent of 'heroin' sold on the East Coast is actually just fentanyl. I mean, it's gotten to the point where people are listing fentanyl as their drug of choice, and while mass overdose events are rare, it's terrifying because even when a bad batch hits the streets, you and I both know the demand isn't going anywhere."

"Well, I don't know about that. It looks like the 'demand' is filling up the morgues." Gabby tapped on Harley's monitor. "I can't believe there's been so many fatal overdoses. Is it just in California?"

"I'm not sure, but we need to find out."

Gabby pushed herself off the desk and stood up tall. "What does this mean for us?"

"For us?" Harley rubbed her hands on her thighs and stared into her screen. "I think we respond based on the worst case scenario because we can't underestimate how hard this could hit the streets. I suppose if there's any silver lining here, it's that we've done our best to plan for events like this—we being medical experts, drug treatment specialists and a number of government officials—but the bad news is that our clients are often left in the dark. But my biggest fear, by and far, is that people won't take this threat seriously because as far as they know, fentanyl is already everywhere and it's just the same shit, different day."

"You think they won't believe us?"

"No, they'll believe us, but put it this way: what options do they have?" Harley didn't wait for an answer. "Those who are physically dependent don't have the leisure to suddenly stop and wait for something like this to blow over. They can scramble to get into detox, find a safe supply or take their chances with what's out there—that's about it. I'm telling you Gabs, this can get real ugly real quick for a lot of people. And as in any war, who gets hit the hardest?"

Gabby tugged on her lower lip. "Those on the frontline. Shit, we need to get the next shipment of fentanyl test strips in right now."

"See, that's where you're wrong. We needed them yesterday." Harley picked up her phone and dialed a number from memory. "Ethan, it's me. I need a favor. Any chance you're able to work tomorrow?" She held her breath for a few seconds. "Thanks. Also, can you meet me here a little earlier than normal? Awesome. See you then." She hung up and leaned back in her chair.

"What's going on?" Gabby asked.

"I think we're going to need extra hands on deck. That, and a part of me is still a little jarred from earlier."

"Do you think she's dangerous?" Gabby asked.

"No, but I've been wrong before."

"Then why don't you take this?" Gabby dug into her purse and pulled out a canister of pepper spray.

Harley studied the can but didn't reach for it. Having survived for so long with no self-defense protection, she didn't see a need to amass an arsenal now.

"What am I supposed to do with that?" Harley asked.

"You don't know how to use this?" Gabby twisted the pepper spray so Harley could see the top. "You flip this tab and—"

"I mean, does this stuff even work? Won't it just escalate a tense situation further?"

"It's hard to tell, but there's nothing wrong with protecting yourself. Besides, having it on you will make us both feel better."

"I don't know about that. I think I'm good for now, but I appreciate your concern." Harley moved her mouse to wake her screen up. "Speaking of concern, do you have anywhere to be right now?"

Gabby sighed. "I'm still missing that extra hour of sleep, but something tells me I'd better get used to it."

"Perfect. Then if you don't mind staying for a bit, why don't you pull that chair around so we can review our response plan. There's no way I can do this alone."

four
transients

"Morning, Ethan. I appreciate you coming in early."

Ethan tipped his paper coffee cup. "You know I'm always here for you." His back was pressed to the front door of the exchange and though it was only half-past nine, he was already rocking a five o'clock shadow. As Harley approached the entrance, he stepped aside and made way for her to unlock it.

"Want to tell me what's going on?" Ethan asked.

Harley opened the door and glanced down the road, making sure the mom hadn't returned. "Gabby and I had a run-in yesterday with the woman who's been creeping on the exchange."

"The same one who almost ran me over?" He raised his hairy arms to adjust his Hooligan snap cap and flashed a freshly shaven head. "Don't tell me she's back."

"I don't think she ever left. Says she's looking for her daughter and thinks this is the best place to find her."

"Did you tell her that's not how this works, unless she's intending to scare her daughter away?" He pulled at his throat, distorting a gray-scale Mandala tattoo. "I'll keep an eye out for her. By the way, do we know who her daughter is?"

Harley forced a smile. "It's Liv."

Ethan didn't respond. Instead, he held the door open for Harley and quietly followed her into the lobby, then locked the door behind him.

In his late thirties, Ethan had spent the better part of his life in Portland. He said that not because he'd been in Bridgetown longer than anywhere else, but because he left Philly and made the move to the city when he first got clean from heroin. He'd been in the city for sixteen years and worked at B-SAP nearly the whole time. But even though he had clocked more time under his belt than Harley at the Bridgeworks syringe access program, he had no aspirations or desires to fill any managerial position. As a person in long-term recovery, he kept it simple and figured he could use his position to mentor any client who was in the market for one.

"And not to be the bearer of bad news, but it gets worse," Harley said, leaning against her door. "The other reason I called you in is because California is experiencing an overdose event. They're seeing a massive spike in fentanyl-related deaths."

Ethan pulled his glasses off. "What's the influx?"

"Four hundred percent and climbing."

"Shit," he whispered. "What a time to be alive. Has any of it washed up into Portland yet?"

"That's what I need to figure out. Last night, I sent out requests for ambulance and emergency room data, so I should have them today."

"Any word from PPB on lethal and non-lethal ODs?"

"Not yet, but I haven't checked my messages." Harley pulled out her phone, scrolled through several voicemails and stopped on one from a friend. She felt bad when she realized she had missed her call, and even worse when she read the transcription:

Hey stranger, it's Sidney.

I know you've been busy lately, but I think I speak for all of us when I say we miss you. Let me know if you're free to get together soon for a girls' night in and I'll gather the gang. We're here for you and miss your face.

Hope to talk to you soon.

"What about HIDTA? Any word from them?"

The question snapped Harley back to the present. She knew that once the High-Intensity Drug Trafficking Areas program got involved, the problem was beyond containment. She shook her head, placed her phone back into her pocket and made a mental note to call Sidney back sooner rather than later.

Ethan wiped his brow. "No news is good news, right?"

"One can only hope." Harley pushed herself off from her door and peeked into the exchange room. "It looks like you're good to go, but will you let me know if you need any help before Karissa arrives?"

Ethan pretended to be insulted and shooed her away.

Harley playfully knocked his hand away, stepped into her office and reached out to her colleague in Tacoma.

A gravelly voice answered on the second ring. "Harley? To what do I owe the pleasure?"

"Unfortunately, I take no pleasure in making this call."

"What's going on?" Wayne asked.

She could tell from his voice that his famous smile had vanished. "I'm wondering if you read Heather's email? I saw your name cc'd on the list."

"I did, and we were just debating how best to mobilize."

Harley felt a tinge of relief at not having to break the news to him. "Has Tacoma or Seattle seen a spike yet?"

"No, and we're praying we won't. What about you?"

"Not that I know of, but it's still early." Harley's words stalled out on her. She hated asking for favors but knew it was inevitable in this line of work. "Wayne, I just checked my inventory on naloxone and I'm worried we're running low."

"How low is 'low'?"

"Lower than I'd like. We're almost out."

"That's not good," Wayne said after a moment. "Do you have any on the way?"

"I don't think so. I put in a purchase order a few months ago for some cases, but nothing has shipped yet. We must still be on back order."

"Join the club."

Harley winced. "You too?"

"You know I would never lie to you. Unfortunately we've been back-ordered for at least nine weeks."

She cursed under her breath.

"I know, but don't start panicking yet. Unless it's worse than what I'm imagining, we're in a good spot and should have more than enough in stock."

A loud knock on the front door of the exchange distracted Harley. She watched Ethan cut through the lobby and head toward the entrance. "Sorry Wayne, I missed that last part. What did you say?"

"I said we're good . . . and so are you. How much naloxone do you need?"

"Without knowing what we're up against, I'll be happy with whatever I can get as long as you can afford to—"

"Harley. Please. I already have a headache. How many vials do you need?"

"If you can afford it, I think a hundred vials would be amazing. But again, only if you have it."

Wayne laughed half-heartedly. "Now, was that so hard?"

"Honestly, yes. How much do I owe you?"

"I'll work it up and send you a bill."

Karissa walked through the lobby and poked her head into Harley's office. "Morning Har—"

Harley held up a finger to cut her off. "You're amazing, Wayne. I'll make it up to you."

"I'm sure you will. So, are you coming up today?"

"I'd love to, but it's probably best that I don't abandon my post."

"I know how it goes. Why don't you send a runner up here and I'll see you when I see you."

"Someone will be on their way soon. Thanks again for everything. You're truly a lifesaver."

Harley hung up the phone and exhaled. Running her fingers through her lilac hair, she caught a small knot and worked it apart.

"I take it you need me to go somewhere?" Karissa asked. She pushed off the doorjamb and slinked forward, dragging her feet across the ground like the belly of a gator. Even though Karissa shied away from makeup, her natural beauty was apparent and at times appeared unwanted. Her demeanor was conflicted as she often was, easy to work with but hard to get to know and a private person who needed everyone to know it. What it all came down to was Karissa kept her circle close, and shortly after she had become a full-time staffer, she began taking her role more seriously than expected. She buzzed her head and told her friends she had made the move for "convenience," but she had stuck with the look ever since.

That made Harley have a soft spot in her heart for Karissa. Even though they were only a few years apart, Harley couldn't help but feel like she had watched her grow up in front of her eyes. It wasn't only her kind face which had conquered a past few knew about, it was how she had pushed through the pain and found the strength to help others do the same.

Harley reached for the keys to her Volkswagen Tiguan. "How do you feel about taking a nice drive?"

"As long as she doesn't die on me again, we shouldn't have any problems." Karissa reached for the keys. "Same place as last time?"

Harley nodded and wrote down a number. "Wayne will be expecting you, but I would still call ahead when you're thirty minutes out."

"Looks like Karissa split on me," Ethan said, leaning his weight against the counter and crossing his arms. "Not that I can't handle it on my own or anything."

"She's off to Tacoma to grab some naloxone vials from Wayne. But don't sweat it, I'm here to fill in for her," Harley said.

"Just like the good ol' days?"

"You could say that, except this time I'm not doing all the

grunt work"—she raised two large Ziploc bags bursting with fentanyl test strips—"and we have a secret weapon."

"You've been holding out on me?"

She lowered the bags. "You know I've been afraid of an overdose event for some time, so I have to keep some tricks up my sleeves."

"Fair play." He moved toward the lobby. "Want me to let them in?"

"Sure, and could you please close my office door while you're at it?"

As he left the room, Harley placed the test strips on the counter and realized how tired she was. It was difficult for her to sleep last night after learning about the waking nightmare her colleagues were facing in California, and since she still hadn't received word back from the local medical examiner, her mind naturally assumed the worst.

Ethan led the first two clients into the exchange room. Jack and Sophia were known far and wide as an inseparable transient couple who came to Portland with little to no backup plan. They had freight hopped a train from Seattle with grand visions of seeing the entire country, but those dreams didn't make it nearly as far as they had hoped. Instead, they soon found themselves stuck in a rut, worn thin by the very streets that would come to grow on them.

Most of their skin was covered up with tattoos and at least two layers of weathered clothing. Like so many others, the couple had made a living on the streets by panhandling, with Jack going the extra mile of facilitating dope deals to support their habits. Even though every day was the same struggle, their future was uncertain and seemingly how they liked it.

Jack reached into the chest pocket of his overalls and pulled out two bundles of needles. Like Sophia, the cuffs of his jeans were rolled above his ankles to prevent water from creeping up his legs. "JAJI-M-0497 and SOHO-F-0299. We have forty-six fulls. Want me to count them?"

"Nah, you're good." Ethan counted out the replacements and tossed them into a paper bag. He held out the bag but didn't let go when Jack grabbed it.

Jack gave it a tug, then caved. "Fuck, alright man. *Hit me.*"

"*'A man who chases two rabbits, catches neither.'*" Ethan let go of the bag and smiled.

"Sounds like some Neo-*Matrix* shit."

"Except this isn't a simulation," Harley said, handing Jack a handful of fentanyl test strips. "Please take these. Also, I'm wondering if you've heard of any recent overdoses, lethal or otherwise."

"It depends. How recently are we talking?" he asked.

"Within the past week."

Jack shook his head. Subconsciously, Sophia followed suit.

"That's a good sign," Harley said. "There's a mass overdose event happening in California as we speak. We believe fentanyl-related deaths have shot through the roof, so I'm going to give you two some extra test strips. Can you spread the word and give these to those who need it most?"

Harley withdrew a packet from the Ziploc bag but didn't open it. "There's a thin test strip in here that will alert you of the presence of fentanyl in your drugs. Just mix a shot like usual and dip the end into it." She flipped the packet over. "Here's the instructions if you need a reminder, but the main takeaway is you're looking for two pink lines—not one."

Jack raised a single finger. "But what am I supposed to do if my dope tests positive for fentanyl? It's not like we can get our money back."

"You can't get your life back, either. Remember, fentanyl can be up to a hundred times more powerful than morphine."

"That's not something you want to take a chance on if you can avoid it," Ethan added.

Harley looked thoughtful. "If you're going to use anyway, there are some practices that can mitigate some of the risks, such as never using alone, which shouldn't be a problem since you two are always together. Another safe bet is to do a test shot."

"A test shot?" Jack raised his chin to show off a number of track marks. "Do you know how long it takes me to find a vein?"

Ethan crossed his arms. "And do you know that two holes in the neck are better than one in the ground?"

Jack looked down and laughed awkwardly. "Is that another one of your ancient Chinese proverbs or something?"

"No, but it's still a safe rule to live by."

Harley nodded in agreement. "As long as you try your best and remember that a 'test shot' can mean many things to many people. Some people do half their normal amount while others do maybe a quarter or less. Some wait a while between shots while others go one right after the other. The point is that math is hard, especially when you're dealing with unknowns. You can never be too safe."

Sophia pulled herself closer to Jack. "Is it only in the dope? Or are they finding fentanyl in meth as well?"

Harley shrugged. "No idea. We suspect it's only in the heroin, but nowadays almost everyone is injecting a mixture of both, so it's hard to say." She then paused for a second. "We'll find out soon enough, but if you're also using meth it's a little more complicated to test. You need to add more water and be sure to test the meth residue—not the shards—and you can always bring your stuff here and have us test it for you." As she spoke, Harley saw an opportunity and arched her back. "By the way, do you have any on you?"

"Any of what?" Jack asked.

"Anything. Heroin? Coke? Pills? Meth?"

Jack shook his head. "We wouldn't be caught dead with meth. That's not our thing, but depending on how much you need, I have some black tar on me if that'll help?"

"Are you comfortable with us testing a bit? I'm only talking about a minuscule amount of residue."

"Yeah, sure," Jack said. "We're both well, so we're not in a rush."

Harley glanced at Ethan, then at the growing line behind him. "You may not be in a rush, but they certainly are. Ethan, would you mind taking them into the drug checking room while I work on getting this line moving?"

"Sorry, partner. Not today," Harley chided, turning around from the counter to face Clay. She placed a bag on the counter and pointed toward the exit.

Clay set his guitar case on the floor and opened the lid. "What do you mean 'not today'? Are you out of supplies or some shit?"

"I meant no cutting in line today. It's time you wait your turn like everyone else."

"But I didn't cut."

Harley crossed her arms. "I'm not doing this with you, Clay. You need to—"

"You think I cut?" he asked, his sour voice cracking. "I didn't, and everyone's right there. We can bring them in and you can ask them yourself."

"In that case it's okay. We don't have to—"

Clay stuck his head into the lobby. "Can someone come in and tell her I didn't cut?"

"Clay, I said it's—"

"I don't have time to go outside. My guy is on his way and—"

"Will you please listen to me!" Harley stepped forward and snapped her fingers to attract Clay's attention. "No one's going outside. Now, what do you need?"

"Same shit, different day." Clay spun around and reached into his guitar case. With his back toward the door, he didn't notice Ethan poking his head into the room to check on them. Harley quietly waved him off and signaled that everything was under control.

"Is that ten fulls?" Harley asked.

Clay nodded and tossed his syringes into the Bio Bin.

49

"I'm also giving you two single-dose vials of naloxone, a few intramuscular needles and some fentanyl test strips." She handed him his paper bag and watched him jam it into his guitar case. "Do you remember how to use naloxone?"

"I see people get hit with it all the time, but it's been a while since I personally administered a shot."

"Do you need a refresher?"

"Nah. I figure it's like riding a bike."

"And what about the test strips? Do you know how to use them?"

"Why? Should I be worried about IMF?"

Harley knew what he meant, but even in her circle of professionals it was rare for anyone to use specific acronyms unless they were giving a presentation or nerding out behind closed doors.

"Why do you look so confused? Is this not what we're talking about?" Clay stood up and studied a test kit.

"Yes, but—"

"And will these check for all forms of illicitly manufactured fentanyl? Because there's also methyl-fentanyl, acetyl-fentanyl, acryl-fentanyl . . ."

Harley nodded along in amazement but realized she was giving mixed signals. "No, they won't. These tests are good, but they aren't perfect. They can detect most of the known fentanyl analogs, but not all of them." She paused for a moment. "Can I ask how you know all this?"

"Because I love it," Clay said, widening his stance. "And I read . . . when I have down time." He shook the test. "I suspect these won't test for potency, either."

"Correct. It would take a little more equipment than what could fit in your pocket."

"That's too bad because there's a ton of fentanyl out there. Not so much pharmaceutical fentanyl as you know—the good stuff is so controlled it rarely gets diverted into the black market— but the streets are flooded with IMF that's been synthesized in makeshift labs. So much so that I'm pretty sure a lot of junkies shoot some every day without even knowing it."

Harley deadpanned, her gaze boring into him. "You know I'm not a fan of that word, right?"

"What word? *Junkie*? Why not? Aren't junkies your favorite people?"

She sighed and shook her head. "They are, but the word is derogatory and stigmatizing. It's often used to imply people who use drugs are irredeemable human waste, or something along those lines."

"But that's not what I meant. Heroin has always been known colloquially as 'junk,' so isn't it a logical derivation like how we get smackhead from smack or druggie from 'drugs'?"

"You can take it or leave it, Clay. I'm not trying to change your language here. I'm only trying to make you aware of how your words matter. It's the same thing when other words stir up shame and judgment such as how 'drug abuser' implies violence or 'addict' labels a person's identity by their disease."

"That may be true, but you're talking like my words mean something. No one gives a fuck what I say, let alone think."

"I don't believe that for a second. Your words do matter and language is a powerful weapon that shapes how we communicate, think and treat one another. And if we ever hope to change how others talk about our community, it starts with shaping how we talk to one another."

Ethan joined them in the room. He glanced at Harley and mouthed "Negative."

Harley closed her eyes but knew that while it was a good start, testing one person's dope was about the worst possible sample size anyone could hope for.

"If you want we can continue this conversation later, but I also wanted to ask if you're using meth every day."

"That's the plan," Clay said, swinging his guitar case onto his back.

Harley waited until he made eye contact with her and

wondered if it was time to play favorites. "I'll tell you what, I'll make a deal with you. Come find me every morning and I'll escort you to the front of the line."

"Really? You would do that for me?" Clay asked, looking at the long line behind him. "Wait, what's the catch?"

"No catch, but if it's not too much to ask, it would be nice if you could meet with your dealer *before* you pop in here so I can test your supply."

five
lao che

Harley stared at the last two vials of naloxone she could afford to give out, then set them into a paper bag and handed the supplies to Asher. "I also included a couple of intramuscular needles and some fentanyl test strips."

Asher scratched at his jaw.

"Do you remember how to respond to an overdose?" Harley asked.

His eyes—set deep into their oily sockets—searched aimlessly for an answer. "Yeah, I think so? First I find a vein, then—"

Harley reached out and took the bag back. "Okay, let's run through it together. It'll only take a second." She unrolled the bag and withdrew the small vial.

"What is it?" Asher brushed his stringy hair away from his face with hands riddled by track marks.

Harley held the vial in front of her and dropped her voice. "'The antidote, *Dr. Jones.*'"

He cocked his head.

"'. . . *For the poison you just drank.*'"

"Huh?"

"*Lao Che?*"

Asher cleared his throat. "What the hell are you talking about?"

Harley set the vial down and marveled at where life had led her. "Are you serious right now? Am I the only one who grew up on *Indiana Jones?*"

Asher turned and looked behind him. "Sorry, I've never been to Indiana."

It took a moment for Harley to realize he wasn't joking, but once she did, she picked up the vial and moved on. "Let's start over. This is naloxone. It's the generic version of Narcan, an opioid reversal agent able to reverse most overdoses in a matter of minutes. You see here?" She tipped the vial to slosh the liquid back and forth. "Each vial contains precisely one dose."

Ethan joined them in the exchange room.

Harley continued. "But before you use this, you should know how to identify an overdose. Do you know what signs to look for?"

Asher licked his chapped lips. "I dunno. Someone not breathing?"

"Correct, respiratory depression is a definite sign of an OD, though of course the goal is to prevent that from happening. Other telltale signs to look for are unconsciousness, labored breathing, pinpoint pupils, blue lips and blue fingernails."

"What about a needle in their arm?" Asher asked.

"Yes, that would be an excellent indicator, and once you identify an overdose, there are three things to do: dial 911, administer naloxone and breathe for the person until help arrives."

"And we always tell people that if they can do at least two of them, there's a good chance they could save someone's life," Ethan said.

"Exactly," Harley said. "If someone's not breathing, you need to act fast, but always be sure to call 911 first."

"Or ask someone else on scene to make the call for you if you're preoccupied," Ethan added.

"That's so I don't get arrested?"

"No, it's so you can attend to the person in need of saving. And you don't have to worry about being arrested during an overdose event." Ethan pointed to Harley. "You can thank her for that law."

Harley dismissed the compliment. "Thanks, but the Good Sam Law was a team effort. I'm just glad I was asked to be involved."

"What's the law?" Asher asked.

Harley touched her chin. "Think of it as a saving grace. The Good Samaritan Overdose Law protects anyone who calls 911 from being arrested for possession of drugs or paraphernalia, violating probation or parole, or even from being picked up on outstanding drug warrants."

Asher stretched his arms over his head. "No shit? I didn't know that."

Ethan nodded. "A lot of people don't, so be sure to pass the word on. Never be afraid to call for help, though I will say when you make the call I wouldn't mention drugs over the phone unless you want the cops to come. All you have to say is that someone is unconscious or had a seizure and isn't breathing, then when the paramedics arrive, let them know the full story."

Harley held up the vial along with the intramuscular needle. "Now to administer this, all you do is remove the cap from both the vial and the needle, turn the vial upside down, stick the needle in here"—she tapped a rubber membrane on the cap—"draw up a cc of fluid and inject the dose into their arm, thigh or butt cheek, but never into their vein."

"Makes sense," Asher said, nodding.

"And if you need to, you can inject right through their clothes," Ethan noted.

"Right, and then if help is on the way, continue breathing for the person until they can breathe for themselves. We recommend one breath every five seconds for at least three minutes."

"That's thirty-six breaths," Ethan whispered. "Give or take."

"What if I don't know where their mouth's been?" Asher asked.

Harley dropped her shoulders. "Even though the risk of catching anything through rescue breathing is low, we had CPR shields with a one-way valve, but we gave them all out on Overdose Awareness Day. Otherwise, it's your right to do what feels comfortable but know that a lot of damage can happen in a short time when a brain is deprived of oxygen. So at the very least, try to put yourself in their shoes."

"Also, if the first dose doesn't bring them back within three minutes, hit them again with dose number two, assuming you have a backup." Ethan did a one-two punch in the air, which made Asher take a half-step back.

Harley smiled. Every time she brought someone up to speed on responding to an overdose, the world was that much safer.

"So are you good to go?" she asked.

Asher smiled.

"Perfect. *Next.*"

A young woman wearing a hoodie entered the exchange room and swapped places with Asher. "OLDO-F-0703. Two . . . four . . . six . . . eight."

Harley had her back turned to the client yet recognized her voice. "Halves or fulls?"

"Fulls, if you don't mind."

Harley rolled up the bag and turned around. "Not at all, and I put some extras in there for you as well."

The client smiled, took the bag and tucked it in the front pocket of her hoodie.

Harley looked at Ethan and then back to the client.

"Do you have a second?" Harley asked.

"Can it wait? I'm kind of in a rush."

"Please, Liv. It's important. Can we talk in my office? It'll only take a second."

Liv glanced at Ethan then stepped to the side, motioning for Harley to lead the way.

"It's been a while. How have you been?" Harley asked, raising an arm to direct Liv into her office.

Liv's tame green eyes exposed a certain fragility as she took a seat across from Harley. When she pulled her hood back, auburn hair slid to the side, revealing a tan rarely seen on someone who called Portland home.

"I'm sure you know how it is," Liv said. "Every day is an endless struggle."

"I know life can get hectic, but don't let it overwhelm you." Harley leaned forward in her chair. "Of course with that said, there's something you should know."

"It's my mom, isn't it?"

Harley pictured Liv's high school photo. "Yes."

"She's still coming around?" Liv asked, stiffening up. "What's her fucking problem?"

"We didn't get into the details, but she's obviously concerned for you."

"So you talked to her? Did you tell her she needs to leave me alone?"

Harley shook her head. "No, I didn't."

"Did you tell her that since I'm no longer a minor, she can't report me as a runaway or sign over parental custody and pass me off to another 'troubled teens' boot camp?"

Harley shook her head again. "Of course not, because—"

"Or did you tell her that I don't respond well to ultimatums and I'm only 'living' on the streets because she forced me to choose between this life and a cold-turkey detox?"

"That's awful, but again, I didn't—"

"Or, better yet, did you tell her that she's the reason I got hooked on this shit in the first place? After all, if she hadn't hurt her back and left pills lying around the house for years, maybe I wouldn't have developed a pill habit just like her. Then one day out of the blue she decides to buy a safe, lock up her pills and expects me to suddenly stop? *Sorry mom*, it doesn't work like that. Did you tell her that she ruined my life, not me?"

"No, I didn't tell her any of that because I had no idea, and even if I had, you have a right to privacy and I will never disclose I know you to anyone without your permission. Not even to your own mother. Also, I wouldn't take it upon myself to put words in your mouth. But look, here's the proble—"

Liv slapped the desk and jerked back in her chair. "She's the problem! She wants to control my life and still thinks she can tell me what to do."

Harley held up a hand, not to cut her off but to calm her down. "I know how complicated family relationships can be, which is another reason why I try not to get involved, unless it is requested of me from both parties. I also don't assume the relationship between a parent and child is necessarily a healthy or unhealthy one, but the one thing I will always do is support you however I can." Harley noticed Liv's breathing appeared to be ramping down and made it a point to tread carefully. "You can tell me if it's none of my business, but because I have to file an incident report for my records, can I ask what your mom's name is?"

"Donna."

"Perfect. Okay, so here's where I see this going: without knowing the details of your specific situation, I've seen this scenario play out time and time again, and the one common thread is that they rarely resolve themselves. Many parents—especially moms—will never give up on their child, which is a beautiful thing, *except* when they don't understand that they can't control others or force someone into detox or treatment."

"And you wonder why I stopped coming around?"

"No, I get it, but that's the last thing we want," Harley said, scooting her chair forward. "I can't tell you what to do one way or the other, but I firmly believe it's imperative you have access to any services you need. So before you leave, is there anything else you need from me?"

Liv thought for a moment. "I know you already hooked it up, but maybe I should grab some more needles if that's okay?"

"Of course, and what about testing? Are you up to date on HIV and Hep C?"

Liv leaned back in her chair. "I think I'm good."

"Are you sure? What about STIs? If you're sexually active, you're here now and they're all rapid tests."

Liv looked away.

"Okay, no pressure. You know where to find us if you change your mind. Now, there's one more thing."

Pushing her chair back, Harley reached into her desk drawer and removed a vial of naloxone and a large needle. She only had a few vials left but knew Liv wouldn't be returning anytime soon.

"I've trained you on this before, right?"

Liv nodded and pulled her hood back over her head.

"Good, and here's some fentanyl test kits too so you can test your drugs. Also remember to do a test shot and if at all possible, never use alone."

Harley rose to leave and like a shadow, Liv tailed her into the lobby. She peeked into the exchange room, saw Ethan serving another client and turned to Liv. "Hang tight for one sec while I grab the rest of your supplies."

Once inside the exchange room, Harley set the vial of naloxone on the counter and started packing up another health kit.

"Hit me," the client said behind her, happy to play along.

"'*We have two lives, and the second begins when we realize we only have one.*'"

"*Confucius*? Isn't he played out?" The client returned his bag and offered Ethan a chance to redeem himself. "Come on, man, you've got to step it up."

Harley smiled, reached for a handful of cookers and did her best to quietly place them in the bag.

Ethan cleared his throat. "What about '*He who returns from a journey is not the same as he who left.*'"

"Doesn't that sound kinda sexist to you?" the client asked Harley.

Harley laughed, then buried everything beneath a shower of syringes and folded the bag closed.

Ethan, never backing down from a challenge, dug through the archives of his mind. "Okay, I got it: '*It is difficult to catch a black cat in a dark room, especially when it's not there.*'"

The client took the bag and hissed.

Harley patted Ethan on his back. "I'll be right back," she said, her tone light.

Returning to the lobby, she smiled at Lurch and the surrounding clients waiting their turn in line, then turned her attention to Liv. "I think this should hold you over for some time, but if not, don't be afraid to come back. If you prefer to send a body double instead, that's fine with me too."

"Sounds good. Thank you." Liv stepped away from the wall and reached for the bag with two hands.

With all of her strength, Harley refused to let go.

Donna was standing in the doorway, dragging a finger down her cheek. She stepped into the lobby, skirted past the line of clients and wasn't bothered with masking her disgust, even after she locked eyes with Harley.

"I'm taking you up on your offer," she said, jostling a thin stack of flyers in the air. "I figured . . . what the heck, right?"

Liv recognized her mother's voice behind her and went crimson. Harley reached out to grab her arm but was too late.

"Why won't you leave me the fuck alone?" Liv cried.

"*Olivia*?!" Donna dropped the flyers and rushed to her daughter, locking both arms around her torso. Her fingers clawed at her daughter's back. Seconds later, she was tearing Liv toward the exit.

"Let me go!" Liv screamed, fighting back. As she thrashed in her mother's arms, her screams echoed throughout the small space.

"Donna, stop!" Harley jammed the bag of supplies under her arm and tried to break Donna's grip with her free hand.

Ethan rushed into the lobby to assist yet he couldn't separate mom and daughter. Donna held on for her dear life, but the harder Ethan pulled, the more Liv panicked and screamed.

"Let go of her now or I'm calling 911!" Ethan shouted.

Donna twisted her grip and dug in her heels. "Call the frickin' cops! Maybe prison would save her along with every other dope fiend in here!"

A dark shadow stepped out of line. Having heard enough, Lurch hooked his arm around Donna's neck and collapsed her with control. As he pulled her down to the floor, Harley and Ethan fought to keep Liv upright, and once Donna released her hold, Liv pulled herself free from Harley, knocking the bag of supplies out of her arm. Syringes tumbled out of the bag, cascading down onto a stunned Donna. Liv stood there shocked, then started for the exit.

"Olivia, stop!" Donna demanded. "Someone stop her!"

Liv slipped on a flyer, regained her footing and bolted out the door. Count barked as she sprinted down the sidewalk, but she never looked back.

"Get your filthy hands off me!" Donna shouted, wiggling on top of Lurch.

Lurch looked to Harley for direction, who waited a moment to give Liv a running start. When she nodded, he eased his hold and Donna couldn't scramble away from him fast enough. Rolling onto her hands, she brushed a clearing in the needles and pushed herself off the linoleum. As she rose to her feet, she straightened her shirt and fought to catch her breath.

"Why did no one think to stop her? What is wrong with you people? Don't you see she needs help?" Donna stared at a number of clients and seemed surprised that none of them wished to be involved. With no response, she turned her attention to the ground. "And look at all this. Is this the '*help*' you've been giving my daughter?"

She was surrounded by syringes, along with a mess of cookers, twist ties and tourniquets.

A small glass vial rested against her shoe.

"And what the hell is this? Are you giving out drugs, too?" Donna raised her foot to get a better look. "Over my dead body."

Without hesitation, she brought her knee to her chest, stomped on the vial and stormed out of the door.

six
bridgetown

"Hey, Harley. You got a minute?"

"For you? Always."

Ethan closed her office door and took a seat at her desk. "You hanging in there?" he asked.

Smiling weakly, she said, "I imagine I'm still in a bit of shock, but yes, I'll be fine. Thanks for taking care of the mess out there."

"Honestly, the clients cleaned up most of it while I served the rest of the line."

She wasn't surprised. After years of working with countless clients, she knew if there was a population she could count on, it was her people.

"I still can't believe that just happened," Harley confessed. She thought back to some of the more memorable encounters with parents over the years, which there was no shortage to choose from. Yet across the board, they were mostly successful and professional, even with emotions running high and parents who openly admitted they couldn't support the idea of their child frequenting a syringe exchange.

"Honestly, I'm a bit surprised that you're surprised," Ethan said. "Are we not talking about the same woman here? The one who nearly ran me over with her car?"

"To be fair, I'm not entirely convinced she saw you."

"So being blinded by rage is a defense now?"

"Look, I'm not trying to defend her, but you have to admit that she showed up with some missing person flyers today. That meant she must have heard what I said yesterday and wanted to work with us. It doesn't make sense that she was trying to ambush Liv."

"Maybe so, but what difference does it make? She not only violated our space but our clients. She doesn't get a pass just because she's someone's mom. " He laid his palm on her desk. "Harley, I understand she's scared, but she's also unhinged. Who knows how Liv is going to react and what wounds of hers might now be reopened? And you know what people do best with open wounds, right?"

Harley nodded. "They fill them."

"What do you think about trespassing her from our premises?" Ethan asked. "We can still try to help her, just not here."

Harley waved him off and sighed.

"That's it? How are you always so nonchalant about these things?"

"No, it's not that. I'm thinking about how hard it is to trespass someone. I think the law requires Donna to be here on the property and refusing to leave when asked."

"Who comes up with this shit?"

Harley frowned. "Don't look at me. I don't write the laws."

He glanced at her with a raised eyebrow.

"Okay, I didn't write *that* law, or any other law, technically. But even with Good Sam, I was an advocate and happened to be in the right place at the right time. You know this."

"Well, maybe this is the right time to think about what other changes we can make here. We have the power to make a lasting impact."

She knew where this was going and would hear him out, but she didn't want to keep having this conversation every time someone stepped out of line.

"I've been here a long time," Ethan stated, "and I have always thought we needed to have security cameras installed. Imagine if we had caught the assault on camera? Liv could use the footage to get a Temporary Restraining Order against her mom if she wanted to."

"She can still get a TRO without the footage, but I don't think that's the solution."

"That's just an example, and I can think of *hundreds* of instances where having footage would have been useful. Think of how many fights we could have prevented after someone in line dropped their dope?"

"You mean after someone *thought* they dropped their dope?" Harley asked.

"Think of how many times a client has picked a fight with someone standing in line? It goes downhill faster than a Zoo Bomber and it could all be avoided by pulling the tape to clear the air. I can go on and on and on."

"I know you could, and I could add to your list if I wanted to. Trust me, there have been many, *many* times where having cameras would have proved useful, but I'm still opposed and will cite the same reason as always."

Ethan leaned back, removed his glasses and scrubbed them with his shirt. "You know the chances of that happening are so unlikely."

"Doesn't matter. It's not a chance I'm willing to take. The only way to guarantee a subpoena can't snatch our footage is if we don't have any footage to begin with. End of story, and ten times out of ten, I would take a random abandoned litter of puppies in the lobby or a whodunit mystery of lost dope over having to turn in evidence that ever assists with the prosecution or incarceration of a client."

"Fine. So what other options do we have?" Ethan asked. He leaned forward and picked up a paperclip. "Would you consider keeping the front door locked during business hours and only allowing known clients onto the property?"

"Like a rub and tug parlor?" She shook her head. "Never. We

have nothing to hide here, and being secretive would imply otherwise."

Ethan started twisting the paperclip. "Do you enjoy shooting down every idea I come up with?"

Harley's face softened. "That's not my intention, but you know me better than anyone else. This is our space, and for us to be the most effective at what we do, we have to keep our doors open to anyone who needs us."

Ethan jerked forward. "But at what expense? To where clients are getting attacked because there's no sense of security?"

"Of course not, but don't forget that you've had multiple opportunities to sit where I'm sitting and have always passed on the promotion. That was your decision, not mine, and I'm only in this position because you didn't want to deal with these types of decisions."

"No, you're there because I know I'm more effective out there," he said, pointing toward the exchange room.

"Agreed, and I'm more effective here, so why are we arguing?" Harley raised a palm. "I'm sorry, we're just . . ."

"Passionate? I know. Perhaps even a bit triggered as well, but where does this leave us? Because with this overdose event looming, my concern is we have enough to worry about without this added drama."

"You're right," Harley said. "It's a distraction, but as much as I hate to say it, I don't think Liv will be coming back soon."

"I think you're right, and who can blame her?"

Harley nodded. She leaned back in her chair, stared at the crumbly drop ceiling and made a mental note that the tiles needed to be replaced.

Ethan looked up for a second as well. "I hope she comes back, but in the meantime let's help those we can."

Harley's eyes dropped. "Are you thinking we can't help Liv?"

"Well, how can we help her if she doesn't come back?"

"We find her."

Ethan rubbed his face. "You don't think that'll—"

"Fine. I'll find her on my own."

"Since when do you chase clients?"

"I get it, but this time it's different. Liv was here for our services and left empty-handed through no fault of her own. It's not fair to her and it doesn't sit well."

Ethan shook his head. "I know you want to save them all and trust me, I do too, but some things are out of your control. What happened today wasn't your fault, my fault or even Liv's. Donna chased her daughter away, not you or anyone else. 'Accept the things you cannot change.'"

"I don't know how I feel about that," Harley said, pressing a hand to her temple. "Do you have plans tonight? Karissa has my car and she should be returning with naloxone in a few hours."

Ethan looked up with resignation. "What exactly are you asking?"

Harley shoved her last bottle of naloxone into her pocket, pushed back her chair and began rolling up the cuff on her right leg. "Can I borrow your bike?"

"Thanks again for locking up," Harley said as Ethan walked her through the lobby. "And depending on how long I'm gone, feel free to take my car home."

"Promise me you'll take care of my baby." He waved goodbye from inside the exchange and placed his hand against the glass.

Harley grinned. She knew damn well he wasn't talking about her.

In the distance, the reliable rumble of the I-5 Freeway brought Harley a sense of peace and assurance that life does go on. Locked to the bike rack near the entrance was a restored Schwinn track bike just begging to be unlocked. Though vintage, the bike was pristine and loved with a period-correct robin's-egg blue frame. As Harley had heard many times before, the only liberty Ethan took with the restoration was to convert the drivetrain into a fixie.

Harley removed the U-lock and dropped it into her backpack

next to the replacement supplies she had stowed away for Liv. She considered adjusting the saddle height but decided against it since Ethan wasn't that much taller than her. She swung her leg over the top tube with minimal effort and wrapped her fingers around the cushy drop bar. With a gentle kick and a wave goodbye from Ethan, she settled in nicely and glided to a slow roll.

After cutting into the road where the sidewalk ended, she hit cruising speed and attempted to become one with the traffic. It had been some time since she had ridden a fixed-gear bicycle and though it wasn't anything she couldn't handle, she knew deep down that she was not about that life. There was a certain beauty behind coasting downhill during a well-earned break that required a free-spinning rear wheel to do so, and pulling her feet from the pedals was a terrifying solution. Cycling, she believed, was never intended to be a recreational form of punishment, except for those who were into that sort of thing.

The snappy Portland air bit at her face, making her feel equally alive and anxious. As she soared down the street, there seemed to be no getting around her bare-bones plan. All she wanted was to find Liv and give her the naloxone she needed, but the problem was determining where to start. Checking over her shoulder, Harley changed lanes and hooked right at a stoplight, then leaned into the hard turn.

Liv had been a regular client at the exchange for a little over a year, and though Harley always strove to get to know her clients better, Liv was less forthcoming than others. Some clients jumped at the chance to share every minute detail of their life while others became withdrawn as soon as they hit the door. Since no memory surfaced from past conversations with Liv about her favorite hide-aways or haunts, Harley figured it couldn't hurt to head for the most obvious hangout.

She rolled up to the first jumping-off point and took in her surroundings. Pioneer Courthouse Square was a massive open-air plaza built from a sea of red bricks that gobbled an entire city block. Set in the heart of downtown, it was also the central artery for the Metropolitan Area Express Light Rail to flow in and out of the city. The MAX attracted all breeds of life, including street dealers who took advantage of its cheap fare and rapid access to the city.

Even though the plaza was vast, there was nowhere to hide, but on the surface Harley wasn't expecting to find Liv there. Instead, she was hoping to stumble upon someone who knew or saw something and was willing to share. As she scanned the horizon, her eyes skipped over the hustlers, corporate zombies and paid petitioners before settling on a group of street kids lounging on the steps across the way.

Her leg swung over the frame and she stepped off the bike. Cycling wasn't permitted in the square and since law enforcement had the power to make her job immeasurably harder, she refused to give them more ammunition than what they already had.

The calm stroll gave her a moment to catch her breath and stretch her legs. As she approached the crowd of street kids, whose ages ranged from early teens to late twenties, Harley smiled at the first recognizable face. A woman in a baggy long-sleeve shirt jumped up and stretched her arms out like a bat. Both sides of her head were shaved, and she sported a spiked faux hawk that could be tamed at a moment's notice.

"Ay-yo!" the woman called out, pointing a lollipop at Harley's bike. "Does Ethan know you jacked his whip?"

Harley looked down and laughed. She raised her foot to look for a kickstand, but there wasn't one to be found. She remembered Ethan had once referred to the accessory as sinful and then proceeded to justify "marginal gains" in an illogical rant. It sounded silly to her at the time, but as she stood there holding the bike upright by the saddle, unable to lay it down for fear of scratching the frame, she was convinced he needed professional help.

"I'm borrowing it for the time being, but that's not why I'm here. You got a second?"

The woman slid her sucker between her lips and bounded

down the steps. As she approached, she scanned Harley up and down, grabbed the handlebars and straddled the front tire with her thighs.

"Gully, I'm trying to find someone," Harley said with a pensive smile. "Do you or Rita happen to know Liv?"

"Let's back it up a sec. This Liv—does she owe you money?" Gully asked, rolling the sucker in her mouth with her tongue.

"No, not at all. I'm worried about her."

"Just checking. I'm not trying to get involved in some beef. But either way, the name doesn't ring a bell. As for Rita, you'll have to ask her when you see her next. We broke up a few weeks ago and I haven't seen her since."

Harley slumped her shoulders. "I'm so sorry. I had no idea."

"Ah, don't trip about it. It's probably for the best." Gully glanced around the plaza. "So what's this Liv look like?"

"Tan skin. Auburn hair. She's about my weight and your height . . . not counting your hair."

"Any idea who she runs with?"

"I don't know. I want to say she has a boyfriend, but every time I've seen her, she's been alone."

"Is she a beauty? Because this 'boyfriend' you speak of might actually be more of a pimp."

"She's attractive, but I don't know if she's a sex worker or not."

Gully let go of the bike. "What about a street name?"

Harley shook her head.

"I wish I could help, but I'm drawing a blank right now. If you want, I can ask the fam. Any chance you got a pic?"

Harley smiled and shook her head again.

"It's all good. If anyone knows her we'll find out soon enough." Gully retreated up the steps, melted into the crowd and poked her head into a few conversations. Someone would occasionally cast a glance at Harley and wave, but nothing seemed promising.

In time, Gully gave up. She stood at the top of the steps and shrugged.

Harley waved for her to come back but on the second time around, Gully wasn't in as much of a rush. "I should have told you this before," Harley said, "but there's something else you should know. Parts of California are being flooded with hot dope and ODs are skyrocketing. Can you put the word out and tell your people to look out for one another?"

"Sure, but you should know that we always look out for one another."

"Perfect," Harley said, smiling at Gully. "Also, I feel like it's been a while since I've seen you at Bridgeworks. Why don't you stop by tomorrow and grab some fentanyl test strips to check your meth, just in case?"

Gully pulled out her lollipop and licked her lips. "The reason you haven't seen me around is because I cleaned up." She beamed with pride, but the light soon faded. "But even though I can pass a drug test, I'm finding it hard to make ends meet. I had hoped to take a crack at this honest living shit, but I'm learning it's not as easy as it looks with certain felonies on my record."

"Job or no job, you should be proud of yourself," Harley said. "Do you want my advice?"

"Sure, fuck it."

"I would say to keep grinding and don't stop. Anything you want will come in time as long as you keep at it." Harley unzipped her bag and removed a few test strips from Liv's health kit, then passed them off to Gully. "I know you're not using, but can you take these for your friends? Also, you can still swing by the exchange to look at any openings we might have at Building Better Bridges. We've always hired felons and do so proudly."

Gully wiped her mouth. "I'll think about it, but no promises." She turned around and headed for the steps. "Oh, and Harley, I wish we could have been more helpful."

Harley swung her leg over the bike saddle. "Don't sell yourself short. Sometimes ruling something out is just as valuable as being pointed in the right direction."

. . .

The longer Harley searched, the less hopeful she became. She knew that tracking a ghost was difficult in the best of times but next to impossible when they didn't want to be found. And with Liv likely running scared, the chances of finding her hanging out in the open were slim.

For the very reason it would surprise Harley to discover Liv on the Waterfront Bike Path, she decided to give it a go. She also couldn't rule it out since benches near any body of water had a long and troubled history of calling out to wayward souls. But as poetic and timely as it would be to find Liv there, with each stroke she took toward the city limits, she couldn't dispel the sinking feeling that Liv had skipped town.

Tires whizzed on the rippled concrete below while Harley skirted around the occasional pedestrian. To her left was the pristine Waterfront Park—a field that paralleled the city and hosted various festivals and events all year round, weather permitting. A blurry guardrail blocking access to the last frontier was on her right, where a steep drop-off gave way to the numbing waters below.

As Harley appreciated the Willamette River, the current swept her gaze away and she caught herself contemplating impressive feats of engineering spanning both the river and the tests of time. Each bridge had its own beloved character, unique in breadth, tone, composition and mechanics, earning Portland one of its more palatable nicknames: Bridgetown.

Some time ago, Harley had gone through a phase and found herself immersed in the history of the collection of bridges. After reading that it was the oldest operational lift bridge in the country, she gained a deeper appreciation for the Hawthorne Bridge— the one she was currently leaving in her wake. Ahead of her stood the Morrison and Burnside Bridges, both double-leaf bascules able to give Evel Knievel's ghost a run for his money when raised. And not one to be overshadowed was the iconic Steel Bridge looming in the distance, a monstrous through-truss design with a double vertical-lift span where horse-drawn carts of old have been replaced by the city's all-electric Light Rail service.

But for all the life the bridges breathed into the city, Harley knew they could take a toll, especially when some of the most desperate and vulnerable called them their home. And because most of the bridges offered pedestrian access, little had stood in the way when jumpers turned to them in an irrevocable act of desperation. She glanced down at the water before focusing on the path ahead. Too often in the past had the cover of night made way for a grim discovery in the morning.

One bridge in particular, on the outskirts of downtown, had become known by its gruesome moniker "Suicide Bridge." Built in the 20s, it took decades of suffering and a series of back-to-back deaths for the city to bite the bullet and install suicide-prevention barriers. They seemed to help and dropped the death toll from two a year to none to speak of, but Harley feared this "remedy" only shuffled the problem elsewhere.

As she thought of troubled jumpers, she scanned beyond the shadows of the bridges for a bobbing carcass. After a quick scare, she pedaled past a log floating on the water and approached the last bench on the esplanade with a sense of relief that it wasn't Liv. She slowed and considered taking a rest, but knew it would be hard to pick up the pace after losing momentum.

Deep down, she feared Liv had boarded a train or bus to flee the city proper, which was what she would have done herself if she were in Liv's shoes. As the final few hours of daylight ran thin, she headed toward the world-famous Saturday Market grounds beneath the Burnside Bridge to try her luck there.

During the week, the market struggled to maintain its purpose, but on weekends, vendors set up shop and breathed life back into the open-air market. Tourists and Oregonians alike celebrated local ales, art, crafts and food while buskers and street performers dueled it out with one another for tips. Walking tours weaved guided groups through a compacted crowd and repeated tattered fragments of history. Drummers morphed into alchemists and turned plastic buckets and pots into a respectable payday—their hypnotizing polyrhythms could be heard for blocks, beckoning those with time to kill to explore the distant racket while it lasted.

Because it was a weekday, it was clear from afar that the market had closed and the neighborhood had resigned to life as usual. As Harley saw it, the unhoused population on the fringes hadn't moved in on the space but returned from being displaced and inconvenienced by the weekend shenanigans. Loosely anchored blue tarps breathed in the wind above wool blankets, camping tents and sleeping bags that were casually sprawled out. People were already settling in for another long night, staking a claim at any spot that was sheltered from the rain.

Harley sensed the onset of depression with not finding Liv and imagined that a change of perspective couldn't hurt. As she dismounted her bike and began walking around, one thing became abundantly clear—there was much more work to do. Year after year, the homeless population continued to grow and many of her clients existed in this world, one that was complex, grueling and challenging. But what Harley saw that others often overlooked was there was no shortage of beauty to be seen.

In front of her was a prominent and ominous concrete landmark with trash littered about. Skidmore Fountain always had a place in her heart, in part because it proved no fountain was ever too grand to double down as a wishing well.

While Harley walked past the treated waters, she couldn't resist glancing in the basin at the tiny treasure trove lying beneath the surface. Were it not so overcast, the pocket change would shimmer in the sun like a diamond mine, but like any natural beauty, one had to look deeper to appreciate the true value. Untouched beneath the prominent landmark—accessible to all and surrounded by so many in need—were countless wishes entrusted to the eternal spring that remained unmoved from where they first landed.

The humanity of seeing the untouched coins gave her a second wind, even though Liv was still yet to be seen and Harley was running out of places to check. She got back on the saddle, and in the middle of deciding where her final stop should be, her name was called out from above.

Harley craned her neck and looked up. Twenty-five feet above her, a head jutted out over the edge of the Burnside Bridge.

"Harley!" the man hollered again, waving a cigarette like it had a mind of its own.

She waved back and placed her feet on solid ground.

"You're never going to believe what just happened!"

She squinted and recognized him as a client of hers. Somewhere behind him, a stream of traffic overpowered his words.

"What's going on?" she yelled, cupping her mouth.

"Take a wild guess!"

Harley gave it her best shot. "You hit the Powerball, took the lump sum and want to donate your winnings to Bridgeworks?"

"No, even better!"

"I don't know, but come on down here. This hurts my neck!" she yelled.

"Can't. I'm in a rush." His hand disappeared, and a second later he was waving a white piece of paper. "I just passed my first drug test with flying colors! And no, I didn't have to cheat!"

She cheered him from below until he disappeared from view, then continued on under the bridge, emerging into gritty Old Town. Her handlebars rattled in her grip as she crossed over the Light Rail tracks. As she zig-zagged back and forth in a slow roll, she wondered where to head to next and ultimately settled on taking the long way home.

seven

city of roses

"I take it you didn't find her yesterday?" Ethan asked, dangling Harley's car keys in front of her eyes.

Beyond a deflated smirk, Harley didn't respond. Instead, she gave a lazy wave to both Mateo and the clients crowded on the sidewalk who were all waiting for Bridgeworks to open. She swapped Ethan's keys for hers and unlocked the front door. "Sorry I'm late, everyone."

"You're not late. You're just not as early as normal," Ethan said as he tailed her inside. "And don't be so hard on yourself. I'm sure she'll show up eventually."

"I take it you're talking about the girl from yesterday?" Mateo asked, following them both into the lobby. "The one who ran away?"

Harley grunted as she squatted to pick up the mail. "Yes. Why? Do you have any leads?"

"Not that I know of, though part of me is wondering if it's always so chaotic here?"

Harley locked the front door and turned around. "Not really, no. Though I will say most people who don't understand what we do assume that every day is some sort of shitshow like what you witnessed yesterday. The reality is much different. Things here have a tendency to remain fairly predictable and calm . . . up until they aren't." She glanced at Ethan, who bobbed his head in reassurance.

"Like I told you," Ethan said to Mateo, "most days are pretty boring, but that's how we like them. It helps us focus on the needs of our clients in real time with less distraction."

"And if you ask me, the most exciting part of this job is not the random drama, it's talking with clients and getting to know their story." Harley headed into the exchange room and the others followed suit. "You know, some of the best human interactions I've ever witnessed have happened right here in this very room."

"A hundred percent," Ethan said. "But don't take our word for it. Stick around long enough, and this place may change your life."

"It has been known to happen," Harley said. "Anyway, those clients outside aren't waiting around for their own health. Why don't you two go ahead and open up. You know where to find me if you need me."

Ethan motioned for Mateo to lead the way. "Want to do the honors?"

Harley hustled out of the room and headed into her office to discover a tall stack of boxes surrounded by a spread of clutter. Her finger tapped each box as she counted her way up the stack, starting from the bottom and ending with the cherry on top. She tore off a pink Post-it note and held it close, admiring Wayne's charm. Somehow, with all the fatherly advice he had readily at his disposal, instructing her to keep her head up seemed to be exactly what she needed to hear.

She stuck the note to her monitor with the intention of drawing strength from it in the coming days, only to realize seconds later that she was already in over her head. Even though she feared that a hundred vials—while more than what she could have ever asked for —was a healthy start, she knew it would be gone in no time and couldn't replace the shipment of naloxone she was waiting on.

Tucking a case of vials inside her drawer and balancing the

remaining boxes in her hands as if her life depended on it, Harley used her chin to steady the tower and cautiously headed back into the exchange room.

Mateo sprung forward when he saw her. "Here, let me help you."

Harley took a small step back. "Please don't," she said, not wanting to risk dropping the boxes. "But if you can open that cabinet for me, that'd be great." She did her best to motion with her eyebrows, then shuffled around the client dropping syringes into the Bio Bin and placed the entire stack into the cabinet, saving one box. Mateo finished counting out the client's syringes, rolled the bag shut and handed it off.

"Hit me," the client said, turning to Ethan.

Ethan pulled at his neck in thought, distorting his geometric tattoo. "Let's see. What's one I haven't used in a—"

"How about '*The best time to prepare for a calamity is when there is none.*'" Harley tucked her hair behind her ears and cocked an eyebrow. "What? You thought you were the only one who knows how to appreciate a good proverb every now and then?" She turned to the client. "Long time no see. How have you been?"

"Could be worse, I suppose."

Harley paused. "I feel you, and it's good to see you again. I wanted to tell you how sorry I am about your friend. From the amount of time I spent with him, I could tell he was a good man."

"That he was." As Pogue mulled over her words, something overtook him. "You know, I still can't believe I got picked up on those bullshit warrants. Had I been there for him, there's no way he would have—"

"I need to stop you right there," Harley said, reaching out to squeeze his shoulder. "I hate to cut you off, but you can't be doing that to yourself. It won't change the past and it won't help you move forward. You were a good friend to Smiley, and he knew it."

Pogue looked down at the floor and shook his head.

"Do you need anything?" Harley asked. "Counseling? A hot meal? A hug?"

"I'm sure I'll be okay."

"How are you on naloxone?"

He pulled out his empty pockets.

Harley flipped the lid of the box back and withdrew two small vials. "Please be careful out there. The last thing you need to do is beat yourself up over something that was out of your control." She held out the vials, waiting for him to take them. "Also, because these are scarce, please be sure to wait at least three minutes before administering a second dose if needed."

Pogue studied the vials for a moment then took them, tucking them away in his pocket. "I will, and if it comes to it I'll be sure to put them to good use."

Harley glanced at the door. "Also, since you're here, any chance you're interested in drug checking?"

Pogue looked around and seemed unsure.

"Because if you are, we can check what you have for traces of fentanyl."

"I would, but my tolerance is so high I need every last bit I have."

"We can test a used cooker so you won't miss out on anything."

Pogue shook his health kit. "Then there's the other problem: these are the only cookers I have. But if it's important to you, I'm happy to go and fix a shot then come back."

Harley thought of all the ways that plan could go wrong. She glanced at Ethan, who appeared to read her mind. "I tell you what. Why don't you follow me into my office so we can discuss this further and get out of their way? Does that work for you?"

Pogue nodded and they both headed for Harley's office.

He sat down at her desk and propped himself on an elbow while Harley cleared a spot to give them room to work with. She pulled her hair back to keep it out of the way.

"Before you begin, I need to explain that during normal times, I would never allow you to prepare a shot in my office. Also, we're only here for drug checking. I can't have you using in here for obvious legal reasons."

Pogue gave her a thumbs up, brought his palm to his mouth and produced a tightly knotted balloon. With his free hand, he pinched the knot and stretched it out until it snapped. Inside the rubber carcass was an orb sheathed in two white circles of plastic. He peeled off the first layer and let it drop onto the desk before transferring the innermost ball into his palm. As the plastic bloomed—exposing a black oily chunk surrounded by brown powder—he leaned forward and exhaled warm air on the powdered heroin. The heat and moisture from his lungs melted it all together.

"I don't think you need to worry about a breeze carrying anything away," Harley said.

"I know, but if I drop it . . ." He took one last deep breath and blew on the dope, then stared at the dark mass as though a hidden message would reveal itself.

Harley reached across the desk and grabbed his paper bag. She withdrew a small metal cooker not much larger than a bottle cap, then wrapped a twist tie around it and set it down in front of him.

"Is this your normal dose?"

He nodded, held his palm out and rotated his hand. The chunk of dope toppled into the cooker with a slight clunk.

Pogue opened a small bottle of water, dipped the tip of the needle into it and with the back of his thumb, withdrew the plunger to flood the chamber. Pointing the syringe at the cooker, he washed down his dope and gave it a second to partially dissolve. Fishing through his pockets, he found a book of matches and set them on the desk.

"Here, use this instead," Harley said, handing him her lighter.

He leaned forward and grunted. A flame snapped to life under the cooker, sizzling the water and melting the dope. He dropped a tiny ball of cotton into the fluid, spiked it with his needle and sucked it up like a sponge. After drawing the shot into the chamber, he set the loaded rig on the table and passed his cooker off to Harley.

She added a bit of water to the cooker, dipped it inside the fluid and proceeded to sing the Happy Birthday song.

Pogue looked at her sideways. "What the hell was that?"

"It was about fifteen seconds, give or take," Harley explained, placing the strip next to the cooker. She made small talk and didn't stop until two minutes had passed. When she flipped the strip over, she focused on a single line staring back at her, then closed her eyes and leaned back into her chair.

"Is it bad?" Pogue asked.

"It's definitely not good. If I were you, I would be very careful with this shot."

"Motherfucker," he seethed, leaning on his elbows. "Does it say how much fentanyl it's picking up?"

"I wish. These tests are sensitive, but they don't tell us whether your drugs were cut with fentanyl or only contaminated by it."

"So it could be safe?"

"Would you bet your life on it?" she asked. "I'll tell you what, give me your shot"—Harley held out one hand and opened her desk drawer with the other—"and take this."

She dangled a twenty-dollar note in the air.

"What's that for?" Pogue asked.

Harley stared at the bill. "This? This is what we professionals call *Contingency Management*. It's an evidence-based practice used to mitigate the risks of SUD."

"I don't know what that means but I'll take it." He reached out, handed her the syringe and grabbed the money before she rescinded her offer.

"While you're at it, take this too," Harley said, sliding more tests toward him. "I can't tell you how to live your life, but if you go back to the same dealer, please be careful. And I hope you consider checking every shot from here on out. It literally can't hurt." She paused for a moment. "Also, do you mind if I ask what part of town this came from? Southwest? Southeast? Northwe—"

"Right around the corner," Pogue said, jabbing his thumb over his shoulder.

There was a knock on Harley's door.

"One second," Harley called out, pointing toward the window. "Do you mean right around *my* corner?"

Pogue raised his palms. "Sorry, I meant around the corner as in down by the Square, not down your block. And it came from some new runner I just met, so don't worry about me"—he held up the folded bill to show it off—"I'll take my business elsewhere." He got up, tucked in his chair and opened the door.

"You guys about done or what?" Clay asked, walking into the room with a cocky stride. He leaned his guitar against the wall and turned to Harley. "Ethan said you wanted to see me?"

Pogue saw his opportunity to escape and took it, shutting the door behind him.

"Thanks for waiting. Please have a seat."

"That's okay. I'm kind of in a rush," Clay said, dripping with sweat.

"Please. I insist."

Clay pulled back the chair and made himself comfortable.

"Any chance you brought something for me to check?"

He held up a small baggie and gave it a shake.

"Perfect. Why don't you go ahead and fix your shot. All I need for testing is the empty bag with the residue."

Clay stalled a second. "With pleasure, but before I start, I just want to say that never in my wildest dreams did I think I'd ever be fixing up with you."

"You're not 'fixing up' with me."

"Sure feels like it." He placed the small baggie onto the table and smashed the contents with the heel of his lighter, then reached for a needle and removed the plunger before dumping the contents of the baggie into the chamber of his syringe. To finish the job, he sucked up a few drops of water, inserted the plunger back into the syringe and left a sizable air bubble inside.

"You don't cook your shot?" Harley asked, tasting a bit of her heart in her throat.

Clay smiled and shook his syringe like a martini. "Not usually, but it sure beats a straight bloodshot. It's also an easy way to fix on the go, and why waste time cooking a hit when water and a little blood can melt the meth in the syringe just fine. And as an added bonus, the shot's less diluted so it hits harder. It's a no brainer."

Harley pulled at her lips. "It almost looks as if you're trying to give yourself an abscess."

Clay rolled the syringe in his fingers. "Abscesses are inevitable, but I will say one downside to this method is that shots can come out a little crunchy."

She covered her mouth and had to look away.

"Sorry if that's TMI." He pushed the empty baggie across her desk and reached for a tourniquet.

"What do you think you're doing? You're not shooting up in here."

"Why not? You just watched me make my shot."

Harley folded her arms against her stomach. "You think I'm joking?"

"Honestly, I don't know what to think. I mean, I'm getting mixed signals over here. Aren't you the one always saying we should never use alone?"

"Yes, but I can't have you using here. Besides, we haven't even tested your meth."

Clay fidgeted in his seat.

"Trust me, if it was legal and we had systems in place to hopefully keep you safe, we wouldn't even be having this conversation. But we're not there yet, and you know this."

Clay stared at the loaded shot in his hand. "Whatever. I can wait, but let's not drag this out any longer than we have to. Just test the bag or do what you need to do so I can get on with my day."

Harley raised a finger. "Hold that thought. I'll be right back."

She jumped up, left the room and returned moments later with a styrofoam coffee cup filled to the brim with water. "As I'm sure you know, meth is water soluble." She filled the used baggie with water, dissolved the residue inside, then dumped the fluid into the cup, swishing it back and forth to mix it. Repeating the same process as before, she gave it a couple of minutes and flipped the test strip over.

She held back a sigh. "The good news is this tested negative for fentanyl, but I would still be careful."

Clay grabbed his loaded needle and slipped it up the cuff of his sweater. "I'll do my best."

"That's all you can do. Be safe out there for me." Harley walked around her desk, opened her office door and followed him into the lobby. She watched as he hustled out onto the street, then turned her attention to the thinned-out line.

"Can I have everyone's attention? I just checked some heroin that came back positive for fentanyl, so please be extra careful out there and pass the word on to your friends."

Heads nodded all around.

"Also, we'll be doing drug checking until we run out of tests." Harley pointed toward the drug checking room and realized she was pointing with Pogue's loaded syringe.

Harley headed into the exchange room and saw a familiar face at the Bio Bin. She excused herself, reached around Sadie and squirted the contents of the syringe into the bin.

Ethan stared at Harley until he caught her attention. Seconds after they locked eyes, she knew he was deeply troubled.

"Sadie," Ethan whispered, "can you please tell her what you just told me? Can you do that for me?"

Harley tossed the empty needle into the Bio Bin. "What's going on? Is everything okay?"

"With me?" Sadie asked. "I'm doing fine, but I can't say the same for the body I discovered this morning down by the river."

Harley took a step forward. "What do you mean you discovered a body? As in a dead body?"

"Well . . . yeah. Is there any other kind?"

Harley blinked slowly. "Was it a female?"

"Nope. Try again."

"Okay, Sadie, I don't want to play games right now. I need to know if you're telling me the truth because if someone is dead out there, the cops need to be—"

"Called? Don't worry. They were."

"By you?"

"Who else would call them? The guy's no longer with us and no one else was around."

"Okay, okay." Harley ran through a multitude of scenarios before something wasn't adding up. "Wait. How long ago was this? I'm surprised the cops let you leave the scene."

Sadie snorted and covered her mouth. "Come on. I may be many things but stupid's not one of them. I waited until I got into town before calling them. There's no way I'm going to get involved in something like that again."

Ethan leaned back against the counter and crossed his arms.

"Okay, so let me get this straight," Harley said, placing her hands on her head. "You came across a body this morning and just left him there?"

Sadie shrugged. "What was I supposed to do? Bring him with me?"

"Please Sadie, I'm being serious here."

"And I'm not? Think about it. How could I have called for help if I don't even own a phone?"

Harley exhaled. "Fine. Now you said this was by the river. Was the victim a jumper?"

Sadie shook her head. "No. I found him in the bushes not too far from where I make camp."

"Can you be a little more specific?"

"Morrison Bridge. Eastside. I'm happy to take you there if—"

"Is there a problem or something?" a client asked, poking his head into the room. "Some of us have things to do."

"Out!" Ethan ordered, pointing into the lobby. He jumped forward and backed the client out of the room.

Harley leaned into Sadie. "How exactly did you know he was dead? Did you check for a pulse?"

Her voice went flat. "Put it this way: once you've seen rigor mortis, you *never* forget it. That, and the flies in his mouth were a dead giveaway."

Harley stared at Sadie and inhaled through her nose. "Do you know his name? Age?"

"Nope to both."

"What about the cause of death?"

"From the looks of it, I'd say he overdosed."

Harley swallowed. "What makes you say that?"

"A few reasons. He's a known user, and there was a syringe in the dirt that looked to be recently used." Sadie held up her arm and tapped the side of her wrist. "And the other dead giveaway was the caked blood on his hand . . . right here . . . right above the ugliest rose tattoo I've ever seen."

eight
john doe

Alone in her office, Harley stared at her phone and reminded herself not to fall into his trap or lead with her guttural response when talking with Chief Deputy District Attorney Kip Morris. When they first spoke many years ago, she chalked up his condescending tone to reflect a sure sign of burnout and compassion fatigue, but as his slights continued—typically without provocation—she became convinced he actively sought enjoyment in talking down to others.

As the head of Division Three, which was one of four special departments within the District Attorney's Office, Chief Morris had his fingers on the pulse of multiple divisions. Division Three aimed to take on white-collar crimes, identity theft cases, gambling rackets, human trafficking operations and the kicker—illicit drug rings. He only answered to his boss, the Elected District Attorney Harry Dalton.

Harley picked up her phone and made the call she wasn't looking forward to. "Good afternoon, Chief. How have you been?"

"I'm well, Ms. Hammond. And you? Staying out of trouble and keeping your clients in check I hope."

"We're hanging in there," she said, rolling her eyes and wishing he could see her. "The reason I'm calling is I just got word about a potential overdose this morning. I'm wondering if you've heard anything on your end, and if so, would you be willing to share?"

"I'm always happy to help, but it depends on what OD you are talking about."

Harley went quiet for a moment. "There was more than one?"

"Two so far. One non-fatal and the other . . . not so lucky."

Harley expelled an audible breath. "The fatal overdose? Was it near Morrison Bridge?"

"Sure was. Eastside, just beyond the bike path."

She buried her forehead in her palm. "Any chance you have the investigation report on hand?"

"I do. Is there something in particular you are interested in?"

"I want to know if any drugs were recovered. If so, I'd like to check them for fentanyl. If no drugs were recovered but any supplies were—such as a used cooker—I'd like to test it to rule out the role fentanyl may have played in his OD."

"Can I ask why?"

"Why what?"

"Can I ask why it matters?"

Harley paused. "You're wondering why I'm trying to confirm how he died?"

"I guess I don't see what difference it makes. An OD is an OD, right? Besides, if you want to do it right and not take short-cuts, it still runs around six weeks to receive the toxicology results."

Harley breathed into the phone. "I know how the process works. Just please let me know if there's mention of either drugs or drug paraphernalia."

"Sure thing," the Chief said. "I'm just making sure we're on the same page, is all. Okay, back to the police report. It appears the classification is 'sudden death' due to a 'possible drug overdose'."

"Do we have a name?"

"Just another John Doe."

Harley tapped her desk with her knuckles. "What about witnesses?"

"My understanding is that this one was called in anonymously. Maybe *that* was your little birdie?"

Harley sighed, making no effort to conceal it. "What can you tell me about the narrative? I'm interested because I need to figure out if this is a one off event, or if we're about to see a surge of tainted dope decimating our streets. Trust me, we wouldn't be having this conversation if we had streamlined toxicology reporting. But for now, all I have to go off on is what I can gather and what you're willing to share."

"So you're expecting an influx of overdoses?"

"I hope not, but California is being slammed so hard it's about to fall into the ocean."

"Well, the good news is that other than this, I haven't seen a notable spike in overdose clusters, so I wouldn't be too concerned yet if I were you."

"Thanks, but I have a feeling I'll always be concerned for my people, especially when sixty percent of overdoses aren't reported and get handled without involving first responders."

"Sounds to me like another statistic we can't do anything about. Let me ask you this: have you spoken to any healthcare practitioners?"

"Not yet, but I will as soon as we're done here. Speaking of which, can we please go back to the narrative?"

"Fine by me. Okay, the officer talks about responding to a reported deceased male on the embankment near the Morrison Bridge. He says the deceased had obvious lividity in his face, but saw no evidence of foul play."

"Nothing about drugs recovered on his body?"

"Not yet, but hold on. Alright, here it goes on to say that the Medical Examiner arrived, examined the scene and determined the death was likely accidental, due to a possible drug overdose." The Chief paused. "Okay, I found what you're looking for. It says, 'Sergeant Wilhelm searched the property of the deceased and found several used syringes. No further evidence at this time'."

"And if they found dope on his body they would have noted it, right?"

"Correct, but I don't see any mention of narcotics anywhere in the report or on the Property Receipt. I guess that's not what you're wanting to hear?"

Harley frowned and considered what to divulge to Chief Morris. Even though they were worlds apart, their ability to work together could ultimately save lives. "Alright, here's what I've heard: allegedly, our 'John Doe' robbed a dealer for a lot of heroin recently. I'm merely trying to understand whether he died from injecting tainted dope or from going overboard."

"Interesting. What more intel do you have on this dealer?"

Harley was quick to respond. "Like I said, that's all I heard."

Chief Morris went quiet on the other end. "Ms. Hammond, I understand you're used to operating in a pretty little bubble over there on the fringe of society, but in case you forgot, let me remind you about how the real world works, okay? For the most part, honest citizens don't protect murderous dealers and enable them to victimize others down the road. I pray that's not what you're doing, especially if you care about your clients as much as you claim."

Harley stared at the phone in her hand and debated how good it would feel to punch it. She also understood there was a greater disconnect between them than what she could ever comprehend, perhaps attributed to the Chief's lengthy career spent prosecuting all manner of drug offenses. But she refused to play into his demonization of street dealers as heartless killers, especially when she knew far too many who turned to selling or facilitating drug deals as a means to support their own habits.

"Like I said, I don't know the dealer's name. I guess for our purposes here, he's just another 'John Doe.'"

"Of course he is," the Chief said. "Anyway, back to the body. I don't think it means anything that the police didn't find drugs on this individual because they weren't the first on the scene. My suspicion is whoever discovered him and phoned in the call likely rolled the body beforehand. We see it all the time. And if that's not the case, then based on the infestation of vagrants over there, the deceased would've been picked over long before the police arrived." The Chief gave it a moment to sink in. "Trust me Ms. Hammond, I know you struggle to see the good in everyone, but I know them better than you think. I've been prosecuting them long before you came around, and I can say with absolute certainty they're little more than opportunists who only look out for themselves. These people only care about two things: not getting sick and not going to jail. Beyond that, nothing else matters."

There were so many things Harley wanted to say, but she believed deep down it would only fall on deaf ears. She considered reminding Chief Morris that the strongest people she had ever met walked through her doors on a daily basis. She wondered if he would be receptive to her experience that those with the least knew how to give the most. There were other choice words she could think of too, but he would only find a verbal lashing amusing from where he sat and so she forged ahead. "What can you tell me about the other overdose? Do you have a name?"

"One sec," he said. "Let's see. Okay, here we go. It looks like it was a 'Jackson Bardot'."

Harley squeezed the back of her neck. "Where was he taken?"

"It doesn't say, but OHSU is the closest hospital to the scene, so I imagine that's where he's at unless he refused transport, which happens more often than what you might think."

For the first time, Harley took no pleasure in hanging up on the Chief.

"No, it's 'D-O-T', as in *Bardot*."

"Okay, I'll try it again." The woman on the other line paused. "And ma'am, I do apologize, but what did you say your name and position was again?"

"Harley Hammond. I'm the Health Services Program Coordinator at the Bridgeworks syringe access program. I'm not sure if you've heard of us, but we're a subsidiary of Building Better Bridges. I'm also involved with a local task force created to respond to toxicological events here in Oregon, which includes members from your own OHSU, as well as other area hospitals and acute care centers throughout the city. We also work with a multitude of medical experts, drug treatment specialists, police participants and government officials."

"You have members here at Oregon Health and Science University?" the woman asked. "I had no idea, but it's relieving to know people are working on this issue because sometimes it feels like a war zone up here. I'm sure you can imagine how frustrating it can be to feel so helpless." The woman went quiet for a moment. "And unfortunately, I'm about to feel helpless again because HIPAA prevents me from disclosing a patient's information without a release."

"I totally understand," Harley said. "More than you know, but can I still leave my name and number in case someone . . . *asks for me*? We're talking about an urgent matter here with potential far-reaching ramifications."

"I can't make any promises," the woman said, "but I'll see what I can do."

"Thank you so much." Harley hung up the phone and took a second to calm her nerves. She rolled her head in a tight arc, then reversed directions and focused on taking intentional breaths. It took another moment for her to gather herself and a few seconds later, she opened her eyes.

For years Harley had done everything in her power to represent her clients who were too often under-served and marginalized. It was a good start, but she feared it was never enough. All the training, organizing, outreach and discussions kept the fire alive, but she knew if a significant overdose event were to blindside the city, most clients would never know what hit them.

She got up to stretch her legs and check on Mateo, even though she knew he was in good hands with Ethan. The lobby had long grown empty and lifeless, with only a scattering of muddy footprints to show for a grueling day's work.

When she stepped into the exchange room, Harley caught Mateo and Ethan sitting on stools, packing plastic bags with little cotton bullets that were added to every health kit. She didn't want to interrupt their conversation but figured they could save their discussions on the terraforming of Mars for a future date.

"Thank you both for planning ahead," she said.

Ethan sealed a bag and opened a new one. "That's what we're here for. Right, Mateo?"

Mateo pointed to his pile of baggies on the counter which overshadowed Ethan's small stack. "A classic example of the student becoming the teacher," he joked.

She did her best to keep a straight face. "Well, that's mighty impressive, *young grasshopper*, but wait until you're pitted against the real master." Her smile burned brightly for a moment. However, it didn't linger. "Hey guys, I have some bad—"

Her ringing phone interrupted her, and she didn't miss a step. She hustled through the lobby and back into her office, grabbing her receiver on the third ring.

"Hello?"

"Harley? Hey, it's me—Jack. And Sophia's here, too," he said, his raspy voice a shadow of its former self.

"Jack? What happened? Are you both okay?"

"Fuck if I know. We were at the McDonalds on Burnside and slipped into the bathroom to fix. I don't remember everything that happened. All I know was I did a shot and it was like I got smacked with a bat."

"Were you able to test your drugs before using?"

He paused. "No. I was in a rush because I was so sick. I'm sorry, I know I'm an idiot. I even had those stupid tests on me too."

"There's no need to apologize and you're not an idiot. No one's perfect, which is why we encourage drug checking and in doing a test shot *when* possible. So I take it you didn't do one?"

"The test shot? According to Soph, that *was* the test shot. It may have been a little on the heavy side, but it still dropped me. She said she freaked out and immediately hit me with naloxone, but by then the manager had already called the PoPos." Jack paused. "I'm just glad neither of us are in jail, even though we're both sicker than shit right now."

It took a moment for Harley to absorb what she was hearing. "I'm so glad you're both safe. I can only imagine how you must be feeling right now."

"Put it this way: every time I feel like it can't get any worse, it does."

"I know it sucks, but at least you're alive and will get through this. Also, because of the naloxone, your opiate binders are blocked and I question if you can get high right now if you wanted to." Harley then chose her next words carefully. "I know you must've jumped through a lot of hoops to get your dope, but if you decide to use again, please do whatever you can to keep one another safe."

"I can promise you we won't be touching that dope again. Soph flushed everything we had before the cops came."

"I think that was probably a wise decision. So what are your plans for when you leave?"

Jack took his time to respond. "Obviously, we need to figure out how to get well, but after that I think it's time for us to get a move on."

Careful not to put words in his mouth, Harley gave him time to finish the thought.

"We were just talking about this before the nurse came in," he said. "I don't ever want to feel like I feel today. I think we want out, and maybe we can pick up where we left off and travel the country like we first set out to do. It's been a long time coming, but I think we're done."

"Done with what? Using?"

"Yeah, but I know we can't do it alone."

"If you're asking me for my help, I'm right here. Is there something specific you had in mind?"

"Can you help us get into detox? Last I heard the wait-list was a week or so. Since we'll have to stay well until we get in, hopefully we get accepted sooner than later."

"No promises, but I can definitely put in a good word for you two."

"Thanks Harley. That means a lot."

"But before I make the call, there's one caveat you need to know about: the detox center has a long-standing policy against admitting known couples. I know a lot of couples don't disclose they're in a relationship during triage, but know that if you go that route you'll be in different wards and won't get any updates on one another."

"I'll talk to Soph, but it should be fine."

"Perfect. Let me make the call. Can you hit me back in ten?"

"Of course."

Harley hung up the phone and hit number six on her speed dial. Tapping her desk helped ease some stress, but based on what she'd learned it sounded like the tainted dope had hit the streets.

A raspy voice interrupted the fourth ring. "Talk to me."

"Serena, how's it going?"

"Peachy as always, but gimme a sec, okay? Don't go anywhere."

Harley put her landline on speaker and set her phone in the cradle. Leaning back in her chair, she rested her hands on her head and listened to the raspy voice lecturing someone on the other end.

"Salvation Army, Tuesday morning, 8:00 a.m., and be there early, okay?" the woman said. "And write that down so you don't forget. They don't hand out second chances over there." The woman coughed loudly and picked up the phone. "Okay hun, how can I make your life easier?"

"I'll keep it short. I have two clients—a male and a female—both hoping to secure a medical detox. They're admitted to a hospital right now following an overdose, and though I would never take a bed from anyone, I'm wondering if you have space for them?"

"Darlin', you know how it goes: we always have open beds, just never the funding to fill them. Last I checked we're scraping by at around sixty percent of our operational capac—" She burst into a coughing fit. "Excuse me. Capacity."

"I understand, though you know I always have to ask."

Serena cleared her throat. "Do you think they're committed?"

"I think they're not only committed, but scared, so I don't blame them. I'll put it like this: I've been serving this couple for years, and this is the first time either of them has asked for help."

"*Couple?*"

"Yeah, this 'couple' of clients."

"Sure," Serena said sharply. "Do you know if either of them have been seen here before? And if so, have they left AMA?"

"Not that I know of, but I didn't ask."

Serena cleared her throat one last time. "Alright, we'll figure it out when they get here. I can't get them in today, but if they can make it here for triage tomorrow, they should have a good shot. Just make sure they're here tomorrow morning at 6:45 a.m. sharp, and have them ask for me."

"Thank you so much, Serena. You're the best."

"Don't thank me. I'm just doing my job."

nine
planeteers

"Are you sure?" Ethan asked.

"It has to be here," Harley said, staring into the Bio Bin. "Jack's been using for years and we both know he's not a lightweight. I imagine his tolerance is through the roof and since he wasn't incarcerated recently, I don't see where it would have dipped." She thought for a moment longer, then locked eyes with Ethan. "You used to use. What do you think? Has a test shot ever dropped you or anyone you know?"

"No, but that's only because we never thought to do them. Back then, fentanyl and other synthetics weren't on our radar."

Mateo tossed his last bag of cottons onto his pile. "At least they're both getting into detox, and I think it's really cool that you're in a position to help them out."

"Well, we still have to see what happens," Harley said. "A lot can change between now and tomorrow morning."

"You can say that again," Ethan blurted. "So do you really think it's here?"

Harley didn't want to admit it and picked up the closest thing within reach. She scanned the clipboard and flipped through page after page of client codes. The seemingly random characters were not lost on her as she translated one line after the other into a face she wanted nothing but the best for. "I do believe it's here. I would have loved to test their dope to confirm, but it got flushed down the drain. However, everything I've heard and seen so far makes me want to say yes."

"Then that's good enough for me. I trust your instincts." Ethan said, turning to Mateo. "And just so you know you're not beating me, okay? I'm giving you practice to perfect your rhythm."

Mateo sneered and turned toward Harley. "So what's the plan? Get everyone into detox?"

Harley tilted her head. "I wish it were that easy, but not everyone who uses drugs has a desire to stop using. And even if they did, there's not enough beds or funding to detox them all at once."

"Not enough funding? Why not?"

"Well, to start we're not in Canada or Portugal, remember? Here in the US, substance use disorder has been criminalized for so long that most of our treatment opportunities are packed with people who don't even want to be there. In fact, as we speak, I'd bet many of the patients at the local detox center are mainly there to stay out of jail and not to get clean. They're jumping through hoops to satisfy some judge, boss or probation officer, which ultimately means they're exhausting the limited resources available."

"Basically, they're taking a bed away from someone who wants it," Ethan added. "But you can't really blame them either, because otherwise they're either fired or back in jail."

"I don't understand," Mateo said. "I mean, I see why someone would want to stay out of jail, but it seems so wasteful."

"I think 'wasteful' is a nice way to put it," Harley said. "In my mind it's disgusting and almost criminal because in a backward way, our system *prevents* people from getting help when they want it. It's one of the main reasons Jack and Sophia would normally have to wait a week to get admitted."

Mateo's face went limp. "That's so broken. Back home, we figured this out decades ago and realized it doesn't make sense for people to enter treatment under duress or pressure. And if the data is there to support this, then why would anyone ignore it?

What's the point of doing the same thing over and over again, expecting different results."

Ethan shook his head. "You do know that's the definition of insanity, right?"

"To be fair though, it helps to be specific about who we're talking about," Harley said, "because the pressure can come from all angles. If we're discussing the rule makers, a lot of them want to get reelected and take a 'safe' position. If we're talking about family or friends who may have been hurt by people who use drugs, they could offer an ultimatum with good intentions but little understanding on how often they result in longstanding resentments. Whatever it is, it's complicated, and guess who suffers the most for it?"

"It goes without saying," Ethan said.

"One would hope, but who knows? Maybe all of it will change one day, but for now we have to do the best with what we have. So while we love the Portugal model and how it focuses on seeing people with drug problems as people with an illness instead of as criminals, we still have no choice but to work with the tools at our disposal, and detoxing everyone is not even *in* the conversation." She lifted her hand and counted out her options. "Naloxone. Overdose training. Drug checking. Outreach. Education."

"In that order?" Mateo asked.

Harley thought for a second. "Not necessarily."

Ethan nodded. "Speaking of which, where are we at with the re-up on naloxone?"

"We're still back-ordered and we're apparently not the only ones. I heard it's because of a recent recall, so we only have the vials from Wayne and any we may have stashed away."

"A *recall*? You're shitting me," Ethan said. "What the hell for?"

"Something about the vials themselves—most likely the rubber. I meant to ask, but I was more concerned about switching our order over to nasal sprays. So we have some on the way and that's good news there, but since they're so expensive we'll still be short on what I would prefer."

"But at least we'll have something," Ethan said. "And how many do we have left?"

"Maybe forty kits, so eighty vials."

Ethan looked puzzled. "So even though we're running low, you're still sticking with two vials per kit?"

"I don't think there's another option, especially with what we're up against. People should have a backup in case one dose isn't enough," Harley said while heading toward her office. "And after talking with Jack, I honestly wonder if two doses may be cutting it close since fentanyl often requires more naloxone to reverse than heroin."

Harley sat down at her desk and struggled to wrap her head around something she never wanted to think about. Every close call was one more reminder her clients existed in a world where second chances were slim. She wondered if Jack understood how lucky he was compared to so many others who didn't share the same fate.

A long-forgotten truth popped into her mind. There once was a time when she had a finger on the pulse of how many clients had passed away each month, week, or sometimes even each day. But over the years it had become almost a full-time job to track each death, even when friends and survivors were forthcoming with what they knew. Added to the workload came the extra step of confirming the purported details—usually starting with arrest reports and ending with the Medical Examiner—because things weren't always what they seemed. While rare, the streets occasionally got it wrong and as unsettling as it was, Harley had grieved a number of clients over the years only to have them show up one day alive and well.

When she was first promoted, Harley had hoped to attend the memorial of each client who passed away but once faced with hundreds of deaths a year, it soon became an untenable situation. The love was there, but her time—as it had turned out—had limits. The solution then was to stage a public memorial twice a year to honor and raise awareness about the countless lives that were lost to the overdose crisis. The installations were scheduled around both Black Balloon Day and International Overdose Awareness Day. They aimed to be impactful and inspirational, serving as both closure and a reminder that the work was far from over.

Harley smeared away the onset of a tear and wiped it on her jeans. She knew it was unhealthy to internalize despair but often failed to hold her ground when faced with such pain, especially in private. To have a sense of responsibility for something beyond her control demolished her in a way that both ate at her and kept her going.

She reached for her keyboard and started an email when frantic yelling made her fly out of her seat. She followed the panic echoing out of the exchange room, and witnessed Mateo in front of Asher, holding both of his wrists to restrain him. Ethan stood behind Asher with a tight grip on his shoulders, hoping to calm him down.

"What the hell is going on here?" Harley snapped. "I leave for one minute and—"

"He's trying to reach into the bin," Ethan called out, refusing to take his eyes off Asher.

Asher turned to Harley with despair in his eyes. "I dropped my balloons in the bin and they're not letting me retrieve them. How was I supposed to know my dope was in my bag?" Asher tried to wiggle his hands free but Mateo was in complete control. Asher twisted his head in an effort to face Ethan. "And he's the one who told me to dump them!"

Ethan turned to Harley and shook his head. "All I said was that I trusted him and he didn't need to count out his syringes. I didn't tell him to—"

"That's bullshit!" Asher cried out, struggling to break free.

Harley stepped forward, grabbed Asher's arm and brushed Mateo's hands away. "Everyone, calm down. Relax and take a deep breath."

Asher panted and slowly lowered his arms.

"Okay. Much better. There's no reason for anyone to freak out and get upset. By definition, every problem has a solution." Harley leaned over and peered into the Bio Bin. It was close to full with an entangled nest of uncapped syringes, used cookers, tourniquets and other paraphernalia, with no dope sitting on the surface.

"Ash, how much dope did you throw away?" she asked.

"All of it!"

"No, how much dope?"

"Four balloons."

"Asher, how much *money* are we talking about?"

"Sixty bucks worth."

Harley relaxed a little. "Okay, that's not too bad. I think I have forty bucks in my desk. If not, I can run to the ATM."

"I have some cash on me too," Ethan said. "It's not a big deal."

"Maybe to you it's not," Asher said as he straightened out his hoodie. "My dealer's done for the day, so where am I supposed to go? Do you expect me to trust the dope these other dealers are pushing?"

Harley thought for a moment before nodding in agreement. "You're right. You can't really put a price on knowing your source," she said, turning to Ethan. "You know, I think this bin is looking pretty full. Want to help me change it out?"

Ethan sighed, then turned around and reached for a pair of latex gloves.

"Mateo, I hope you don't mind, but our insurance only allows trained staff to swap out the Bio Bin for liability reasons. Can you and Asher wait in the lobby for a moment?" Harley gave Asher a slight nudge toward the door. "Take it easy, okay? We won't be long."

Asher shuffled backward and Mateo closed the door behind him.

"What a day, huh?" Ethan asked as he opened the door on the side of the Bio Bin to remove the sharps disposal container. He set it down on the linoleum and peered inside.

"Can I squeeze behind you?" Harley asked.

She opened a cabinet, removed a replacement container and set it next to the other one on the floor. With a quick yank, she pulled a drawer out and fished for a set of tongs.

"This is probably a one-man job," she told Ethan, taking the gloves from his hands.

"Fine by me," he said, taking a step back.

Harley widened her stance and peered into the container. She wasn't sure what to expect, but as she began transferring syringes from one container to the next, she caught a flash of two red balloons that immediately disappeared from sight. Her eyes burrowed deeper into the pile. Each needle told a story, some of pain and frustration, others of tension and release. In a perfect world, each needle would have only been used once, but she knew this world was far from perfect.

Her tongs snapped, and she stuck to the plan by withdrawing one small pile of syringes at a time. She noticed many of the needles were worn down to where the markings had rubbed off. A multitude of uncapped syringes bounced light off their barbed tips, tips that tore and tugged on flesh depending on the direction they were headed. A number of needles were caked with coagulated blood while others had unknown fluids inside. She transferred them all into the bin as her tongs took a final bite.

"Did you find them?" Ethan asked.

Harley looked down. The bin was empty, except for a few stray tourniquets and four red balloons. "Sure did, and now Asher won't resort to unfamiliar dope."

Harley snapped her tongs and extracted the balloons from the bin, one at a time, inspecting them for any punctures. She placed them on the counter and locked the tongs. "Would you like to do the honors, or should I?"

. . .

Harley shut her office door, leaned against it and fluttered her eyelids closed. Even though she wiped the balloons with an alcohol pad and Asher was ecstatic to get his dope back, it still felt like she was handing him a loaded gun. The moment reminded her there were certain aspects of her job that would always be challenging and there was no getting around it.

When the compulsion to open her eyes hit her, Harley looked around her office and studied the items she so often overlooked. Scattered about were gifts from clients she'd accepted over the years, little tokens of gratitude that meant the world to her. Behind her desk was a series of homemade thank you cards sporadically pinned to the wall, along with unframed photographs held in place with the edge of a thumbtack to avoid puncturing the picture.

Some of the photos featuring her as the subject were taken when a client threw an arm around her and caught her off guard. But as much as she loved those live-action memories, her favorites were the pictures she wasn't featured in. These were photos of clients who had made it out and took it upon themselves to report back from the other side. One showed a former client attempting to wrap her arms around a giant sequoia on a national park road trip that she had always dreamt about. Another was of a newborn nestled in the arms of a shocked new dad who survived years of self-medicating his suicidal ideologies. Every photo was an inspiration she could draw upon whenever her motivation was lacking, and knowing some clients would make it out in one piece was reason enough to never give up.

Harley sat down at her desk and reached for her phone to call her boss and bring her into the loop. April's approach was about as hands off as they came, and would've rubbed Harley the wrong way had she not understood the standoffishness was not born of a lack of interest. Harley knew her syringe access program was only one branch of Building Better Bridges, a broader non-profit corporation under April's control. The mother organization had fingers in various social enterprises, from providing housing to jobs and recovery outlets to healthcare. In many ways, because daily operations at Bridgeworks were often uneventful, April was afforded the ability to turn her attention and focus elsewhere.

Harley made the call and placed the phone to her ear.

"Hi. This is the voicemail of April Cartini, Director of Operations with Building Better Bridges. If this is an emergency, please—"

Click.

She hung up on instinct without leaving a message for April. It was a habit she had developed after realizing April rarely listened to her messages in favor of returning any missed calls directly. But she decided this was a message worth leaving and punched in April's number once again.

Beep.

"Hey April, it's me. Can you call me when you get a chance? I'm worried we may be seeing a surge of heroin contaminated with abnormally high levels of fentanyl as reported in California. If this is the case, the sooner we get on the same page, the better it is for everyone."

Harley placed her phone in the cradle but didn't withdraw her hand because she'd been meaning to call Wayne back. He was another one she also never left a message for, but only because she couldn't remember the last time he had missed one of her calls. She lifted the receiver and waited for Wayne to answer.

"Harley? To what do I owe the pleasure?"

"The pleasure is all mine, Wayne. I wanted to call to tell you just how much we appreciate the naloxone down here. It couldn't have come at a better time, but there's one minor problem . . ."

"Oh yeah? What's that?"

Harley shuffled some papers on her desk. "I'm not seeing an invoice anywhere."

"That's what I was forgetting. Thanks for the reminder—I'll add it to my list."

She knew exactly where he was going with this. "Wayne, I don't expect these for free. If you don't want me to repay you, then at least allow me to return the favor with some intranasal sprays? I have a rush delivery coming in tomorrow."

"You're sweet, but unfortunately I just don't have the space to store them. I promise you though, if it turns out we could use the help, you'll be the first to know. And about the bill, we can always figure that out down the road but right now, I'm much more concerned with how you're holding up down there."

"I'm scared to death but I also know you're trying to change the subject on me. Haven't I told you that your old tricks won't work on—"

"There's no shame in being scared. None at all. It's a perfectly natural response to the stressors we're surrounded with. After all, we exist in this unnatural existence that forces us to face our fears and come to terms with the great unknown. It's even happening as we speak: just this morning we caught wind of a few overdose clusters and it doesn't look pretty."

Harley rubbed her face and gave up on going backward. "Same here. We had at least one fatality, but it's too early to tell if it's because of fentanyl or not."

"I say if you can't rule it out, you have no choice but to plan accordingly. Unfortunately I think we lost a few clients, not to mention a flood of overdoses presented to the emergency room," Wayne said, his voice turning nostalgic. "I know it's been a long time, but do you still remember what I told you on the first day you walked into my exchange to volunteer?"

"All I remember was that it was a lot to take in."

"I warned you that this profession would be taxing but I made the promise that as long as we stuck together, we could get through anything."

Harley shut her eyes and nodded. "I know you'll always have my back, but maybe what I'm really scared about is not getting the community support we need. Or maybe that's not the problem and what I'm really worried about in the end is . . . no one cares."

"I wouldn't say no one cares, though let's be honest—many don't. But you know this already. People who use drugs are stigmatized to no end and there are enough people out there who have been hurt in ways that blind them from being able to see the mental health crisis for what it really is."

"I wish your words made me feel better."

"Sometimes the truth hurts. Listen Harley, like it or not we both know there are people who still assert the disease of addiction is a choice, and therefore people who use drugs deserve whatever fallout comes their way, up to and including death. They are happy to disregard trauma as the common thread tying so many underlying issues together. They are content to continue on with their closed minds. Why? Because it's *easy*. For these people, they've discovered it's more convenient to turn a blind eye to the issue because it *doesn't affect them*. That is, until it hits too close to home, of course."

Harley filled her lungs and held her breath until an airiness permeated her mind. Tension in her neck eased, and her head draped forward with controlled release, pinning the phone to her shoulder. She had no words. Instead, she listened to Wayne's steady breathing and admired his calmness.

"Harley, it's important to not let something like someone's faulty worldview stand in your way. Besides, I've seen you at all the conferences, tabletop exercises and simulations. You should know that even if everyone's hearts were in the right place, the community is under-prepared to appropriately respond to a crisis like this. It is what it is and our efforts don't need to be appreciated to be critical."

"But don't you ever feel like our efforts aren't enough?"

"All the time, because truthfully they're not. Remember, we exist in an ever-changing climate with new threats that require new solutions and new ways of thinking, yet the reality is we're restricted by laws and perceptions that often work against us. And after thirty-five years of service, we still find ourselves in situations that require us to be reactive, where we are not in the seat of power. We are not the dealers and we don't have a safe and legal supply to distribute, though the case can be made that safe supply is not the perfect answer since Big Pharma will get involved and do what they do best." Wayne took a deep breath, then slowly exhaled. "Either way, I'm not trying to be a downer here because we as a community have a lot to be proud of. Remember, a lot of things we get away with today used to be illegal a decade ago, so we're making real progress here and standing on the shoulders of giants. So my advice is to follow their advice: keep your ears to the streets, keep doing what you're doing and like I always say, keep your head up."

Harley hung on his every word and sat upright in her chair. "Wayne, I'm so glad I caught you today. Thank you for being you."

"That's what I'm here for. Be safe down there, okay?"

"You got it."

Harley put down the landline, reached for her cell and scrolled to a group text with Ethan, Gabby, Karissa and Mateo. She flipped through a special keyboard and sent out an "Our Powers Combined" GIF with Captain Planet reigning in the Planeteers.

ten
do not resuscitate

"Now that's a sight to see!" Harley exclaimed as she slowed her stroll toward Bridgeworks. The whole team was gathered on the sidewalk near the entrance, their backs pointed toward the cool breeze. As she got closer, she noticed all four of them were crowded around a box of donuts, haggling over their favorites.

"May I?" Harley asked, peeling back the lid to the box. "Seriously? No one saved a Bacon Maple Bar for me?"

Ethan turned his back on her and swallowed the evidence.

Feigning disappointment, Harley reached for a Raspberry Romeo and closed the box. "On the bright side, it looks like you all got my text yesterday. I'm glad to see everyone could make it this morning. You have no idea how much this means to me."

"Actually, we do." Karissa opened her purse and pulled out a small paper bag. "That's why we wouldn't miss it for the world. Care to trade?"

Harley's eyes welled. "I love you so much." She exchanged her donut for the Bacon Maple Bar while she had the chance. "Alright, let's do this."

Ethan wiped his hands on his pants and backed away from the door.

As the first one inside the exchange, Harley cleared the mail off the floor so no one would slip. She popped into her office, dropped the mail and donut on her desk, then returned to meet her team in the lobby.

"Alright, here's where we're at: I don't want anyone to panic, but I'm fairly confident that the hot batch of heroin is in the city. In fact, I stayed up most of the night trying to work out a game plan to complement the task force's response because I'm concerned it won't be enough. So this is what I came up with, and as always I'm open to input." Harley pointed at both Gabby and Mateo. "Can you two handle the exchange room today? It's business as usual, except let's ensure every client who doesn't have an overdose kit leaves with one. Each kit should include two vials of naloxone, a couple of intramuscular syringes and some fentanyl test strips."

"You sure you still want to go with two vials per kit?" Ethan asked.

"I think we have to, but the good news is we're overnighting in nasal sprays and they should arrive today. But as you know, they're significantly more pricey than the injectables so we can only afford so much." Harley turned back to her team. "In case anyone is upset about the switch, just tell them the injectables were back-ordered so it's the best we can do."

Mateo looked at Gabby and raised his hand. "I'm sorry, but I'm confused. Why would anyone have an issue with the sprays? Aren't they easier to use and more effective?"

"They can be, but people are creatures of habit and are often resistant to change, especially if they've been saved by the injectables before. It's that old 'if it ain't broke, don't fix it' mentality."

Ethan turned to Mateo. "Not to mention, once the sprays run out and we revert to stocking the injectables again, clients will spend the next year riding our asses over no longer carrying the sprays."

Harley agreed. "Now that's something I won't lose sleep over. Okay, so while Gabs and Mateo run the exchange room"—she turned to Karissa—"can you help out with messaging on the line? I worked up some drug alert flyers last night for you to hand out.

It would also make sense to start asking about any recent overdoses and compiling what data we can."

Karissa nodded. "I think that's a great idea."

"Perfect. Also, please do your best to keep the line flowing so no one is put off by a long wait." Harley pointed toward the closed door next to the exchange room. "And Ethan, that leaves you to do drug checking in the testing room if you don't mind."

"Sounds like a plan," he said. "And if any dope pops for fent, I'll try to pinpoint where it was bought so our clients can steer clear."

Harley didn't seem hopeful. "It sounds great in theory, but remember not to press for dealer names. We don't want to put anyone in a hard spot, now or ever."

"But what if they volunteer the information?" Karissa asked.

"That's beyond our control, but in the event that happens, keep it between us, okay? In fact, it'll probably happen since most of our clients truly care about one another. I can't tell you how many Hep C tests I've done where someone said they wanted to get tested to prevent passing something on to their friends."

"So true," Gabby said mildly.

"It's too bad our dope's not branded out here like it is on the East Coast," Karissa said. "Imagine how easy it would be to isolate this whole thing."

"It would definitely help." Harley looked down and rubbed her chin. "I think that's pretty much it. I'll be available for any counseling or referrals as needed, especially if anyone is trying to get into detox. If that happens and I'm talking with someone, feel free to interrupt us. Any questions?"

Mateo looked around and raised his hand. "What happens when we run out of naloxone? Should we plant the seed that clients should think about detoxing?"

"That's a rough one because a key principle to harm reduction is accepting that drug use is a part of our world, which also means accepting that some people will continue to use drugs despite certain risks."

Mateo glanced at the other team members to judge their response.

"Think of it this way," Harley continued. "I'll talk to any client about community resources all day long if they want them, but our job is not to condemn or condone people for the decisions they make. So instead of suggesting to a client that they stop using drugs and hightail it to a detox or methadone center, we give them information to be safer as they go about their business. This is where tools like drug alerts, drug checking, doing a test shot, never using alone and learning rescue breathing come into play, and that's where we're most effective. Make sense?"

Mateo shrugged. "I suppose."

"I tell you what: give it time and decide for yourself. Just remember that if someone is looking to get into detox, it's a different story. Bring it to my attention and we'll work it out." Harley looked at the clock. "Alright, we have a few minutes before we open up. Let's do our best to start and finish strong."

After finishing up with the clients in the lobby, Karissa made her way outside to work down the line. Beyond the string of clients snaking down the sidewalk, the street was dead with no passing vehicles or foot traffic to speak of.

"Lurch!" Karissa hollered as she spotted her favorite client. She rolled up a paper and shoved the rest of the stack under her armpit. Gripping the tube with both hands, she swung it mindlessly through the air like a lightsaber. "Ffffkrrrrshhzzzwoom . . . woooom . . . wooooooom."

Her eyebrows sharpened as she swatted down imaginary laser pulses flying at her head. As she moved in for the kill, the Force spoke to her and her blade stopped inches from Lurch's face.

"Bbvvvvvnnn," she hummed, disengaging her imaginary weapon with a straight face. Karissa transferred the paper hilt to her palms and raised it to Lurch's eye level as a peace offering.

Lurch plucked the scroll from her hands and unfurled it.

"I know you already know most of this," Karissa said, "but thanks for humoring me. I'll sleep better tonight if you review it and let me know if you have any questions."

Lurch squinted and read the ordinance.

Drug Alert! There is toxic dope in the city. Fatalities have been reported. Follow these steps to reduce the risk of overdose:

1. *Start low, go slow and do a test shot.*
2. *Use drugs from a trusted supplier.*
3. *Check your drugs for fentanyl BEFORE using.*
4. *Never use alone and when possible, stagger your shots 15 minutes apart.*
5. *Carry Narcan or naloxone on your person and know how to use it.*
6. *Call 911 if you witness an overdose. The Good Samaritan Act will protect you from drug possession charges and certain warrants.*

Please report any overdoses, fatal or non-fatal, to Bridgeworks. Contact us at 503-555-1239.

When Lurch finished reading, he rolled the paper up again and tried to hand it back to Karissa.

She held up her hand. "It would make me feel better if you kept it," she said. "But if you really don't want it, maybe you can hand it off to someone who does?"

Lurch shrugged and placed the paper in Count's mouth like a bone.

"That works too, but in all seriousness please be safe out there, okay? I know you fly solo, but it wouldn't hurt to find a using buddy. And sorry, Count doesn't count." She crouched down, threw her arms around the dog and looked up. "Also, if you happen to have any dope on you, Ethan is doing drug checking in the testing room." She turned her attention back to Count. "Now *who's a good boy?*"

After giving Count a final scratch, Karissa passed Lurch and stepped toward the next client. The man—craggy-faced and frail—rested his weight on a hand-carved walking stick. Damaged silver hair poked out of a bandana cinched around his weathered scalp.

"Here you go. Please look this over and let me know if you have any questions," she said.

"What's this?"

Karissa looked down at the paper she was holding. "It's a drug alert with a number of ways to stay safe and—"

The man brushed the paper away with the side of a calloused palm. "Not interested," he mumbled.

Karissa stood there puzzled. "Are you sure? It's just a few tips that could possibly save the life of you or your friends."

The man sneered at her with what little teeth he had left. "What makes you think I've got friends?"

"Friends, enemies . . . doesn't matter, but even if you're a lone wolf it's still good information to have." She gave the paper another shake but he refused to take it. "I bet if this saves your life, you'll come back to thank me."

"Oh yeah?" the man crowed. He leaned his walking stick against his hip and scratched at the top button of his flannel shirt. With arthritic fingers, he yanked his shirt open and exposed a faded DNR tattoo. "Can you read? Like I said," he hissed, "I'm not *interested.*"

"Why in the world would I lie to you?" Ethan asked, leaning forward in his chair. He reached out, flipped the foil packet over and tapped on the instructions. "See this part labeled 'Result Interpretation'? One line is *positive.* Two lines are *negative.*"

"I see that, but I don't understand why this shit keeps happening to me." Pogue gazed at the packet, then back at the test strip. "Can we test it one more time?"

"We could, but I barely have enough tests to go around and it won't change the results. I hate to say it my friend, but this is where we're at."

"That's such bullshit," Pogue mumbled.

Ethan sat back and raised his hands in the air. "Hey man, don't shoot the messenger."

"Sorry, it's not you I'm mad at." Pogue slid a hand under his hair and clutched the back of his sweaty neck. He looked around the cramped space, which had the makings of a repurposed closet. In the center of the room was a stainless steel table and two maroon plastic chairs. The walls were windowless and draped in posters encouraging all visitors to get up to speed with their HIV and Hep C status.

While Pogue sat there steaming and pondering his next steps, Ethan leaned forward in his chair and started disinfecting the table. Centered before him was a roll of antibacterial disinfectant wipes and a pair of rosette succulents Harley had purchased from the Saturday Market. Her reasoning, she had explained, was that adding a splash of color might offset the distinct and very prominent interrogation room vibes.

Plants or no plants, it was a familiar setting for Ethan, who over the years had tested hundreds of clients for blood-borne diseases and sexually transmitted infections in the confined space. Recently, Pogue had worked up the courage to sit through a finger prick antigen and antibody test. Though he got the news he had hoped for, not everyone was afforded the same fate. Many of the clients had no choice but to come to terms with life's rapid curveballs, and Ethan often admitted it was one of the hardest parts of his job.

Suddenly despondent, Pogue hunched over in his chair and allowed his hair to flop onto the table. "So what am I supposed to do? Everywhere I turn it's bad dope after bad dope."

"I wish I had the answer," Ethan said. "But unfortunately the best I can do is reiterate these recommendations." He tapped the drug alert flyer on the table.

As Pogue scanned the handout, he could hear laughter seeping through the thin wall from the exchange room. "What does this mean, 'Stagger your shots'?" He flipped the paper around and tapped the list of safety tips.

"It's part of never using alone. The idea is to find a buddy to use with so you can watch out for one another. The two of you would then space out your shots at least fifteen minutes apart and alternate back and forth. That way if one of you ODs, the other can administer naloxone or call for help."

"But this assumes I have friends."

"Right, but you can still space out your shots if you're alone. However, don't forget that in today's world, technology is your friend." Ethan whipped out his cell, brought up his contacts and wrote down a number on the drug alert flyer. "For example, you can always call the Never Use Alone organization at 1-800-484-3731. If you reach out to them before you use and give them your name and location, they'll stay on the line and send an ambulance your way if you stop responding."

Pogue flipped his hair out of his face. "That's really cool, but it also assumes I have a phone."

Ethan rubbed his forehead. "If you have any access to the internet, you can also reach them through Facebook Messenger. But the takeaway should be that there are options out there. You just need to find the one which works best for your current situation."

"So what other options do I have? If it's so important that I should never use alone, can I use here?" he asked, looking around the room. "I'll be quick, and trust you won't call the cops on me if I overdose."

Ethan twisted in his chair. "Actually, I would. Assuming I'd let you use here, which I won't."

Pogue crossed his arms and leaned back. "You'd really call the cops on me?"

"Maybe I should clarify," Ethan said. "We call 911 *any* time there's an overdose because it's dangerous to assume opioids are the only factor. We always ask for EMTs, but once we make the call the response is out of our hands and based on our location, they typically send the police too."

"Okay, so if B-SAP is out of the question, what about you?"

"What about me?"

"Can you be my using buddy? You're in recovery and I'm sure you know how to respond to an OD."

"Being in recovery means a lot of things, and having strong boundaries is at the top of the list."

"So why not turn your back on me and not watch?"

Ethan sighed and smiled weakly. "That's not the issue here, Pogue."

"Oh, it's not?" Pogue asked, stuffing his hands into his pockets. "I bet it must be hard, huh?"

"What must be hard?" Ethan asked, his eyes narrowing.

"All these years clean and you still don't trust yourself. Can I ask how often you feel like using?"

A commotion in the room next door distracted Ethan. "You're out of line, Pogue. I think it's time for you to go."

Pogue pushed his chair back and stood up. He reached for the drug alert flyer, studied it for a moment and tossed it in the trash as he saw himself out.

Mateo looked up and greeted a couple as they strolled into the exchange room. Lean and confident, the boyfriend's dark hair dangled out from beneath a black mesh trucker hat with a curled-up bill. Front and center of his cap was a circular embroidered patch with an oddly alluring image—a flying saucer abducting a featureless human silhouette, all encircled by stitched letters that read "I want to leave." A barbell septum piercing dangled from his nose and bounced off his mustache every time he smacked his chewing gum. Both he and his partner wore matching sleeveless vests covered in patches that one of them had hand-stitched to the denim. His was buttoned up the front, but there was no way she was closing hers any time soon.

The girlfriend was short and wore a Bridge City Sinners shirt that barely stretched over her belly. She was well into her third trimester and clasping her stomach between both hands. Her boyfriend had an arm hooked around her neck, but he wasn't putting weight on her. Balanced in his free arm was a water-logged skateboard that had lost its pop ages ago.

"Oh. My. *God!*" Gabby cried, shuffling forward. "*Juju?* Look at you! I haven't seen you in forever! And what is this?" Gabby tugged the flaps of her vest and opened them up to get a better look at her bulging belly. "May I?"

Juju bounced her chin excitedly, grabbed Gabby's wrist and placed her palm onto her belly. Gabby went quiet for a moment, then looked up at the boyfriend. "This is so amazing. Congrats, Mack!"

He beamed with pride and smacked his lips.

"So? Do you know yet?" Gabby asked.

"Looks like we're having a mini-Mack," Juju said.

"I bet you're so pumped!" Gabby tucked in her chin and clutched her hands to her chest. "Did you already have a baby shower? If not, I'm happy to help plan."

"I think the girls are planning something special," Juju said, shifting side to side. "You're invited, of course."

"And speaking of showers"—Mack whiffed his armpit—"I could use one after today's jam at Burnside." He laughed and nudged the nose of his skateboard at Mateo.

"So a happy, healthy boy," Gabby said. "I'm so happy."

"He came as a surprise, but he's in good hands. He'll have a large street family that'll have his back."

"Oh, no doubt," Gabby said, patting Juju's belly once more. "Thank you so much for popping in to see us. Will you promise to bring him back when the time is right?"

"Of course we will," Juju said as she leaned into Mack.

"And before you go I'm sure Harley would love to see you two if you have time."

"We always have time for Harley. Is she here?" Juju looked into the hallway at Harley's closed door.

"Yeah, she's in her office. Want me to grab her?"

Juju dismissed her with a wave. "That's okay, we'll catch her on our way out, right after we grab a couple of kits and exchange these." Juju opened her purse and pulled out a plastic bag of dirty needles. Her belly nearly bumped into the Bio Bin as she counted out her syringes.

Mateo glanced at Gabby.

"That's twenty-six," Juju said. "Fulls please."

Gabby wiped her mouth and forced a smile. "Do you remember your client code?"

"God, it's been so long. I think it was JUSA . . . F . . . 0914?"

"Perfect, thank you." Gabby turned to Mateo. "Twenty-six fulls, please."

Mateo didn't respond.

"Mateo?" Gabby whispered.

He crossed his arms. "Who are they for?" he asked.

Mack stopped smacking his lips and smiled. "Who are *what* for?"

"The syringes," Mateo said. "Who are the syringes for?"

"What the . . ." Mack turned to Gabby and chuckled. "Is this guy serious right now?"

"He's new, Mack. Let me handl—"

"Are they for you?" Mateo asked Mack as he took a step forward. "Or are they for her?"

Gabby held an arm out to cut Mateo off. "Alright, that's enough, Mateo. I'll take it from here."

Mateo reached over her arm and pointed at Juju's belly. "For your baby's sake, these better not be for you."

"Gabby, what the fuck?" Juju muttered.

As Gabby spun around to press Mateo back, Mack grabbed Juju's shoulder and pulled her out of the way, taking her place. "Listen *asshole*, how we live our life is none of your fuckin' busi-

119

ness, okay? We've been coming here for years and that's not how this shit works. You work at a fuckin' *syringe exchange* for fuck's sake. We bring you needles, you exchange them. Got it?" He lifted his skateboard and pointed it at Mateo.

Gabby covered her head and ducked under the board as Mateo brushed it out of his face.

"You might not care if she kills your baby, but I do," Mateo growled.

Mack grimaced and shoved Mateo with his free hand. At the same time, Gabby lunged at Mateo and wrapped her arms around him, tying him up.

"Mack! Stop it!" Juju begged, tugging at the collar of his vest.

Hearing the commotion, Ethan scrambled into the room. He struggled with Mack for a moment and jumped in front of him.

Mack raised his skateboard again but Ethan blocked it. "You have no fuckin' idea who the fuck I am!"

Harley appeared and approached Mack from behind, taking control of his arm. "Mack. Mack! Hey, *Mack*! Relax, okay? It's me. I need you to relax."

Mack jammed a finger at Mateo. "Fuck you, motherfucker!"

Mateo raised his fists but Gabby slapped them down. "Don't even think about it. I'll take you out myself if I have to."

"Let's go, Mack," Harley urged, pulling him back into the lobby. "It's not worth it. You're about to be a dad."

Gabby jammed a finger in Mateo's face. "Don't you fucking move," she snapped, scrambling to make two kits while Mateo leaned back against the counter. She shoved a number of needles into the bags without counting them, ducked around Ethan and ran into the lobby.

A minute later, she returned with Harley.

"What the fuck was that, Mateo?" Gabby asked in disbelief.

"Do you really expect me to give needles to a pregnant woman?" Mateo asked, turning to Harley. "How could I live with myself?"

Harley shot a glance at the next client in line before turning back to Mateo. "If you sincerely want to know the answer, follow me."

"Go ahead and have a seat." Harley ripped the chair back harder than what she intended to, and Mateo lunged forward to catch it. Out of the corner of her eye, she watched as he settled into the chair, then she turned her back to him while circling her desk.

She gave him all the time in the world to get comfortable, but he seemed incapable of processing what had just happened. Her eyes tracked his palm while he rubbed small circles on his temple before he finally caved to the thick silence.

"I couldn't do it, Harley. And if that means I'm not the right man for the job, so be it." He spread his knees and studied his Chuck Taylors.

"Mateo, look at me. I only caught the tail end of what just happened, but if you were picking a fight with my clients or passing judgment on them, that's the last time that ever happens, understand?"

Mateo slowly shook his head. "That's not how I see it, but don't worry about it happening again. I quit."

"You can quit if you want to and I won't hold it against you, but if that's really your decision, at least hear me out so you leave with all the facts. Otherwise, the real tragedy here would be for you to miss out on a painful learning experience."

Mateo cocked his head. "What could there possibly be to learn? We both saw how far along she was, right?"

"I know it's a difficult situation for all involved."

"Well, it doesn't seem to bother you much," he said, scooting his chair forward. "I know you must be jaded to this line of work, but I'm certainly not. I have no problems serving clients who are consenting adults, but there's no way in hell I won't stand up for a child who doesn't have a voice."

"I understand how you feel, and this is exactly why we need to be having this conversation right now."

Mateo crossed his arms and leaned back in his chair. "What is there to talk about?"

"The *bigger picture*, even if it's painful and unsettling to see."

"What are you talking about?"

Harley leaned forward. "I understand what you're feeling because it was very difficult for me to serve my first pregnant client, but I hope you can trust me when I say the situation is more complicated than you may think. For example, are you a doctor?"

He hesitated. "Of course I'm not, but I don't need to be a doctor to know she's endangering her baby's life."

"We'll get to that in a second, but first, what about NAS? Ever heard of it?"

Mateo slowly closed his mouth.

"Neonatal abstinence syndrome?" Harley asked, cocking an eyebrow. "It's when heroin passes to the fetus through the placenta during pregnancy and a baby in the womb becomes physically dependent on the drug." She gave him a second for the information to sink in. "It's potentially lethal to the baby, and the same goes for placental abruption and preeclampsia. I know it's hard to hear, but there are reasons no pregnant mother should ever quit using drugs abruptly. The effects from withdrawal can be deadly—dangerous to both mother and child—and requires medical supervision to get through it safely."

"I don't want to hear this," Mateo said, shifting in his seat.

"No one does, but that's the point." Harley sat up straight in her chair. "I've known Juju for years, and if I had to guess I would say she most likely relapsed before getting pregnant and then couldn't quit. There's also a chance she relapsed after she got pregnant, but I would still bet she didn't know she was with child at the time. Either way, I know it's never easy for a pregnant client to walk into our exchange, but I'm grateful she had the courage to show face because it affords us the chance to help her, not to mention the opportunity to have the discussion we're having right now. So with all of that in mind, what would you rather do? Pick a self-serving hill to die on, or jump at the opportunity to help her protect her child by minimizing risky behaviors *while* connecting her with professionals who know how to navigate this situation."

Mateo sunk into his chair.

"I'm not trying to make you feel bad, but this is how I came to terms with this dilemma so many years ago," Harley said. "Another way I learned to 'live with myself' was by realizing how dangerous it is for a woman to contract Hep C or HIV while pregnant because there's a chance she can transmit the virus to her baby."

Mateo touched his forehead and nodded in agreement.

"Lastly, if there's even the slightest chance someone is considering treatment or detox, we want to be here with open arms and referrals. For example, just this morning I heard that two of our clients are now in detox after one of them overdosed recently and almost died. That came from a referral, and if Juju decides she wants the same opportunity I can connect her with professionals to get her on either methadone or buprenorphine like that." She snapped her fingers. "And she can get the prenatal care she needs at the same time, too. Who knows? Maybe Mack checks himself into detox while she's at it? But if none of that happens, and all we do is educate them on the dangers of using while pregnant, that's still a win. Do you see where I'm going with this?"

Mateo took a deep breath. "Honestly, none of this crossed my mind. I don't know what to say."

"You don't have to say anything, but for what it's worth I do feel like I owe you an apology. Normally we'd run through these scenarios in orientation, but as you know we've been a little distracted with a—"

There was a loud knock on the door.

"See what I mean?" Harley asked. "Let's end with this: only you can decide where you go from here, but I speak for everyone when I say we can use your help. If you want to leave, at least you have a better idea of the challenges we face here. If you decide to stay, know that there's a real opportunity within these walls to make a difference."

"I think it's pretty obvious I have a lot more to learn," Mateo said. "I'll see myself out for now, but I'd like to rescind my resignation if that's okay with you."

Harley pushed back her chair. "Actually, I think we could both use a little fresh air."

Mateo stood up, opened the office door and found himself facing a leaning tower of boxes. Somewhere behind it, Karissa was determined not to be buried alive.

"Thanks, Mateo," Karissa said as he helped lighten her load. They set the boxes of nasal sprays on the floor next to the door and she dug in her pocket for a delivery receipt. "I signed your name for you, Harley. I hope you don't mind."

Harley's eyes glistened as she sized up the delivery. "As of right now, that would be the least of my worries."

eleven
street team

The instant Mateo stuck his neck out onto Market Street, a determined breeze hit him in the back and billowed his shirt. A sudden shiver tore through him, but he recomposed and instinctively fell in line behind Harley to block her from the hounding wind.

"That's mighty chivalrous of you," she called out over her shoulder while her hair blew free every which way. "But not needed really. This weather's grown on me."

Mateo heard her but still followed in her footsteps, holding his backpack at his side as a wind block.

"I'm serious," Harley insisted, waving her hand at her side, demanding he join her as an equal. "Knock it off and get your ass over here!"

The assault didn't let up until they turned onto Park Avenue and as if on cue, the pummeling immediately died down. They found themselves flanked by condos and buildings on both sides that gave way to a dark corridor ahead. Shadows grew long in the few remaining hours of daylight where sun rays struggled to penetrate the dense canopy above. Historic oak and maple trees muffled the rumble of distant vehicles. Their leaves, like a riot in the sky, drizzled dew on pedestrians each time a healthy gust shook their limbs.

"Have you been here before?" Harley asked. Her eyes were

drawn down to a puzzle of concrete pavers breeding moss between their seams.

"Only in passing unfortunately."

Harley's gaze leveled out. "This is the South Park Blocks. It's like Portland's own mini version of Central Park." She pointed uphill. "It runs from College Street to Salmon Street, eleven city blocks in all. I know I'm probably not the best tour guide, but if I'm not mistaken, this is considered Portland's first 'official' green space."

The two continued on, occasionally bumping shoulders until they approached an old man feeding pigeons from a bench. Once again Mateo fell in line behind Harley, but even in their efforts to proceed with caution, it only took a single startled pigeon to spook the whole group and their collective consciousness burst into an amorphous cloud. Harley ducked and covered her head, apologizing as she ran ahead, but the man barely noticed. Instead, he stuck his fist into a paper bag and cast a handful of maize onto the path to reclaim his scattered flock.

Mateo caught up to Harley. "So are you really here to get fresh air, or are you looking for someone in particular?"

"I'm still hoping we find Liv, but I also figured since Bridgeworks is in good hands I could show you how effective a good street team can be." She reached out and tapped his backpack. "Thanks again for carrying these overdose kits. Outreach is so important to what we do not only because it's where it all started, but because not everyone takes advantage of our services. Believe it or not, these are the people I worry about the most because it's a struggle to get information to them in an emergency."

Mateo slapped a light pole and scanned ahead. Damp leaves were scattered everywhere and in the distance, he made out a larger-than-life bronze statue encircled by a series of benches. Most were unoccupied, but one bench in particular drew Harley in. Mateo settled into her periphery as she approached the three men.

"Here you go. Take this and thank me later." Harley handed

each man a copy of the drug alert flyer and asked if they knew Liv. When the men shook their heads and studied the handout, Harley realized Mateo had drifted away, so she beckoned him to join them.

Upon approach, she grabbed his shoulders and spun him around, then unzipped his backpack and withdrew three small boxes, each containing a pair of Narcan nasal sprays. She started handing them out, but when she reached the third man, he flicked his cigarette.

"Imma pass on that," he said. "Thanks tho."

Harley looked confused. "These aren't illegal to possess."

"I never said they were, but I'm on paper. If I get rolled by the pigs, I have to report it to my PO and explain why I had it on me."

With her free hand, Harley stroked her throat. "Why not tell your probation officer I gave them to you and explain how you care about your friends not dying. It's not a crime to be prepared."

"Maybe for you it's not," he said, "but if I get caught with those"—he glanced at the box in her hand—"shit, it don't matter what I say. I'll get violated like a muthafucka."

Harley didn't argue her case any further. Instead, she turned to the second man and offered him the extra box. "On the off chance your friend changes his mind. Now before we leave, do you guys have any questions?"

The first man raised his hand. "Since you asked, do you have a phone I can use?"

Harley reached into her back pocket and removed her iPhone. She unlocked it, blocked her number and forked it over.

The man hopped off the bench and began strolling out of earshot. As he drifted further and further out of reach, Mateo began bouncing on his heels. Harley placed a hand on his shoulder to help calm him down.

"Don't sweat it. He's not going anywhere."

"On second thought, I have a question," the second man said. He unzipped his jacket and peeled his left arm out of his sleeve.

The area in question was a patch of tender flesh with redness spreading above and below his elbow. He lifted it up to show off the extent of the damage, then hung his arm between his knees. "If it's not bulging, it's not an abscess, right?"

"It doesn't look like one, but I'm no doctor." She crouched down to take a closer look. "Is it painful and hot to the touch?"

The man gripped his arm and nodded.

"When did it first show up?"

"A few weeks ago."

"And do you have a fever?"

"You tell me." He leaned forward, and Harley placed the back of her hand on his forehead. "Hmm. You don't feel hot." She dropped her hand to his cheek. "What about sick in other ways?"

"Just the usual," he said, leaning back in the seat.

"I can't say for certain, but it looks like cellulitis—a bacterial infection known to cause a whole host of issues when left untreated. In bad cases when the rot runs deep, what starts as tissue damage can develop to gangrene, shock, amputation—sometimes even death. I've seen it before and you want to avoid it at all costs."

"So what should I do?"

"Were I you, I'd see a doctor sooner rather than later, but I wouldn't necessarily go to the emergency room unless you believe your life is in danger. My suggestion is to take care of this as soon as possible, but I feel like you may get better treatment if you can be seen by a regular doctor at a clinic or urgent care center."

"Then that's what I'll do. I just have some business I need to take care of first."

Harley took a slight step back. "Your business is your business, but if I were you I'd make this my number one priority. I once lost someone very close to me who put off a similar infection. It's hard to say if the infection ultimately killed him, but I'm sure it didn't help."

The man tucked his arm away and motioned behind Harley. She turned around and saw the man returning with her phone.

"Is everything good with you?" she asked.

He flashed a winning smile and returned her phone. "Not quite yet, but in a few minutes it will be."

Harley smiled and wished the three of them well, then tapped Mateo on the shoulder.

They carried on for a few steps until Mateo turned to Harley. "Can I ask a question? Back there, were you talking about your brother?"

Harley stared ahead and kept walking.

"I'm sorry, I forgot about the whole trauma-inform—"

"No, it's not that. I was just thinking about our friend back there and am wondering if he'll actually seek out help." She exhaled and wiped her lips. "Like I told you earlier, I said we'd revisit it when we have some time and I always keep my word." She looked up at the impenetrable canopy overhead and smiled. "When I think back to my childhood, the first image that comes to mind is a fractured home with failed father figures. My mother remarried twice after my dad left. Her second husband gave her a reason to get out of bed, but as good as he was to her, I don't think he had a clue what he was signing up for. After he wised up and left, she dated for a bit before settling with someone who loved her for who she was, which unfortunately gave her no motivation to change."

"What was wrong with her?"

"It depends on who you ask, but she was hooked on pills as far back as I can remember so I'm sure that played a role. Thankfully she's doing better now, but it was tough growing up thinking someone you loved used drugs because they couldn't stand to be around you. Of course today I know better, but a younger me was judgmental and resentful to a fault. And to put it in context, this was during a time in our country where programs like DARE were everywhere."

"What's that?"

"Drug Abuse Resistance Education. It was a program founded in the eighties that pushed ridiculous ideas like addiction was contagious, marijuana is a gateway drug and that other drugs can cause flashbacks for life. But the scary part was cops would show up at schools and drop a whole spiel demonizing drug use—what we now call the 'DARE scare'—then after befriending an entire group of students, a couple of kids would always confide in them as unwitting informants about their own parents, relatives or siblings. As you know kids are impressionable, and while I can't speak for the rest of my generation, I imagine that one experience alone made it difficult for me to see my mom as someone who needed help, love and support."

"That's crazy, but I'm glad to hear she's doing better. Do you get to see her often?"

Harley shook her head. "I check in with her from time to time, but I'm sure I could do better."

"I bet she would like that, especially if she's alone."

"I suppose that depends on how you look at it. She's still with her third husband so at least there's a body there for warmth, but I wouldn't say she's in particularly good company. Sure, he gave me a step brother, which was great, but he's also the reason we bounced around as a family. Our final move was during the middle of my freshman year of high school, and losing the last of the few friends I had turned out to be my breaking point. I took to missing school and partying more, which ultimately set off a trajectory of failure, leading to heavy drinking and other shenanigans."

Mateo stared ahead but didn't add his thoughts.

"I know it's a lot to take in and I'm all over the place, but that's my story. It was rough, but it could have been worse had my step brother's death not forced me to reconsider my own path. Around the time he passed, it was as if I was standing at a precipice ready to jump. But somehow despite the grief, I was able to take a step back and find my footing in this life." She slowed down but didn't stop walking and continued. "Remember when I told you that he overdosed? That was true, because his Toxicology Report showed a lethal combination of drugs, but I later learned there was more to the story. He was in rough shape and had multiple abscesses on his body, along with a severe case of cellulitis that was similar to what we saw back there."

"Do you mind if I ask his name?"

Harley smiled. "His name was Taylor, and unfortunately he wasn't taking care of himself or getting the medical care he required. It's possible he could have been scared, or what we sadly see too often is people having one bad experience in a healthcare setting where they get mistreated or judged, and then they simply refuse to go back. But whatever Taylor's reasoning, I can only imagine how painful it was for him, even while self-medicating. Then a few months after his memorial, I found the courage to dig through his personal effects and discovered his journal. Ever since that day, I've struggled with whether his death was accidental or not."

Mateo turned back to Harley. "You think someone killed him?"

"No. I mean I've always wondered if he took his own life." She wiped her eyes and rubbed them on her sleeve. "At first I didn't know what to think or believe. All I knew was what I was told, and none of it made sense. In hindsight, I believe my mom and stepdad were doing their best to protect me, but even back then I knew that being 'sick' shouldn't have prevented Taylor from returning home to visit his family for over a year . . . especially when Seattle is less than an hour's drive from Tacoma."

Mateo kicked a rock and watched it bounce aimlessly. "So he was isolating."

"A hundred percent, which makes perfect sense because there's so much shame and stigma surrounding substance use disorder. It can be really painful, and some would rather crawl into a hole and die than deal with it. Now this was all happening behind the scenes, but once I read Taylor's journal, it became clear just how lonely and depressed he was, especially when he alluded to a recent diagnosis as a nail in his coffin."

"Did he say what it was?" Mateo asked, waiting a moment for her response. "Was it HIV?"

Harley shrugged. "Perhaps. He didn't say, but whatever it was, the problem with not talking about something is that it's hard to reach out for help." She clenched her jaw for a moment. "And while I didn't find a suicide note per se, I flipped through a series of dark verses which planted the seed in my mind that he believed his life was over. I'll never know for sure. That's just something I have to live with, but in the end I tell myself it doesn't change the fact that he's gone."

Mateo studied the path passing slowly beneath his feet. "I can't imagine going through something like that."

"And I hope you never have to, even if you ultimately draw strength from it like I've managed to do. Now it's hard to say if his death brought me here, but I do know I don't want others to know my pain if I can help it." Harley stepped off the path to let a dog walking an older woman pass by. "The other thing that stuck with me is about grief and how it's a process. I watched from a distance as my stepdad couldn't break out of the denial phase, and because he couldn't move on, I was never encouraged to seek professional help. I didn't know any better, so I bottled it up for the first year, which almost destroyed me. When I couldn't take it any longer, I started looking for answers and those led to questions and the more I learned, the less I understood. It was through that process where I believe I ultimately found my calling in harm reduction. Or as they say, it found me."

"And that's when you started your internship?"

"Sort of. But before all that, I didn't know where to go to make a difference. I was taking classes at a community college and had considered applying for nursing school, but I was scared of taking on so much debt. Instead, I volunteered at a local Food Bank, and though it was an impactful experience, it wasn't until I took a population's health class where everything changed. I can wrap my head around numbers and what I learned there ultimately led me to my first job with Building Better Bridges. The rest, as they say, is history."

They arrived at Pioneer Courthouse Square and Harley motioned for Mateo to hang tight. She covered her brow and slowly began scanning the plaza for Liv, but knew deep down that she couldn't see her being there. Mateo had joined in the search as well, but Harley gave him a nudge, called it off and pointed ahead.

The pair approached the top of a large curved staircase made of bricks spanning the width of an entire city block. A thin stream of water from a food truck snaked down a wheelchair ramp and flowed into the open plaza below. Harley pointed to a small group of street kids at the bottom of the ramp and began walking their way.

When they were at the bottom of the steps, she waved a hand to grab Gully's attention. Gully held up a finger, cutting off her conversation mid-sentence and then started heading toward Harley.

Harley reached out and tapped Mateo. "Do you like magic?"

"It depends. If we're talking Juan Tamariz of course, but black magic?" Mateo screwed his face. "Not so much."

Harley grabbed his shoulder, turned him around and unzipped his backpack. "And for my next trick, I will make the contents of this entire bag disappear into thin air. Et voilà!"

"I can't believe how fast they swarmed us. It was like a feeding frenzy," Mateo said, tugging on his straps and bouncing his empty backpack. "Do you think it'll all go to good use?"

"One can only hope, right?" Harley glanced behind her and scratched her neck. "But even if a client sells or trades their Narcan, it would still end up in the hands of someone who needs it."

"People do that?"

"I'm sure it happens now and then, but it has to be pretty rare since we give them out for free."

Mateo looked up the Park Blocks as they headed back the way they came. "This sort of reminds me about something else I don't understand. Have you seen the meme on Facebook with the roadside sign asking 'Why is Narcan free to a drug addict but'—"

"'My insulin costs $750 a month'?" Harley palmed her face.

"Yeah, why is that? Doesn't seem right."

"It's not right because it's not true. Or, at least it's false logic framed in a way that's missing context."

"How so?"

"Well first of all, *Narcan isn't free*. In fact, it's pretty damn expensive and last time I checked prices weren't going down. Now, we *give* it out for free, but only after we pay for it out of pocket. On rare occasions we may receive a small donation like what Wayne sent to us, but even then Wayne paid for it and I offered to reimburse him."

"I guess I didn't think of it like that."

"Most people don't, and you know what else most people don't think about? How the cost of insulin in America is criminal. Most countries charge a fraction of what we do and some even give it out for free. So that's the real tragedy and something everyone should be up in arms about. The other thing I'll say, because I've thought about this a lot, is that Narcan is a one-off, life-saving medication. Insulin on the other hand is more of a long-term maintenance drug. That's an important distinction because insulin helps people survive whereas Narcan helps people survive *an overdose*. No one is taking Narcan every day and if they are, that's a whole other problem."

Mateo kicked another rock and watched it ricochet off the path. "By the way, that was really cool of your Batman friend to step up and save the day."

"Batman?" Harley's eyes brightened. "You mean Wayne?" She laughed off the idea of Wayne in tights. "Yeah it was, but I have to say I'm not surprised. While we all try to help one another out whenever we can, I have to say Wayne's special, and I'm not just saying that because he's my mentor." She paused and craned her neck to admire a massive banner billowing on the wall of the Art

Museum. She made a mental note to catch the exhibition if she could find the time.

"So if Wayne's your mentor, does that make you Robin?" Mateo asked.

"No, it makes me lucky. That's because I first met Wayne when I volunteered at his syringe access program in Tacoma. Not only did he teach me most of what I know, but he also helped me unlearn a number of miseducations and prejudices, similar to what I'm working on with you."

Mateo shoved his hands into his pockets. "Do you think Juju will forgive me?"

"Knowing Juju . . . probably, but Mack's another story. I will say though that if you feel the need to apologize, do so, learn from where you went wrong and move on with your life."

"Let me take a guess, Wayne taught you that lesson."

"No. I learned that one the hard way which is probably why it stuck." Harley smiled. "You'll have more hard lessons too, but my hope is that with each new generation, the lessons are less painful and the stakes aren't as high. That way, you can build on the work of those who came before you. That's how it was for me with Wayne because even though harm reduction is relatively young, when I entered the field he was nearly burned out after a decade-long battle to get his exchange licensed. Before that, he had been operating an illegal exchange program out of his van, which wasn't an uncommon thing in those days. In fact, it was the same story all throughout the country, and a lot of people risked their freedoms to make a positive impact, including our own predecessors right here in Portland."

"Wait, so people could have gone to jail?" Mateo asked.

"People *were* going to jail. There was even a case in New York where the entire staff at a syringe exchange got arrested. It was a risky business to be involved in and the pushback from the police didn't help. It has gotten better, but even today many places are fighting to keep their doors open, but not like the early years. Back then, cops were harassing staff and clients all across the country. Their ignorance, combined with the War on Drugs, has led to a tumultuous relationship for all involved."

"Have cops ever harassed you?"

"Of course, and we still see lazy policing from time to time, like a rogue cop who parks across the street to gain intel on someone. There was even a sting operation against us a few years back that hoped to catch us giving needles to minors." Harley turned to Mateo and grinned. "But that's why we're strict on policy and can't afford to get caught slippin'. I'm not saying you won't see it happen from time to time, but if it does and we get caught, I always try to remind the police chief that it's in his best interest for us to remain open."

"How so?"

"Because after medical personnel and hospital staff, first responders are at the highest risk of needlestick injuries. There's just no sense in them wanting to shut us down since we take so many needles off the street."

Mateo closed the gap between them. "I can see that. Also, I'm sure that with or without you, people will still find a way to get syringes."

"Exactly, except if we're not around, take a wild guess where they all end up." Harley scanned the park and halted in her tracks. Far off in the distance, walking away from her new friends on the park bench, was the same street dealer with jet-black eyes from the robbery three days earlier. She pulled out her phone, opened her recent call list and saved his number.

Mateo waited to respond until they started walking again. "I imagine they would all end up on the streets."

"They would end up everywhere and no one wants that, not after how far we've come." Harley slowed down and tiptoed through a shallow puddle. "We still have a ways to go so let me give you a quick history lesson. To understand the progress we've made, you really have to go back to the late 80s when the City and County first gave our exchange the green light to operate. By every definition, it would have been a major win, except at the exact same time Oregon's Legislature was preparing to pass the Drug Paraphernalia Law."

Harley looked both ways and motioned for Mateo to cross the street with her.

"Long story short, the proposed DP law had the potential to decimate clean syringe access, but thankfully like-minded people from across the country lobbied their little hearts out and succeeded in getting syringes excluded from the paraphernalia list." Harley paused for a moment and then continued. "You want to talk about an uphill battle? Sometimes I still can't believe they pulled it off, especially with all the public hysteria at the time thanks to Nancy's 'Just Say No' campaign."

"I see," Mateo said, gripping the straps to his backpack.

"Are you familiar with her campaign?"

He shook his head. "No, not really."

"It's another one we need to put into context like the insulin meme. The way I see it, the 'Just Say No' campaign started by former First Lady Nancy Reagan was a disastrous movement that downplayed so many issues relating to substance use disorder. In line with DARE, something about the idea behind the campaign seemed off. On the surface, it looked like an educational program aimed to keep kids off drugs, but their approach vilified people who used drugs and promoted vast anti-drug policy and thinking. The stigmatization from that one campaign alone has made it exponentially harder to get people the tools, supplies and information they need to be safe."

"Is that what started the War on Drugs?"

"Okay, now we're really getting into the weeds. The War on Drugs actually officially started a few presidencies earlier with Nixon, and has been escalated by almost every president since. It's been going on longer than I've been alive, but if the past fifty years have taught us anything it's that the time to end the drug war is now because it has failed in every sense of the word. We've seen high arrest rates that directly lead to mass incarcerations, unthinkable violations of human rights and civil liberties—often aimed at communities of color—and an ungodly waste of money, time, energy and resources. I can keep going but ultimately, if we want to move the needle, there needs to be a higher appreciation for health-centered approaches, which is where we come in."

"So at least things are moving in the right direction since places like Bridgeworks are completely legal."

"I don't know about completely. Technically, Bridgeworks is *legalish*," Harley said, making air quotes. "It gets sticky because of the syringes we take in."

Mateo looked baffled. "I'm confused. If syringes aren't paraphernalia, then why would it be illegal to reclaim them?"

"Because once they're been used with a controlled substance, they contain drug residue, which technically puts anyone in possession of used syringes in possession of a controlled substance."

"Now I'm really confused. Does that mean I could be arrested for working at the exchange?"

Harley tilted her head back and forth. "Put it this way, technically we could have been arrested for jaywalking back there, but it's highly unlikely, right?"

"Don't you think that's something someone should have mentioned?"

Harley grabbed Mateo's arm to stop him. "Look, there's a lot of nuances to what we do and it's hard to touch on them all. Even after everything we just ran through, there's still a million other discussions I'd love to have with you, but again this isn't your standard orientation here."

They started again and walked in silence before turning onto Market Street and coming full circle.

"I also hope you can appreciate that harm reduction is forward-thinking, which often lands us in these types of legal gray areas where being compassionate can get you in trouble. And as long as there's an inconsistency between the criminal code and the state's public health goals, there's a good chance we will land somewhere in the middle, hopefully on our feet. But with that said, try not to get too worked up over it. Remember, we're talking about technicalities and for the most part—at least where we're at—the days of being arrested are long behind us."

They turned a corner and Mateo immediately froze. He lifted a shaky finger and aimed it at Bridgeworks. "How confident are you again that we're not at risk of being arrested?"

twelve
nimby

Harley sprinted down the sidewalk and tried to piece together what she could through a jostled vision. She made out an officer in the road directing traffic along with a transport ambulance and a fire truck parked in front of Bridgeworks. Her team was chatting with an officer by the front door and not a single client was in sight.

As Harley and Mateo closed in on the exchange, the officer registered their stamping and spun around.

"Whoa!" he hollered, raising his hands to cut them off.

Harley screeched to a stop and Mateo nearly took her out.

"Road's closed," the officer said. He towered over Harley, his polished badge shining in her face.

"What the hell is going on here?" she asked in a panic, side-stepping to get a better view.

"Road's closed, ma'am."

"I need to know what's going on. This is my program"—she sidestepped to the right and pointed behind him—"and those are my people."

The officer looked over his shoulder. "They work for you?"

"We work together, but yes, I'm the supervisor."

"What about him?" The officer pointed his pen at Mateo.

"We all work here. Please tell me what's going on."

The officer dropped his arms. "We're responding to an OD.

You can join your employees, just don't enter the property until the scene is clear."

Harley's face went flush as she joined her team. "Is everyone okay?"

Ethan removed his hat and wiped his brow with the back of his hand. "EMS is inside, but unfortunately our friend wasn't being very cooper—"

The exchange door flew open with a loud bang, causing everyone within earshot to flinch.

"Get your fucking hands off me!" a teenager demanded, thrashing on a stretcher. First responders kept a hand on him and with every flailing kick, they fought to keep the gurney upright. His wrists were strapped to the rails with soft restraints, which enabled him to flip off the cops standing on either side of him. His shirt collar was soiled with chunky fluid and a trail of crusted blood had hardened on his arm.

"Is that really necessary?" Karissa yelled. She moved to step off the curb but Gabby caught her by the arm.

Emboldened by Karissa's plea, the teen worked to sit up but a hand calmly pressed him flat, then gently patted the teen's chest. Harley noticed the compassion, saw where it was coming from and immediately recognized that the teen was in good hands.

John was more than a paramedic. He was a hero in her eyes who had responded to more overdoses around Bridgeworks than what she liked to admit, and how he had avoided compassion fatigue after a decade on the force was a mystery, perhaps even to himself.

"Why am I being detained?" the teen yelled. "Why am I being de—"

"You're going to be okay," John said, pinning him back down onto the stretcher again. With his free hand, he helped guide the gurney off of the curb toward the back of the ambulance. As he passed Harley, he gave her the slightest nod.

Harley turned to her team. "Can someone tell me what happened?" she whispered.

"He was dumped," Karissa said, checking her phone. "About twenty-five minutes ago. His friends pulled up, dropped him on our doorstep and peeled out."

Gabby lit a cigarette. "It's a good thing you were out here," she said, blowing her drag upward like a smoke signal. "He was really cutting it close."

"Yeah, I've seen some close calls, but the kid's lucky to be alive," Ethan said. "He wasn't out completely, but by the time we got him inside and situated, he was well into respiratory arrest. And I have to give it to you, Harley. You were right. One dose wasn't enough."

Harley stared at the teen and tightened her fists.

Gabby reached out and tapped her shoulder to get her attention. "Hey, have you seen what they have now when naloxone sprays aren't powerful enough? Or when they can't find a vein? With the drills?" She took another drag. "What did John call it? Intra—?"

"You mean an *intraosseous* infusion?" Harley asked. "Please don't tell me he gave the poor kid an IO."

"He didn't because he wasn't in cardiac arrest, but his partner showed me how it works. It's this tiny little drill that drives a needle directly into the bone"—Gabby leaned down and tapped below her knee—"so they can push liquid naloxone directly into his bone marrow."

"We should look into getting our hands on one of those," Ethan said.

"For what purpose?" Harley asked. "Do you have any idea how painful an IO can be? Or how much tissue inflammation it can cause? I'd rather hit someone with a second or third dose before boring into their bones."

"Believe it or not, you sound just like John," Gabby said. "He called the drill a last resort and said he hopes to never have to use it."

"It still might be useful to have if we're ever low on Narcan and want to stretch our supplies," Ethan said, leaving it at that and focusing on the teen again. "Either way, I will say he wasn't out of control like this when he first came to. It was only after he realized they wanted to take him to the hospital that he became defensive."

"Can you even blame him, though?" Karissa asked. "Wouldn't you be pissed if your 'friends' dumped you on a sidewalk somewhere?"

"Well, better here than on some backstreet in the boondocks." Harley placed her hands on her head and watched as a cop approached the gurney. John finished taking the teen's blood pressure and after running through a series of mundane questions, he finished his assessment and turned to the Fire Captain. "A&O times two."

The cop leaned over the teen. "You don't know what day it is?"

"I never know what day it is! All I know is I woke up here and feel like shit," the teen said, tugging at his restraints. "Please let me go!" He retched again and turned his head to the side.

John moved toward the back of the stretcher, looked up at the officer and shook his head.

The officer leaned over the teen. "Look kid. I wouldn't be doing my job if I let you walk in an altered state where you don't have your wits about you. The heroin in your system may—"

"I don't know what you're talking about."

"You can keep talking like we don't do this every day and see how far that gets you. My concern is that the *heroin* in your blood may outweigh the Narcan in your system, so it's possible you're not out of the woods yet. It's in your best interest to go with these fine people and get yourself checked out."

The teen shook his head. "I don't know what you're talking about."

"Son, I'm talking about your safety here, not mine. Don't play stupid with me. If you didn't have any opioids in your system, the Narcan wouldn't have done a damn thing."

The teen laid his head back.

"Exactly. Now, just a few more questions. Any chance you're feeling suicidal?"

He shook his head.

"What about any thoughts of hurting yourself or others?"

The teen rocked his head from side to side and relaxed his arms.

"In that case, I'm sure you'll be released in no time." The cop placed both hands on the rails of the gurney. "You would be wise to take this as a wake up call. Let these guys do their jobs and help them help you."

The teen gave one last kick in protest.

"That way," the officer said, "we don't have to mess around with a 5150 hold."

The teen stopped moving and lifted his head up. "What's that?"

"Baker Act, aka involuntary commitment services. It means you can be treated against your will if you're emotionally disturbed or a danger to yourself."

"But I'm not disturbed, or a danger to myself."

The officer reached out and patted his foot. "I know you think that, but to me you are, and that's the problem."

"So no one recognized his friends?" Harley asked while pacing back and forth in the lobby as the room became a blur. Her team leaned against the wall where the client line should have been.

"I swear I've seen the driver in here before, but that's about it," Karissa said, rumpling her forehead. "But you know I'm not here as often as I'd like to be since school started again."

Gabby tapped Mateo's arm. "We were in the exchange room so we didn't see anything."

Mateo looked at her but kept his thoughts to himself.

"At least he went to the hospital." Harley stopped pacing and turned to Karissa. "What about the license plate? Any chance you got a good look?"

"I was a little distracted at the moment."

"I don't blame you," Harley said.

"You know, if we had cameras we wouldn't have to wonder who—"

"Ethan, can you please stop it with the cameras?" Harley asked, pulling at her cheeks. "Sorry, I didn't mean to snap at you."

"You're okay," he said. "I know it's nothing personal."

"No, it's not. I just wished they would have talked to us to give us an idea about what his drugs were and where they came from."

"I have a question," Mateo said. "Is it unusual for two doses of naloxone to not bring someone back?"

"In my experience it's pretty rare," Ethan said. "Though I will say the teen showed a slight improvement in respiratory function after the first dose, just not enough for the paramedic's liking. We would have hit him again if they would have let us."

"So it is uncommon?" Mateo asked.

Harley cleared her throat. "Needing two doses or more? It's definitely unusual but not unheard of, especially when the opiates are uncommonly strong or mixed with fentanyl. Also, sometimes fentanyl isn't evenly distributed throughout the dope which creates a hot pocket."

"That makes sense. I guess I was getting concerned we might be spinning wheels over here, or worried that these nasal sprays won't cut it."

"No, they'll definitely help, but don't forget we also don't know what was actually going on with him. For example, if he had recently relapsed he could have a much lower tolerance than what he's accustomed to. The same goes if he was recently released from jail because the chances of overdosing shoots up significantly after any injection user is locked up. It's not a slow drop either—the numbers suggest a seventy percent increase after forty-eight hours of incarceration."

"And speaking from experience," Ethan said, "when you're dope sick, nothing will get in your way. That's when people turn to new dealers or take risks where they don't really know what they're getting into."

"Not to mention that most people get released at odd hours, often in the middle of the night and when no dealers are working. To make matters worse, people suffering from withdrawal often drop their barriers, sometimes taking the first needle off the first person they can find. But with that said, we shouldn't change our game plan based on what we just saw because we don't know all the facts of his situation."

"But it's not the only case, right? Don't forget about Jack," Ethan said.

"True, which was especially worrisome since we believe Jack's using pattern wasn't interrupted. But either way, we're still holding onto some naloxone which isn't doing any good for our clients out there."

Gabby glanced at Ethan. "And just to confirm, we're sticking with two vials per person? Same goes for the sprays?"

"I think for now, because even if it proves to not be enough, it's a safety net that buys people time until help arrives."

"Makes sense to me because not everyone has the means to call for help," Karissa said.

"Plus, there's always a chance our first responders can get overwhelmed," Gabby added.

Harley glanced at the front door. "It's important to remember that most people don't call for help when there's an OD, especially in the rural areas." She turned to Gabby. "And as for a delay in response, it's hard for me to picture what that would look like outside of a natural disaster. Portland Fire and Rescue has thirty or so stations with fifty units in service on any given day, and if I remember correctly, the company contracted to transport medical calls has twenty plus ambulances staged across the city with a long list of hospitals to choose from."

"I guess that makes me feel a little better," Gabby said, wiping her brow.

"But that's not to say they can't be overwhelmed," Harley

said. "Though according to John, it would take a lot to cripple their response time goal of four minutes or less."

"Really? That's faster than I would have expected, though it all still feels reactive," Mateo said.

Harley cocked her head. "How so?"

"It's like how clean supplies are good for preventing the spread of diseases, but they won't stop dirty drugs from entering someone's system. Or how naloxone only helps someone once they've overdosed. It's like we can't get ahead of the ball."

"True, but since we're not dealers, the supply is out of our control," Harley said. "And even if we had access to a safe, legal and regulated supply, Big Pharma would price gouge it out of reach to most, especially for people without insurance. But with no safer consumption spaces for people to use in, we'd still have overdoses all over the place to respond to."

Ethan turned to Harley. "By the way that reminds me—Pogue asked if he could shoot up in the testing room and I turned him down."

"I told Clay the same thing," Harley said. "Though that's where we could make a real difference. Imagine if we had a safe consumption space or overdose prevention center like they do in Canada, where people can use in a clean and supervised environment. Last year alone, they had over two-hundred thousand visits and reversed around two thousand overdoses. Think about that number for a moment. Two *thousand* overdose reversals. And the best part? *Not a single death.*" She couldn't help but smile. "But that's what you get when you have trained staff who can offer first aid in the event of an overdose. And of course, all the needles are safely disposed of."

"So what's stopping us from doing that?" Mateo asked.

Harley held up four fingers. "Insurance, laws, funding and NIMBY."

"*NIMBY?*"

"Not In My Back Yard. It's when some people want a solution as long as it's not in their neighborhood."

"But there have to be other options, right?"

"Sure, there are plenty of solutions, though many are off the table for us here in America. For example, London started prescribing immediate-release hydromorphone tablets to clients—what you might know as Dilaudid—though it's not a perfect substitute for heroin. Their medical model also requires a prescription, which is one more hurdle for people trying to get onboard. I say it's a decent start, but if our country was really serious about making a difference, we'd go beyond MAT and take an honest look at HAT."

"I'm not familiar," Mateo said, frowning.

Harley turned to Gabby. "You've researched this a lot. Want to bring him up to speed?"

"Sure," Gabby said, pushing herself off the wall. "Medication-assisted treatment is when someone is prescribed drugs like buprenorphine, methadone or naltrexone to replace their drug of choice. Often it's paired with counseling and behavioral therapies, though the medicines work fine on their own without added interventions. HAT, on the other hand, is heroin-assisted treatment, which prescribes pharmaceutical-grade heroin to people who have struggled with traditional MAT. Studies show it reduces crime and overdoses because patients don't rely on the black market for their fix."

"I think we actually have that in Spain, but I never quite understood how it addresses the problem." Mateo paused for a moment and stretched his jaw. "You don't think using heroin to treat heroin addiction just prolongs the pain?"

"It all depends on how you want to look at it," Gabby said. "Personally, I think it addresses the issue head on because it all starts with seeing substance use disorder for the disease it is."

"And SUD is not a blanket diagnosis that applies to anyone who dabbles with substances. It's defined by the recurrent use of substances in a way that is specifically harmful to a person's well-being," Harley explained.

"Exactly, and that's where moving someone to a regulated and controlled use can actually do wonders for their health, much in the same way that operating a safer consumption space can. But the barrier still remains political and public buy-in is hard to secure. Most people have a hard time seeing the benefits of safer consumption spaces, at least when it comes to drugs. The irony though is when you really think about it, it's not so different from the millions of bars and restaurants throughout the country that serve alcohol day in and day out."

"Except," Harley added, "the one major difference is that at least bartenders are serving their customers an approved, regulated and 'safe' supply. But go back to prohibition when alcohol was outlawed and look at what happened. Amateurs started concocting bathtub gin and people were being poisoned and dying all over the place."

"True." Gabby turned back to Mateo. "And no one wants that, which is why Spain, along with Switzerland and a few other countries, saw what wasn't working and decided to give heroin-assisted treatment a try, at least for those who MAT didn't work for. In fact, Switzerland requires patients to attempt treatment twice before they are eligible for HAT, right?"

Harley nodded. "Not only that, but they require patients to have suffered from opiate use disorder for at least two years."

"Oh, that's right," Gabby said, snapping her fingers. "Anyway, the data has been in for some time, and these clinics have been able to stabilize their clients more than anyone could have imagined. Not only were the clients able to sever their disease from the sticky web of criminal activity, but they showed monumental gains in mental health and social reintegration that no one thought was possible."

"Actually, some thought it was possible," Harley said, checking the clock. "I think the main takeaway is when you have an epidemic that impacts as many people as what we see, you need to keep it unemotional, stick to the science and not rule out possible solutions. That's what Canada did. They took a human rights-based approach to drug policy and it's been incredibly successful."

Mateo leaned back against the wall, bumping shoulders with Karissa. "I can see how much you all care, and I want you to know I do, too. If there's anything I can do to help, I'm in."

Harley smiled. "I think for now, our efforts are best spent educating our clients and trying to see if we can't pinpoint the source of the hot batch. Speaking of which"—Harley turned to Ethan—"how did drug checking go? Are there any areas we should tell people to avoid?"

"Yeah, actually. Let me grab my list." Ethan stepped into the testing room and grabbed a sheet of paper. "So far, all the meth I tested was clean, but I did test a few cookers that were used to make goofballs. Some of those popped for fent, but we couldn't tell if it came from the meth or the heroin. Other than that, for the heroin that did pop, most of it came from deep Southeast, the Hollywood District and of course, downtown."

"So all along the MAX line?" Harley asked.

"Correct, and a handful of pissed off clients also outed their dealers."

"Why am I not surprised?" Harley asked. "Anyone we know?"

Ethan nodded. "I'm not familiar with this Armando person, but Dylan and Luis have been around for a while now. Also, there was someone else that kind of caught me off guard, though it could easily be a mistake."

"What makes you say that?"

"Because I've known Gully for a long time, and as far back as I can remember she always steered clear of selling heroin."

Harley pedaled right through the open plaza and coasted to a stop at the bottom of the staircase. She dropped one foot onto the ground to balance herself, wiped sweat off her brow and called Gully over.

"You're really putting them miles in lately," Gully said. "Everything good with you?"

"Gully, please forgive me if I'm overstepping, but I want you to know that relapse is common and you're always welcome to come back and see us if you need supplies."

Gully studied Harley and twisted a sucker between her blueish lips. "What makes you think I relapsed?"

Harley shrugged. "I heard you might be dealing and figured it was to afford a habit."

Gully mouthed an expletive and looked away.

Harley leaned over the handlebars of Ethan's bike. "Look, I don't care about the dealing. I'm only here because it sounds like something you may have sold tested for fentanyl and—"

"What did you just say?" Gully asked.

Harley squeezed her grips. "We were doing drug checking all morning and trying to pinpoint the source of this hot batch. Your name came up and—"

Gully cocked her head. "What do you mean my 'name came up?'"

"Look, you saw us down here earlier handing out overdose kits, remember? I wasn't at the exchange when they were doing drug checking. It's also possible this could all be a mistake. But if not, I'm hoping we can test your supply just in case. That's all."

"And I'm hoping you can tell me who the fuck is throwing dirt on my name."

"Like I said, I wasn't there, but I'm sure it wasn't anything like that."

Gully stepped forward. "I don't think you understand how important it is to maintain my reputation out here. Tell me who it was so I can address it."

"Please, Gully. Don't make this about you. People are fucking dying."

Gully bit into her sucker and started walking away. "People are always fucking dying."

Harley watched as Gully headed for the steps to rejoin her

street family and couldn't help but panic. "Wait," she called out. "I can send them your way. If your supply checks out."

Gully paused, then stopped walking and spun in place. As she looked down on Harley, something came over her. "You think this is about money?"

Harley didn't respond.

"Because you know me better than that. The reason I'm so pissed right now is because I've never set out to hurt anyone," Gully said, walking back toward Harley. "And I'm not saying that because it's bad for business. I care about these people, more than you'll ever know."

"Of course you do, and I do too. Why else would I be here?"

Gully cast a hand behind her. "*Don't make this about you,* remember? We're a family, Harley, and for some of us we're the only family we've ever known." She grabbed hold of Harley's handlebars and squeezed tight until her knuckles turned white. "Since I only service my family and friends of friends, I make it a point to be the type of dealer I always wanted when I was using. I'm not here to treat anyone like a customer or a doormat. Do you know how demeaning that can be for someone?"

"I can only imagine."

"No. You really can't." She rested a knee on top of Harley's front tire. "When someone has something you need, they have all the control in the world. It's sickening really, which is why I take care of my family and they in turn take care of me. It's also why I can't have someone lying on me and saying I'm selling that shit, because I would never sell anything I don't know is safe."

"Speaking of safety, I understand the importance of clients having a relationship with their supplier, but when you say you don't want to hurt anyone, my only response is that these tests don't lie. I completely understand you didn't make the drugs you're selling and that they could have been cut anywhere along the supply train. Them popping for fentanyl is not a reflection that you did anything wrong."

"Well, now I'm not only pissed off but confused because nothing I've sold has popped for fentanyl."

Harley struggled to take in what she was hearing. "Hold on. You're telling me you've been testing your drugs?"

"You gave me the tests, remember? And unless I'm doing it wrong, everything I've tested so far has been negative."

Harley frowned. "Are you sure? Sometimes people get confused when reading the results. You know one line means positive and—"

"Two lines are negative. Yes, I know," Gully said, shifting her stance. "I may not have finished high school, but I can fuckin' read basic English."

Harley scratched her head, finding herself at a loss for words. "I don't get it. We were told your heroin tested positive for—"

"Heroin?" Gully pulled her knee off the tire and took a step back. "Is that what this is about? Harley, I only sell meth, remember? Maybe now and then I'll middleman a balloon or two of black if someone's sick, but otherwise I stick to what I know best."

Harley smacked her handlebars. "Why didn't I think of that?"

"Hey, take it easy on yourself. You're under a lot of stress. But just so you know, if I'm hooking someone up with dope, it's a quick flip and I'm not testing or pinching it. It's in one hand and out the other. I make a few bucks, if that, and go on with my day. That's about the best I can do because it's not like I'm working out of a cushy office out here."

Harley looked around the plaza. "Sorry about the mix-up. If there's any good news here, it's that at least your meth is clean."

"True, though I'm sure if I wanted to I could make a call and get my hands on some clean dope to sell as well. But why risk doubling my charges when I found myself a nice niche out here, especially when the Honduran runners are dominating the market."

"Is that where the heroin came from?"

"Of course. I won't give a name though, but it shouldn't make a difference. It's all the same shit."

"That's what I was afraid of." Harley looked around and watched as a number of street kids let the day slip away. She ran her fingers through her hair and accepted what she was about to say. "I can't believe this is coming from me, but perhaps it's time you thought about broadening your horizons? If you can get your hands on some heroin that's 'safe', I'm sure I could send a lot of clients your way."

Gully cocked an eyebrow. "You're not serious?" She pulled the lollipop stick out of her mouth, leaned in and studied Harley's face carefully. "Holy shit. You are fuckin' serious, aren't you?"

Harley unlocked her apartment door and bumped it open with the front tire of Ethan's bike. After squeezing into the entryway, she steadied the handlebar against the wall, dropped her bag on the floor and made a mental note not to trip over it in the middle of the night.

She locked her door and took a deep breath. Her one-bedroom apartment on the fourth floor of her building was reminiscent of her office at the needle exchange. It was cluttered with half-read books, literature and a hamper filled with washed but unfolded clothes. Since Harley couldn't help but bring her work home, cleaning always seemed to take a backseat to the work that mattered most. Rinsed dishes teetered in her sink and though not dirty, none of them were clean enough to be put away. And in case she ever felt truly alone, she could always count on spotting a few fruit flies hovering above the counter, languishing in the light rays slicing through her window.

She popped open a bottle, tilted a pint glass and filled it with an IPA she'd been meaning to try out for so me time. She had made a pit stop at a local brewery before heading home and reached out to place her second bottle inside her fridge. While poking around, she reached for a loaf of sharp cheddar, which won out as the most logical pairing for dinner on the fly. She sliced off a few thick slabs and placed them on a paper towel, balanced a beer in her grip and made her way to the couch.

Balancing her MacBook on her thighs, she sank into the cushion and wiggled the laptop charger to get it working. It took her Inbox a moment to refresh, and she organized her emails as the messages poured in, dragging and dropping message after message into their appropriate folder. With her free hand, she reached for her beer and took another sip. When her eyes returned to the screen, Harley read the subject line of the following message a second time:

FWD: Are you seeing a spike in overdoses too?

Harley felt her cheeks burn and heat flourished behind her eyelids. After promising herself she wouldn't cry, she closed her laptop, finished her beer and returned to her fridge to finish what she started.

thirteen
shadowbox

"Hi. This is the voicemail of—"

Harley hung up. She reached for a sip of coffee and dropped her elbows onto her desk. It took a moment to remind herself that voicemail wasn't dead before she removed the phone from the cradle and called April again.

". . . if this is an emergency, please hang up and dial 911. Otherwise, please leave your name, number, reason for your call and I'll get back to you. Thank you!"

Beep.

"April, it's me. I need to talk to you ASAP regarding an email I received last night. If you can please call me as soon as you—"

A green light flashed on her landline, and Harley switched to the incoming call.

"Sorry for the phone tag," April said. "I've been meaning to connect with you lately, but things have been pretty hectic around here. Anyway, I saw you just called so I assume it's a good time to talk?"

"It is. We don't open our doors for a bit."

April paused for a moment. "Correct me if I'm wrong, but anytime you start your day off this early it's because you couldn't sleep."

"I think you know me too well," Harley said, tapping her desk with her fingernails. "The reason I called was to see if you received the email I forwarded last night?"

"Last night?" April asked. "Probably not. I've been running a day behind lately, but give me a sec here and I'll pull it up."

Harley took another swig of coffee and licked the back of her teeth. She would never say it aloud, but that wasn't the response she was hoping to hear from her boss.

"Is it this 'Critical Emergency Room' report?" April asked.

"Exactly. It should be flagged as urgent."

"Just give me a second to once-over it." April mumbled a bit until she reached the exciting parts. "Twenty-eight patients . . . treated and discharged . . . five were admitted to hospital . . . patients required higher than normal doses of injectable naloxone . . . four transferred to the Intensive Care Unit . . . three of whom subsequently *died* . . ."

For a moment, Harley thought the call got dropped.

". . . and this is all from *yesterday*?" April asked.

"Not only just from yesterday, but that's just from OHSU."

"Harley, this is bad."

"I know. Did you see how much they were upping the doses of naloxone?"

"No, let me—"

"It was 3 mg, if you can believe it."

"And that's what? Four times the normal dose?"

"Try seven and a half," Harley said. "I'm pretty sure that was all intravenously too."

April thought for a moment. "How prepared are we for something like this? Do we have enough?"

"Enough of what? Doses? We have some injectables left and I brought in some nasal sprays with my emergency budget, however it's nowhere near enough to make me comfortable. Especially if hospitals are pushing over three times the amount we're handing out in our overdose kits."

April groaned. "No wonder you're working early."

"I figured if I was going to be awake, I might as well make myself useful."

"You know you're always useful. I hope you know you can't beat yourself up over these numbers. Remember, as troubling as they are, don't lose sight of the fact that we're finally seeing real-time reports from the emergency rooms. When I first started, no one was talking amongst themselves, so at least all of our overdose response planning efforts are making a difference."

Harley appreciated the sentiment, especially when fatigue was setting in and the day was just starting.

"There's one more thing," April said. "As far as toxicological emergencies go, this may be the first actual event we're facing since our last regional Tabletop meeting. At the very least, we'll see where the modeling and assumptions fell short to improve our response. Or, if the system gets overwhelmed, we'll discover where the weakest link is and shore it up in the future."

Harley took another sip of coffee. The last thing she wanted was for any part of the system to break down. Nothing good could come from paramedic services being overrun with calls or the hospitals being flooded with clients. She didn't want any more updates from Chief Morris, and she didn't want her or her clients to run out of naloxone.

"April, I don't want anyone to die," Harley uttered. "Not for any reason, *especially* not to teach me where I fell short."

April paused and lingered on the line. She cleared her throat and said quietly, "I'm sorry, Harley. I didn't mean to jump straight into systems thinking and future planning. There's a time and place for all that, but I understand it's not now and it's not why you called. I'm here to support you any way I can. Just tell me what you need."

Stepping out of her office, Harley unlocked the front door to Bridgeworks and welcomed most of her team into the lobby. Gabby and Karissa filtered in first, followed by Mateo who started to pull the door shut, but Harley caught it with her hand. She poked her head outside, looked around and smiled at the clients on the sidewalk waiting for the exchange to open.

"Ethan's not with you?" Harley asked as she stepped back into the lobby. "I thought he was on the schedule today."

"He is," Karissa said. "Is he not here? We figured he was since his bike is out front."

Harley shook her head. "No, we swapped rides yesterday because I had to run by the Square."

"Maybe that's why he's late? He couldn't figure out how to drive anything with more than one gear."

Harley chuckled and turned to Mateo. "Speaking of the schedule, I wasn't expecting to see you here today."

"I found a classmate to take lecture notes for me and figured you could use the help."

Harley smiled. "It means a lot. Thanks for coming in."

"So what's the plan?" Gabby wondered aloud. "Same shit, different day?"

Nodding, Harley pulled out her phone. "Except I'll fill in for Ethan and do the drug checking until he shows up. Also, we need to let our clients know things have gone downhill fast. I got a report last night from OHSU and there were three fatal ODs." She shot off a text as she spoke, then turned to Gabby. "We only need a very small backup of naloxone for ourselves. Let's get the injectables and sprays into the hands of anyone who will take them."

"You got it," Gabby said.

"On second thought, when you get to the tail end of the stack it makes sense to give higher priority to clients who camp out beyond the city limits. They're the ones who face lengthier response times from paramedics if they even get a response at all."

Gabby nodded. "Agreed, but I don't know how I feel about using my discretion to pick favorites."

"I don't see it as picking favorites, but about using rationale. My thinking is that there's hopefully enough naloxone floating around downtown so that if someone needs it, it's only a shout away." Harley glanced at the clock and took a step back to address her team as a whole. "But that brings up a good point. I want to remind you all that when it comes to things like this, the only decision you ever have to make is the one you're comfortable with. It's never my intention to put any of you in a hard spot or to make you uncomfortable, so if that ever happens, please say something so I can either explain my reasoning or we can formulate a new plan. That's how we keep our team effective. Our clients depend on us being on the same page."

"That works for me," Gabby said. She stepped forward and rubbed Harley's shoulder. "And as for being on the same page, we're with you, Harley."

Karissa reached out and gave Harley a light pat on the arm. "You know I was about to say the same thing but Gabby beat me to it."

"I appreciate that," Harley said. "Because I'm just not sure where I'd be without you all."

In the background, Mateo smiled.

Gabby dropped her hand. "Since you're filling in for Ethan, do you want me to let them in?"

Harley nodded and turned to open the door to the drug checking room but didn't step inside. Instead, she took a moment to admire her team and wondered where she would be without them. The truth was, she wasn't drawn to this field in search of camaraderie, but once she was exposed to the companionship she knew she was home.

As Harley hung back, she watched as Gabby held the front door open for the morning rush and welcomed each client with open arms. Mateo was quick to take his place inside the exchange room and confidently stood his ground behind the Bio Bin. Karissa pulled a stack of drug alert flyers from her bag, stepped out onto the street and disappeared out of sight. Harley watched with amazement as her team broke apart. She realized that even though they had each gone their separate ways, they were closer and more in sync with each other than ever before.

．．．

"Again? What is wrong with these fucking people? I swear they're trying to kill me." Asher slammed his fist on the table and pushed his chair back. "If I see Armando again, I'm swinging on him." He got out of his seat and shadowboxed an imaginary opponent. By the fifth punch he was out of breath.

Harley held up a hand to calm him down. "I understand you're upset, but remember that violence only begets more violence."

Asher threw a sloppy jab-cross-hook, followed by a slow-moving uppercut.

"You said this came from Armando?" Harley said, turning her attention back to the test strip.

"Yeah, I don't know why I try anymore. He's probably pushing the same shit as Luis and Tony." He rested his hands on his head and fought to catch his breath. "I'm surprised they haven't leveled out their supply by now. It can't be good for business to kill off all your loyal customers, right?"

Harley looked around the small room. "I would hope that would go without saying."

"Me too," he said, shaking out his hands. "Alright, I'm out of here."

"Wait," Harley said with urgency. "If you're planning to do these drugs, do you have an overdose plan in place?"

"Well, I don't have a buddy to use with, so the next best thing is to go low and slow, right?" Asher grabbed the doorknob, opened the door and stepped back.

"Gully?" Asher glanced at Harley as he backed into the wall. "What are you doing here?"

Gully stepped forward and closed the door behind her. "That's none of your business, now is it?"

"You're right. Well don't mind me, I was just making my way out." Asher tried to step around her, but Gully snatched the collar of his t-shirt like a python.

"Funny I should find you here," she said, twisting her wrist to

161

cinch down on his collar even tighter. "Where's my money, Ash-hole?"

Harley shot out of her chair, knocking it back. "That's enough you two. This is not the place."

Gully held her hand out. "Sorry Harley, but I've been searching high and low for this piece of shit. Funny I should find him here."

Harley lunged around the desk and bumped shoulders with Asher. She reached out to separate the two, but Gully beat her to it, released Asher's collar and slapped him across the face.

Harley took a step back and covered her mouth.

Asher clutched his cheek and held his hand out to fend her off. "What the fuck was that for? I told you I didn't steal from you. I got robbed!"

"And somehow that's my fault? I don't think so. Now, one last time. Where's my money?"

"I have a plan to make it up to you. I just need more time."

Gully raised her palm again and Asher backed into the wall. "You said the same shit two weeks ago and have dodged me since."

"Gully, wait!" Harley pleaded. "How much money does he owe you?"

"One seventy," Asher answered.

"Plus fifty for interest."

"That's not so bad," Harley said. "I'm sure we can all figure something out."

"I don't want your money. I want the money this piece of shit owes me," Gully snarled, looking at Asher with disgust. "And when will you stop trying to save everyone, Harley? You're not doing anyone any favors in this life if you bail them out every time they fuck up."

"Trust me, this will work," Harley said. She opened a cabinet and pulled out a box of fentanyl test strips and placed them on the table. "Gully, I take it you've expanded your operations?"

Asher looked at the box then turned to Gully. "Are you selling black now?"

"Shut up," Gully snapped. "Now empty your pockets."

"Gully, please," Harley said. "If what you have checks out, why not use him as a runner?"

"Because he can't be trusted."

"Oh, come on. You know I've never done you dirty before," Asher exclaimed, reaching out for a truce. "Put me on again and let me work off my debt."

Gully waved him off. "The second I start giving out second chances is the second people will start asking for them. Have my money by the end of the today or you're 86'd from downtown." She reached into her pocket and pulled out a chunk of sticky black tar heroin wrapped in plastic. The dope was the size of her fist and resembled a large piece of rat poison. She dangled it by the knotted end in front of Harley. "Do what you need to do, Harley."

"You know," Harley began as she took the bag, "people are dying in the streets as we speak." She circled the table, set the dope down in front of her and got to work. "If this is fentanyl-free, you can make a lot of money *and* make a difference, especially with help."

Gully didn't respond. Instead, she slipped a scale out of one pocket, a knife out of the other, then set them both on the table. A few balled-up plastic shopping bags came from her back pocket, along with a pocketknife and a variety pack of water balloons from the Dollar Tree.

Asher clapped his hands. "I knew this exchange was a front! It makes so much sense!"

Harley held a hand up to calm him down and stared at the tools of the trade. "I'm glad you came prepared, but I'm sorry if I gave you the wrong impression. I can't have you breaking down your dope here. If word ever got out, not only could we get shut down, but we could take down the rest of our organization as well."

Gully bit her upper lip. "Well, what the fuck, Harley? You

think I enjoy walking around with more than enough shit on me to catch a distribution charge?"

Asher opened his mouth before Harley could respond. "I can carry it for you," he said. "What do you say?"

Gully scratched at her jaw for a moment, then started packing her things up.

"Wait, where are you going?" Harley asked.

"To try and find a place where we can break this shit down. Come on Ash, I can use your help." She reached for the door, but Harley pressed it closed.

"What I meant to say was that we can't do it here, but I also don't want you going somewhere you can get arrested." Harley dropped her hand and studied Gully. She couldn't determine what she admired more: that Gully went out her way to make a difference, or that she trusted her enough to show up at her exchange. Realizing they were incomparable, Harley cleared her throat and spoke up. "I have a spot in mind. It's not perfect, but it will have to do."

fourteen
the breakdown

"You can leave your shoes on," Harley said as she leaned Ethan's bike against the wall and closed her apartment door. "Do either of you want something to drink?"

"I'm good," Gully said while heading for the couch. "I'm not gonna lie, Harley. Your spot is a bit smaller than what I imagined."

"Is it?" Harley snapped the deadbolt and turned around. "I've always felt like it's perfect for my needs, especially since I rarely host."

"So I haven't been missing out on any parties?"

Harley smiled. "Not that I know of. I like to be accessible at work but prefer to keep my private life private. I need time to unwind."

"It must be nice."

"What's that?"

"Being able to unwind. I can't get a good night's sleep without someone rolling up on me and begging for a handout." Gully tossed her backpack on the coffee table and used the back of her hand to brush off the couch cushion. "I promise to respect your privacy and never stop by unannounced."

Asher opened a small door next to Harley's bedroom and poked his head inside. "Do you mind if I use your bathroom?"

Harley's eyes went straight to his pockets. "Not at all, but please leave your dope kit out here with us. This is my home, and I don't want you getting loaded here."

He pulled the door shut. "In that case, I think I can hold it."

"I appreciate that," Harley said, heading into the kitchen.

Asher worked his way around the room and ran a finger over a rippled patch of wallpaper before straightening a photo of a young Harley hugging an older boy. Moving on, he circled the coffee table and plopped down next to Gully with so much force that she toppled into him. She jabbed her elbow into his ribs and as he sat upright, he noticed a stack of books beneath the coffee table. Sitting on top was a ragged copy of *Papillon* by Henri Charrière. "This looks interesting," he said, holding it up. "Any chance I can borrow it?"

Harley reached out and removed the autobiographical novel from his hands. "Normally I'd say yes, but not this one." She stared at her brother's favorite book before placing it back on the stack. "I'm sure Powell's or the library has a copy, or you're welcome to any other book if you want."

"Hmm. What about this one?" He held up a memoir with dog-eared pages. The cover was bold and striking, depicting the shell of a man running for the hills.

"That one's not too shabby if you don't mind reading about recovery."

"Hey Ash. I got an idea. How about you quit fuckin' around and make yourself useful," Gully said. She leaned forward, unzipped her backpack and set her scale and knife on the coffee table. She removed a plastic shopping bag from the small zippered pocket and pinched a portion between her fingers. Next, she cut out a small circle—about two inches wide—and repeated the process, stockpiling the circles of plastic like a stack of pancakes. She handed the bag and scissors to Asher. "Here, make yourself useful."

Asher started slicing away until the bag was riddled with holes like a fishnet stocking. Harley dropped a pillow on the carpet and thought about setting her coffee mug on the table, but opted for the floor instead.

"Come to help?" Gully asked.

Harley shook her head and groaned as she took a seat. "My help here is limited to moral support," she said, her mug stopping short of her lips. "And Ash, please remember what we talked about on the train. This is a means to an end and it stays between us."

He nodded and sliced another circle from the bag.

Gully leaned across the coffee table and slid her scale in front of her. She unsnapped the clear acrylic lid and flipped it upside down to use it as a tray. After turning the scale on, she placed a plastic circle on the tray, zeroed the scale and held out her hand. "Dope?"

Asher dug into his pocket and pulled out the large bag of heroin. He watched curiously as Gully sliced the knot off, then— using the lid as a cutting board—took her pocketknife and scraped off a chunk of the gooey substance. She smeared the dope onto the plastic circle and gave the scale a second to register. The piece weighed a tad over a tenth of a gram, so she trimmed off a sliver, folded the plastic around the dope and twisted it closed. "Balloons?"

Asher leaned forward and grabbed the bag.

"Have you done this before?" Gully asked him, dumping the balloons on the table.

Asher shrugged.

"I'll take that as a no." She picked through the pile and separated the red balloons from the stack. "Save these for the half grams."

Asher set them aside.

Harley placed a test strip on the table. "While you two do that, do you mind if I run another test? Just to be safe."

"Be my guest," Gully said, turning back to Asher. "So once the dope is wrapped in two circles, stuff it into the balloon like this and stretch it out as you knot it. That way, when it snaps back, the knot is tight and you have enough rubber left to make a second knot." She dangled the latex balloon so Asher could see, then ripped the balloon open and handed him the wrapped portion of dope. "Your turn."

Asher was slower than Gully but the outcome was the same. His knot was pulled tight and importantly, he avoided trapping any air inside which meant they could fit more balloons in their mouths.

"Not bad," Gully said. "Now with the first knot in place, invert the balloon to double it back on itself. This way there's two layers of protection once you make the second knot."

"In case there's a hole somewhere?" Asher asked.

"That and it also helps if we accidentally bite them. But more importantly, if the cops run up on us and we need to swallow them, we don't want our stomach acid eating through the rubber as they work their way through our system."

Asher stared at the balloon in his hand.

"So take your time and get it right." Gully turned to Harley. "Are you sure you don't want to help? You've already come this far."

Gully had a point, but what she didn't know was that Harley had been struggling with the right answer since they'd first left Bridgeworks. It made sense to expedite the process and help Gully get up and running, but something stood in her way. She watched Asher struggle to tie a knot and wondered what was really holding her back. Regardless of what he said, it went without saying that he couldn't keep a secret, but Harley imagined that while some might listen to him, few would believe him.

Harley's cell phone rang and afforded her a moment to step away from the table. She glanced at the incoming call from a blocked number and excused herself to the bathroom. Closing the door behind her, she sat down on the toilet without dropping her pants and took the call.

"Hello? This is—"

"*Hello,*" a pre-recorded female voice began. "*This is a prepaid debit call from*—'Harley, don't kill me,'—*an inmate at the Mult-nomah County Jail. This call is subject to monitoring and recording. To accept this call, press zero. To refuse this call, hang up or press—"*

Beep.

"*Thank you for using SuperMate. You may start your conversation now.*"

". . . Ethan?" Harley asked in a low voice. "Why the hell are you calling me from jail?"

He breathed into the phone. "Before we start, this call is being recorded."

"I heard. What's going on? Is everything okay?"

"I'm fine, I'm just, what's the word I'm looking for? *Fucked*? I think that pretty much sums it up. Yup. I'm *fucked*."

"Why? What happened?" Harley hunched over and dropped her elbows to her knees. "And feel free to leave out the specifics."

"Actually, I hope someone's listening in right now because you're not going to believe this shit. This morning, on my way to work, I was at a red light and saw . . . POJE-M-0186 crossing the road. Do you know who I'm talking about?"

Harley nodded and pictured Pogue's face. "I do. Go on."

"Well, he came in yesterday to get his stuff checked out and of course it popped dirty. We went through the whole Never Use Alone spiel only for him to call me out for not letting him use at B-SAP like I'm some type of hypocrite."

"Really? That doesn't sound like him."

"I know. I think he's struggling with finding F-free shit. But here's where I messed up. I figured since I had your car, I'd offer him a safe space to get down."

Harley leaned back on her toilet and felt it rock slightly. "No, you didn't."

"I know it was stupid, but I felt guilty and thought that if he fell out, the least I could do was dose him and breathe for him. But of course that's not what happened. Instead, right as we parked, a cop pulled in behind us and lit us up. I'm sure the cop knows him and probably thought we were in the middle of a transaction. All I'm going to say is somehow a kit got stuffed into the center console, along with a stash of M30s and my DOC. I refused a warrantless search, but the cop claimed probable cause and now I'm facing possession and delivery charges like I'm some dealer."

"Are you serious? You couldn't convince the cops it wasn't yours?"

"You don't think I tried?" Ethan asked. "I don't want to throw anyone under the bus, but it wouldn't have mattered either way since neither of us stepped up to claim the drugs. And you know how it all goes. When no one takes the fall, everyone goes down."

Harley shook her head. "I can't believe he did that to you."

"I don't think it was personal, but there's one more thing. They've impounded your car for evidence and possibly even forfeiture."

"Of course they did." Harley sat up straight and covered her eyes. "What the fuck is wrong with them? Don't they know who you are, or where you work?"

"Oh they know, but honestly I don't know if it helped or hurt my case."

Harley shifted forward on the toilet seat. "This is making me sick. So are you both there in booking?"

"He's here. He mentioned how he thought there was no way they would have arrested me, but I have no idea what gave him that idea."

"Whatever it was, we shouldn't hold this against him. Can you tell him to come and see me first thing when he gets out? Please reiterate that we're not upset with him and—"

"Oh, we're not?"

"It doesn't matter what we are. We don't want him afraid to come around once he gets let out, and you know exactly why. Now let me work the phones and figure out what's happening. I can contact April and talk to legal if you want. Do you know yet if you qualify for pretrial release, and if so, will they release you on your own recognizance?"

"I doubt it. Also, there's no need to bother April with everything else since she has enough going on right now. I just have to wait for a bail hearing and hope it happens before getting hauled out to Inverness Jail, though I'm confident that these charges won't stick, even with my priors. The cop didn't have a warrant or consent to search the center console so he shouldn't have a case."

"Case or no case, this is such bullshit and I'm going to do whatever I can to get you out of there."

"I appreciate it, but I'll be fine. I don't want this to be a distraction for you either."

"Ethan, they had no right to—"

"Harley. Stop. Like I said earlier, I can handle this. Do you remember my favorite proverb? *'If you've survived a storm, you won't be bothered by the rain.'*"

"I do, and it's beautiful, but I really need your help out here."

"I'll be out in no time. Which reminds me, I'm not sure how much longer we have here but there's something else I need to tell you."

"I'm really hoping you have good news for me."

"Are you sitting down?"

Harley looked down at her toilet and sighed. "Let's get it over with."

"When I first arrived in booking, they sat me a few seats away from this guy who seemed to recognize me. We started talking once I realized he was a former client of ours, though I haven't seen him around the exchange for a while."

"Do you remember his client code?"

"Not off the top of my head, and he was only here for a petty shoplifting charge so he's already cut loose. He was really upset and hoping to get back to his girlfriend at the hospital. Apparently, they both overdosed yesterday and when he came to, she was still unconscious and not breathing. He mentioned he tried to breathe for her but she kept falling in and out, even after the paramedics arrived. I hate to say it Harley, but he didn't make it sound hopeful."

Harley rose from her seat and paced back and forth. "Who's the girlfriend?"

He didn't respond.

Harley froze. "Ethan, who is she?"

"OLDO-F-0703. I'm sorry."

"What hospital is she at?"

"OHSU."

"I'm on my way. Call me when you can and keep me posted." Harley hung up, rushed into her living room and struggled to find her center. She glanced at Gully and Asher. "I'm really sorry, but we have to pack it up."

Gully handed a twisted ball of plastic to Asher and waved her knife over the table. "What the hell are you talking about? We're just getting started."

"I know, but we have to go. We finally found Liv."

Gully placed her pocketknife down. "Is that the girl you've been searching for? Everything okay?"

"I'm not sure, but I have to find out." Harley combed her fingers through her hair and checked the time. "How much longer do you think you need?"

Gully dropped her chunk of heroin on the scale and did some quick math. "Forty-five minutes, maybe? Thirty with your help."

Harley blew her cheeks out. "I can't. I have to go." She rubbed her face and looked up. "Here, take this and please lock up when you're done." She pried open her key ring and removed her apartment key. "Also, I don't have a spare so please drop it off at the exchange sometime today."

"Wait, you're taking off?" Gully asked.

Harley went over to Ethan's bike and spun it around. "I don't have a choice. You can stay as long as you need to, as long as you respect my home. And Ash, no using in here, okay? This isn't another notch in your belt."

Asher nodded and tied another balloon.

"Is that a yes?" Harley asked. "Because if not, we can all just lea—"

"That's a yes," Gully said, whacking him on the arm. "We'll respect your home. Do what you need to do and don't worry about us."

Not knowing Liv's last name or date of birth, Harley filled out what she could on the Visitor Registration Form and returned the pen. The receptionist glossed over the paper and set the clipboard on her desk.

"Is the patient's decision-maker expecting you, ma'am?"

Harley shook her head.

The receptionist smiled and reached for her phone. "Okay, let me call the unit and see if they're accepting visitors at this time. Please, have a seat."

Harley sank into a squishy chair and pressed her palms into her eye sockets. She sat there motionless while her mind ran through a series of best and worst-case scenarios.

"You said someone is here to visit Olivia?" a woman asked. "It's not that 'boyfriend' of hers again, is it? If so, this time I'm calling the cops."

Harley pulled her face away from her palms and looked up to see the receptionist pointing at her.

Donna turned to face her. Her arms, sapped of energy and life, dangled at her side as she walked over to where Harley sat and towered over her. "What's your name again?"

"Harley Hammond."

"And what exactly are you doing here?"

Harley tilted her chin up. "I'm so sorry to hear what happened. I came to check on Liv."

"I think you mean *Olivia*." Donna took a step back and crossed her arms. "And I don't know what you're hoping to see, but there's not much left to 'check on'. And by the way, who told you what happened to my daughter?"

"Someone who works for me heard about the overdose from another inmate in jail," Harley said.

"Any chance it was Olivia's boyfriend? Because that son of a bitch will face a manslaughter charge if things don't turn around soon," Donna said, then pinched her lips together for a moment. "And why the hell is an employee of yours in jail?"

"It was a misunderstanding."

"Oh, I'm sure. I bet that whatever it was, someone else is to blame."

Harley popped out of her chair and stood tall. "Do you not see that all we want is for your daughter to be safe?"

Donna pushed back with a finger in Harley's face. "Do you honestly expect me to believe that enabling my daughter to use drugs is a good thing? Do you not see where we're at?"

"Donna, I know you're angry."

"*Angry*? I'm so far beyond angry that I may never find my way back."

"Is everything okay?" the receptionist asked, waving her phone. "Or do I need to call security?"

"Everything is great," Donna said sarcastically. "My one and only child is on life support and I'm dying inside, but sure, nothing to see here."

"It's not her fault," Harley said, glancing at the receptionist. "She's only trying to help."

"And let me guess, you're only 'trying to help' too? Well, it's too little, too late."

"I'm here to help, Donna, and it's never too late. I want to support Liv any way I can."

"How? Are you going to breathe for her?" Donna bit her lower lip and looked up. "You really have some nerve showing up here. And to think you can help . . . after all the damage you've done."

Harley took a step forward. "I know you're hurting Donna, but I didn't come here to fight with you. I'm here because I'm worried sick about Liv and can't stomach the idea of her fighting for her life."

"Fighting for her life?" Donna asked. "Do you have any idea what that even looks like?"

Harley stared into Donna's eyes, not only void of sleep, but of life and hope as well. "Because if you don't know what it looks like," Donna continued, "maybe it's about time you find out."

Harley held her head up. "Like I said, I'm not here to battle with you or to make this about me. I'm here for Liv and no one else."

"And *like I said*, there's no 'Liv' here." Donna gestured to the receptionist to buzz them into the Intensive Care Unit. When the door clicked open to the locked ward, she flung it open and charged through. Catching it with her palm, Harley slipped around the door and into the busy corridor.

A distant intercom cackled with an otherworldly language as Harley tailed Donna past a nursing station and down a cluttered hallway. They passed placard after placard before stopping at a closed door, but Donna didn't immediately enter. She took a moment to straighten her outfit, mouth a quiet prayer and dry her eyes with the back of her hand.

"You know, some parents can't believe something like this could happen to their child," she said, not looking at Harley. "But somehow I always knew this day would come."

Donna took a step forward and entered the room, leaving Harley to catch the door before it slammed in her face. This time though, rather than follow in her footsteps, she froze at the threshold and prepared herself to be strong for Liv.

Harley put on a brave face and pushed the door open with her thoughts collected and emotions in check. She braced herself to meet Liv, along with any family members who desperately needed someone to blame, but was surprised to see that the room was free of visitors and hope. The curtains were drawn and someone had dimmed the bright lights overhead to replicate dusk and keep reality at bay. *Family Feud* was playing on the television with the volume turned down just low enough to make one wonder whether or not they were hearing voices.

Donna was sitting on the edge of her seat next to a lonesome hospital bed. The attending nurse sensed the tension and excused herself to continue on her rounds. Harley stepped aside to let the RN squeeze by and watched as Donna looked down on her daughter with pity. Her fingers weaved through a mess of cables, lines and breathing tubes as she stroked Liv's hair with one hand while beckoning Harley closer with the other.

"Anoxic brain injury," Donna whispered, hoping her daughter wouldn't pick up on the fear in her voice. "You may think she looks peaceful, but there's nothing peaceful about it." She winced at the thought, then pulled her elbows in as if to hug herself. "The doctor said that with suppressed respiratory function, there's a very narrow window before sustained organ damage or brain death occurs." She turned her head as if to cough but buried her mouth into her shoulder, then wiped her tears on her sleeve. "Who's to say if she'll ever wake up? And if she does, will she even be the same Olivia? Will she know how to talk? Eat? Function? Laugh? Love? It's enough to make the goddamn devil cry."

Donna stayed silent for a moment longer.

"The doctors mentioned breathing and awakening trials, testing for electrical activity and something about fighting the vents, but all I need from her is to wake up so we can all go home." Donna twisted in her chair to face Harley. "Since you're here, you might as well be useful and say a prayer that she comes to and can follow simple commands without being in distress. Once that happens, they can extubate her and we can get the hell out of here."

"As long as she's alive, there's still hope."

"*Hope*? We don't need hope. What we need is a miracle."

The image of Donna crushing Liv's naloxone flashed in Harley's mind and her heart hurt to relive the memory, especially since it wasn't the first time she'd been bedside to someone with an anoxic brain injury. Harley knew from both experience and the data that the likely outcome was never what anyone wanted to hear.

She also knew that when compared to fentanyl, it was accepted that heroin was the lesser of two evils. It was often thought of as more forgiving because fentanyl could hit like a shot in the dark, depressing the brain's respiratory drive and paralyzing the very muscles needed to breathe. On a good day, the human brain could survive for maybe ten minutes without oxygen, and that was pushing it. Brain cells were often laid to rest in about half that time and even in the most optimistic cases, the damage was dire and irreversible.

While Harley kept her thoughts to herself, Donna sniffed and struggled to embrace the silence. She pushed back from the bedside and twisted in her chair. In the absence of light, the heavy circles under her eyes became more apparent. "You know what kills me?" Donna asked, not leaving space for an answer. "How this, how *all of this* could have been avoided. It didn't have to be this way." She paused and hunched over. Tears carved through her trembling lips and she blindly reached out to grip her daughter's hand. "I don't care what anyone says, I won't meet with Donor Services."

Harley couldn't tell who she was talking to. "Donna," she said, "I won't pretend to imagine what you must be going through, but if it comes down to it and you want me to stay, I'm willing to help you talk with them." She placed a hand on Donna's shoulder to comfort her, but Donna brushed it away and motioned for Harley to see herself out.

fifteen
safeguards

"Can you do me a favor and close the door, please?" Harley sat down in her chair and waited for Gabby to turn around.

"You were gone longer than what we expected," Gabby said. "Is everything okay?"

Harley held off responding until Gabby settled into her chair. "No, not really."

"Do you want to talk about it?" Gabby leaned forward and placed Harley's key on her desk. "Gully dropped by and left this for you. She said they were good to go."

Harley took the key and twisted it in her fingers. "I don't want you to worry, but Ethan got arrested and is in jail for unlawful possession of a controlled substance and—"

"What?" Gabby shifted uncomfortably and leaned forward. "Our Ethan?"

"Uh huh. He was trying to help Pogue and it backfired on him. The cops impounded my car for evidence, maybe even forfeiture . . . but that's not the worst of it." She then took a deep breath. "I found Liv."

"What do you mean you 'found Liv'? Where? *How*? Is she alive?"

"Barely. She's with her mom in the ICU on life support."

Gabby leaned back and covered her face.

"Ethan will be okay," Harley reassured her. "What he did was stupid, but his heart was in the right place. As for Liv, you know I always try to stay positive, but her injuries are serious. I'm not a doctor, but I've seen brain death before and I can't help but feel like I just saw it again."

Gabby dropped her hands. "Brain *death*?"

"It can occur when an overdose leads to oxygen deprivation and the brain stops functioning."

"So she's vegetative?"

"I can't say. They still have tests to run so there's no diagnosis yet, but either way they're not the same thing. If Liv is in a vegetative state, that's actually a better prognosis because at least there's a chance of regaining consciousness. But with brain death, the brain stem actually dies and there's no coming back."

Gabby stared down at her hands. "Poor thing. And her poor mother, too."

"I know. It was devastating and took everything I had not to fall apart." Harley picked up a pen, twirled it and placed it back down. "I think the fact that the doctors didn't medicate Liv to keep her under was very telling. She's unconscious on her own and that's never a good sign."

Gabby stood up and leaned against the wall. "How does something like this even happen? We have all the tools at our disposal to prevent this sort of tragedy from occurring, yet it *still* happens."

Harley shook her head. "I wouldn't say we have all the tools we need, and the longer our country continues to criminalize substance use disorder, the longer we'll have to wait to get them. That means people will continue to exist on the fringes of society where they are easily passed over and forgotten. It's the whole out of sight, out of mind trap, and people who get caught up in it are the ones who suffer the most."

Gabby stared at her hands as if they held the answers. "So then what's the solution? What more can we do to stop this from happening to anyone else?"

"I honestly don't know what we can do to prevent it." Harley picked up her pen again and tapped it on the desk. "At least not with the way the current laws are written. I think we're doing everything we legally can to minimize the pain, but it's clearly not enough." She rubbed at her eyelids as a weak laugh escaped her. "I can't believe I'm saying this, but maybe it's finally time to switch gears."

As soon as the words left her lips, she knew what it implied and recognized that she couldn't take it back. Not because Gabby hung onto every word or that Harley regretted what she had said, but because she knew it was the truth and that there was no way around it.

She had always believed that a commitment to patience was critical to advancing social justice issues yet recognized that time was always working against her. It took time to change the system, educate the lawmakers and garner public support. It took time to write grants, craft petitions, implement policy and coordinate outreach. Those were just some of the methods credited for transitioning harm reduction out from the underground and into the light and while they were all powerful, they were slow to take effect.

"Do you really mean that?" Gabby asked, stepping forward. "About it being time to switch gears? Because I feel like I know you too well to think that you would ever do anything to jeopardize this place or our people."

Harley exhaled. "I meant every word, but you're right. I've never wanted to expose our program to legal issues since we're not autonomous from Building Better Bridges. It's not my place to interfere with anyone else's mission, but that's also not what I'm talking about."

Gabby crossed her arms. "Go on."

"What if, instead of risking our program, we looked for a blind eye to bend the rules in our favor?"

"Who are you, and what have you done with my friend?"

"Look, from what I've just witnessed, I'm convinced something has to give. Supporting Gully and anyone else who can move safer dope gets the needle moving, but it's barely a start. Providing naloxone is a lifesaver, yet there's not enough to go around. In my mind we're in crisis mode, but I know we can get through this if we think outside of the box."

"I'm with you every step of the way," she said, placing her hands onto Harley's desk. "Where do we start?"

"First things first, I need to talk to April and if she green lights my idea, we go from there."

"And assuming she's on board, then what?"

Harley shuffled her feet beneath her desk. "I think the only solution at this point is a pop-up SCS."

Gabby dropped her hands and sat down in the chair. "No fucking way."

"I wouldn't get too excited if I were you. I'm still wrapping my head around the logistics of how we could pull it off. But like I said, it's not up to me. It would be contingent on April's approval, and she may even defer to the Board of Directors. But it never hurts to ask, and it's the only thing I can think of that could make an impact in the coming days. It's also sort of the same reason Ethan is in jail right now—he thought he was rising to the occasion when he offered to let Pogue fix up in my car."

"I can't believe this is you talking," Gabby said.

Harley sat up straight. "Really? You know I've always been a proponent of safer consumption spaces. I know the data and have studied how they work, and have always dreamt about what the first SCS in Portland would look like."

"And it sounds like your dream may come true," Gabby said.

Harley shook her head. "This isn't the same thing and it can easily turn into a nightmare if we don't pull it off. One, it won't be legal, regardless of how we spin it, and two, if it backfires on us, this has the potential to prevent the real deal from ever happening down the road."

"That won't happen, Harley. We won't let it."

"I hope you're right, but let me connect with April before we spend any more energy on this."

. . .

"In the future, may I suggest getting a drink or two inside your boss before dropping a bomb like this on them," April said lovingly, her voice blaring out of the speakerphone. "It would still be a hard pass, but at least I would be cheery about the ordeal."

Harley stared across her desk at Gabby and pinched her lips together.

"April," Harley said, "I am confident we can do it safely, or at least a lot safer than what's going on out there."

"With everything we just discussed, I would have to say safety is the least of my concerns." April paused. "That came out wrong. Safety is always a top priority, but you've been with us long enough to know how the system works. We have safeguards in place to keep the doors open, along with insurance, a landlord, neighbors and an image to uphold. These are all necessary evils, but necessary nonetheless."

"I understand," Harley said, "but we're talking about an emergency here."

"Which is even more reason to stick to the script. Can you imagine the fallout if word got out that we were letting clients use our facilities to consume heroin that's contaminated with high levels of fentanyl? It could make us complicit, especially after the recent dumping at Bridgeworks, because there's proof we're aware of what's happening."

"But you know people get dumped at hospitals, detox centers and fire stations all the time. The only reason it happens so often is *because* there is no safe place to use."

"I don't disagree, but think about this: do you know what happens when a bartender serves a patron too much beer?"

"No, but Gabby's right here. Want me to ask her?"

April sighed. "What I'm saying is there's a certain culpability when someone is over-served alcohol at an establishment. Meaning that if a bartender gives alcohol to a visibly intoxicated patron, they can be held liable for events that occur after someone leaves their premises. If the customer hops in a truck and smashes into an SUV with a family of four, it can fall back on the bartender. You see what I'm saying? How is this any different?"

"Well, we wouldn't be serving our clients alcohol or drugs. Instead, we'd be present to hopefully ensure that if an individual does overdose, they don't die. We can follow proven protocol and keep them here until they're cleared to leave. Think about the SCS in Canada. Last year, they had over *two thousand* overdoses occur on their watch without a single death. How can you say no to that? Don't you always say once something is done, it's no longer impossible?"

"Harley, I trust you and your intentions and I know you would do anything for your clients, but this is not something I can wrap my mind around. What you're talking about exposes us to unimaginable liabilities if someone were to get hurt. I can't in good conscience allow this to happen or turn a blind eye to it like I have with certain things in the past. I hope you understand my position, even though it's not what you wanted to hear."

Harley stared at Gabby, then dropped her head.

"I'm sorry, Harley, but if your heart is telling you this is the only way, maybe there's somewhere else you can take it? To a park, perhaps? Or maybe find someone who will open their apartment or business after dark? I know you have allies and supporters out there. Maybe it's time to call in some favors?"

"I understand, April. Thank you for hearing me out."

"Of course, and I wish I could have been more supportive but the only way I would have even considered this was if you somehow got a nod from the Health Department and the DA's office. And we both know, even in a progressive city like Portland, that's never, *ever* going to happen."

sixteen
all the best

Harley reached for her wallet, but Chief Morris already had his card pinched firmly in his grip. He shooed her away with the back of his hand and tapped the white lid to his Grande Pike Place Roast. "Good morning. Just this please," he said to the barista, then waited for her to remove Harley's drink from the order. Once the price dropped, he inserted his chip into the card reader, punched in his pin and passed on tipping.

Embarrassed to follow in his footsteps, Harley paid for her own coffee and offered a decent tip to compensate. After declining a receipt, she turned around and scanned the café before realizing Chief Morris had helped himself to a seat outside. She weaved through the cafe and bumped the door open with her hip, then slowly approached the table, though not for fear of burning her hand. The two of them had rarely met in person, but on the few occasions they could justify a sit-down meeting, it had always started and ended as a dreadful experience.

Harley set her coffee down and offered a smile, but Chief Morris's face remained unchanged. As she took a seat across from him, she noted how his appearance remained remarkably forgettable for a Deputy District Attorney of such stature. His suit lacked personality and seemed no different from the next, at least, not to someone like herself who wouldn't be caught dead in one. He was old enough to be her father—were her father still around

—and likely used their age gap to justify the way he spoke to her. He was partially balding as well, yet still attempted to pull off a military fade even though Mother Nature had different plans.

Together they faced the great expanse of Pioneer Courthouse Square, and in the early morning rush hour Harley was impressed the table was not only unoccupied but bussed. As she looked across the sea of bricks that were still glassy from the morning's dew, she caught the stretched reflection of street kids scampering about in full force, staking their claim before the day grew long.

She removed the corrugated sleeve from her cup and warmed her palms. "Thanks for meeting me on such short notice."

"Just doing my job," Chief Morris said.

Harley knew from prior interactions that unless she carried it, their conversation wouldn't make it very far. She cleared her throat and said, "So, do you have a busy schedule today?"

"One would think that goes without saying." Chief Morris took a sip of his coffee and savored the bitterness. "As long as crime never stops, our work doesn't stop. And speaking of crime, how are things holding up at that little exchange of yours?"

Harley forced a smile. She needed something from him and they both knew it. "Not so good."

"I bet. It sounds like it's an inconvenient time to be a junkie in the city, not that there's ever a good time to be one, though." He took another sip and set his cup down. "Your message was a little vague. What brings us here?"

Harley sat up tall in her chair. "I have to ask a favor of you, and since it's a big ask I wanted to do it in—"

"Hold on, Ms. Hammond. I'm a Deputy District Attorney, which means I don't do favors and I don't ask for them, either. Unlike your job, my profession is on the straight and narrow. Favors lend to expectations of reciprocation and eventually animosity if the 'favor' is not returned in kind. This can get sticky and is best to be avoided at all costs."

Harley looked past the Chief. Across the plaza, she could make out Gully and Asher amidst a blur of bodies. "Let's not call it a favor then. Perhaps what I'm after is your discretion in the upcoming days."

"*Discretion?*" he asked, his eyes narrowing. "I like the sound of that even less."

Harley reached into her cardigan, withdrew a piece of paper and placed it on the table. She tapped it with her finger and waited for Chief Morris to break eye contact. "These are the latest stats compared to normal times. Even before this toxicological event, too many people were dying. Now the numbers are off the charts. Hospitals are seeing an unprecedented increase in overdoses. Intensive Care Units are packed, and that's only for those lucky enough to make it that far. People are dying in their tents, being found under bridges and discovered in doorways. Yesterday, I visited a client at OHSU who is around your daughter's age and is on life support."

"It sounds to me like you have quite the disaster on your hands." Chief Morris took another sip. "What's this have to do with me?"

"With your help we can turn it all around. So much of this can be avoided if we set up a pop-up overdose prevention center at our exchange to make our way through this event." Harley observed his reaction to determine where to take it from there. Every move she made around Chief Morris was calculated, down to the term *overdose prevention center*, which polled better with politicians than any other name.

"'Pop-up' sounds like a slick way of saying illegal," Chief Morris said as he leaned back in his chair and crossed his arms. "And call it what you want, but I know what you're getting at. You may think justice is blind, but if you're asking me to turn a blind eye to the formation of a state-sponsored shooting gallery operating in the heart of downtown, during the middle of an overdose crisis, the only answer I have is—"

"It would only be for a few days until this passes."

Chief Morris stared off into the distance and rubbed his temple. Seconds later, he was shaking his head. "Not only does it sound like a terrible idea, but based on your own figures, why in the world would I encourage such a thing? If the problem is as bad as you make it sound, how would enabling the insanity to continue fix it?"

"Because you're missing the point. It's not enabling, and it's not condoning or endorsing either. Most of our clients are physically dependent and will use with or without us. At least this way we can have trained people present to protect and save lives."

"Ms. Hammond, even if I were to agree with you, which for the record I most certainly do not, why are you having this conversation with me and not the Chief of Police? His boys don't work for me, so if you're asking for a pass to engage in flagrant criminal misconduct, he's the one you want to have sign off on it. Not me."

Harley fought to keep her voice even. "My understanding was that the police focus their arrests on who the DA intends to prosecute."

"That is partially correct, though your understanding is limited. Our priorities are targeted toward offenses, not people. After all, doing otherwise would be discriminatory, right?" He shook his head and leaned forward. "Either way, I couldn't turn a blind eye to something like this because it's not my place to do so. What you want is a nod from my boss—the Elected DA—and if you think that I'm tough to work with . . ."

"Is that something you could help me with? I've worked with Harry Dalton before. He knows who we are and he has always seemed to be a strong supporter of our efforts."

Chief Morris leaned forward and drummed his fingers on his cup. "Being a strong supporter is a start, but as I'm sure you're familiar with, public perception is king. Even if Harry agrees this is a good idea, it doesn't mean that he *agrees* this is a good idea. Let me know if you need me to repeat that."

"But I can't imagine either of you would prefer the alternative. Don't you realize we're talking about our mothers, fathers, brothers, sisters, children, friends and family here? This is our community and this is a moment we can help them live to fight another day. Why would politics be involved if we're talking about a matter of life and death?"

"Oh, Ms. Hammond, you're smarter than that. Politics are *always* involved. You can't escape it. I can't escape it. It's what makes the world spin, but if you want me to jump on a different ride, you need to sell me on why I should get on board." He scooted forward and straightened his tie. "If you want something from me, I want to know what you are offering in return."

"Offering?" Harley asked, disgusted. "We're talking about saving lives here. Is that not enough for you?"

"No, it's not, mainly because I'm not convinced saving lives will be the outcome. In fact, I believe people will die under your watch and you will have to answer for it," Chief Morris said while scanning the plaza. "Look, if this is something you truly believe in, then offer me something concrete. But it has to be actionable, tangible and worthwhile. For example, I would take the names of three dealers and call it a day. They can even be small fish, too . . . doesn't matter since we can always work our way up the food chain. Do that and I'll take care of the DA and the Chief of Police."

"You know I can't do that," Harley said.

"Can't? Or won't? Because I imagine there's at least three dealers behind me watching us right now." Chief Morris waved his hand at the crowd in the square. "But if you can't do three . . . fine. I'm a reasonable man. I'll take two and you can thank me later."

"I can't do it."

"Oh, really? And why not? Aren't these the same people selling the same drugs that are killing off your precious clients? Are they not the root of all your worldly ills? Are they not the reason we're here?"

"Dealers are a dime a dozen and you know this, Kip. You lock one up and they're replaced by two more within the hour. As long as there's demand, there's supply, and not the other way around."

"So suddenly you're an economics professor too?"

Harley stared out over the plaza once again. Gully was sitting on a ledge banging her heels against the stone while pigeons swooped overhead. Asher was running amok and breaking a sweat in the far distance, hoping to play it cool in a world so cold.

"I'm sorry, but I can't give you what I don't have."

Chief Morris tried for a last sip, but his cup was empty. "Well, you can't blame me for trying, right?"

"You know what? In this case, I can." Harley picked up her coffee and got up to leave. "Have a nice day."

He leaned forward and grabbed her wrist. "Please, sit back down. This is not how negotiations work."

Harley pulled her hand away and leaned over the table. "You think I came here to *negotiate*? This isn't business to me."

"Perhaps not to you, but this is how I operate. Please," he said, motioning toward her chair.

She sat down on the edge of her seat and waited for him to make the next move.

"I know you may not believe me, but truthfully I want to help you. However, I am telling you—and this is coming from someone who is responsible for everything from fraud to assaults to human trafficking—that where there is a give, there has to be a take. Otherwise people in my position don't last. Now think, Ms. Hammond. What can you bring to the table that justifies me declaring a shift in priorities from my office?"

The word rolled off her tongue. "Data."

"Data?" Chief Morris opened and closed his mouth.

"Yes, *data*. It's the most powerful weapon we have. Numbers don't lie, and we will track every single overdose we reverse so you can defend your decision if need be. Remember, this is about saving lives," Harley said. "Nothing more. Nothing less."

Chief Morris twisted his cup on the table. "Out of curiosity, if it means so much to you, how long are we talking?"

"As long as it takes."

"No. This is not an open invitation," he said, leaning back in his chair. "But just so I can tell you I told you so, you have two days."

Harley kept a straight face and fought a burning impulse to celebrate. "Three is better."

Chief Morris cocked an eyebrow. "One day."

Harley grimaced. "Fine. We'll take two, but we need a day to prepare. That means finding a paramedic who can—"

He raised a hand to cut her off. "Save me the specifics. The less I know, the better." He reached out to shake her hand and Harley accepted. She noticed a looseness in his grip which reminded her the deal was useless without the addition of one final caveat. "One more thing," she added. "Can I get it in writing? An email is fine, or even a handwritten note."

"Sorry, Harley, but I won't be publicly tied to this when it blows up in your face like I expect it will.

Harley couldn't pull her hand back fast enough.

"Anything else I can do for you?" Chief Morris asked.

She wiped her sweaty hand on her thigh. "Since you asked, there is one more thing. It's about my coworker."

"Any word on Ethan?" Gabby asked. She stood tall at Harley's office door, twisting a thick tuft of shiny black hair around her finger.

Harley glanced up from her computer monitor. "I'm hoping he gets out soon. Morris implied he would look at his case, so we'll see how that goes. Otherwise Ethan either needs to wait for his day in court or needs to start digging a tunnel."

"And you think Morris is good for it?" Gabby asked.

Harley mulled it over for a moment. "I don't think it matters what I think. Either Ethan gets out soon or he doesn't, but right now we need to work with what we have."

"I guess you're right," Gabby said as she stepped into Harley's office. "Also, what about the SCS? I know you've had some time to think about it since yesterday, and the three of us were wondering if—"

"You're wondering if I changed my mind?"

"Yeah. Kinda." Gabby dropped her shoulders. "I know you had time to sleep on it last night. Perhaps you even calmed down a bit. I don't know. Maybe my fear is that we've talked about this before and there are so many complications we need to work out for it to all come together."

Harley started by pointing at her tired eyes. "First of all, in case you can't tell, I didn't sleep much last night, but you're absolutely correct about us having the same barriers as before." She pulled her hands back from her keyboard and started counting on her fingers. "We have logistical concerns, time restraints, safety issues and legal ramifications to worry about, especially with none of this being sanctioned. But the good news is I just got off the phone with the Health Department and they heard me out. While they didn't say yes, they didn't say no, which is good enough for me. As for Morris, he's in the loop too, so to answer your question—no, I haven't changed my mind."

"Are you sure we really want to do this?"

Harley jerked her head back. "You know, to me it sounds like you might be the one changing your mind. That's fine if you are since it's your right to do so, but aren't you the one always saying I should do more?"

"I am, but that's my go to response anytime someone jeopardizes our mission. I'm worried this can get us shut down or even tossed in jail with Ethan."

"Listen Gabs, I can assure you that we would never suffer the same fate as Ethan."

"How can you be so sure?"

"Because Inverness doesn't house female inmates. If we get sent away, they'd take us down to Coffee Creek Women's Prison."

"The real joke here is that you seriously think you're funny," Gabby said, a thin smile crossing her face. "Whatever. Maybe it's just nerves, but like I said earlier, I'm with you all the way. Do you want me to grab Karissa and Mateo so you can walk us through what you need from us today?"

"No, not yet. We still need time to prepare. I'm thinking we start tomorrow which still gives us the rest of today to get the word out. We should also hold off on handing out any more naloxone unless someone can't make it back here tomorrow." Harley looked around the room and struggled with finding words to convey her next thought. "If we can help it, I don't want anyone else to end up like Liv."

Gabby took a step closer. "I hope you know you didn't fail her." She stood there for a moment, then looked over her shoulder toward the front door. "I know it's not quite ten, but we have a decent line forming outside. How do you feel about us opening up a little early? We're all set and ready."

Harley centered her keyboard in front of her. "I still need a few more minutes to wrap up this email, but if you're good to go, then I say go for it." She smiled as Gabby left her office and then she turned back to her monitor.

. . . and based on our discussion, I appreciate the support of the District Attorney's office in allowing us to implement an emergency overdose prevention center at the Bridgeworks syringe access program. Per our discussion, our impromptu overdose prevention center will run for a duration of two days, starting tomorrow. Thank you for assisting us during this public health crisis and for seeing the value of this endeavor. Please let me know if you have questions.

All the best,

Harley S. Hammond, BSW. Pronouns: She/Her

Health Services Program Coordinator, Bridgeworks SAP

503.555.1239 | 1576 #B SW 11th Street, PDX, OR 97201

Harley read the email aloud, cc'd April and let it rip. She hoped April would accept the message at face value—assuming she ever opened it—but she also knew that April might question why the email wasn't originating from Chief Morris. Knowing April, this technicality may very well elicit a red flag but would likely not be a deal-breaker, assuming that Chief Morris didn't hit "Reply All" and publicly refute Harley's take on their conversation.

Suddenly, the lobby roared to life with a rush of clients reeling to enter the exchange room. It was a sea of familiar faces, but one stood out the most.

"Loooochhh!" Harley called out. "You got a quick second?"

Lurch was fourth in line and turned around to inspect the long string of clients behind him.

"You won't lose your spot, I promise," Harley said.

He mulled it over, then stepped out of line and into her office.

"How are you? And how's Count?"

Lurch gave the question the attention it deserved and after a long moment of searching for the perfect response, responded with a thumbs up.

"Good. I hope you stay safe and don't disappear on me. Also, since you're always in and out of the city, I wanted to let you know that starting this time tomorrow we're going to let clients use here on site so no one has to use alone. We'll open up the drug checking room and go from there. Is that something you might be interested in?"

Lurch paused for a moment and shook his head.

"And that's okay, too. If you happen to change your mind, I plan to run it for two days, but we'll see how it goes. Otherwise, I know you have a wide orbit and cross paths with people who gave up on downtown long ago. If it's not too much to ask, can you do your best to help us spread the word? Or if that's outside of your comfort zone, maybe you can help them out and point them in the right direction?"

chilean rose-haired tarántula

"Here you go, and please be sure to come back tomorrow if you need a safe space to use." Mateo handed the client a bag and motioned for the next person to enter the exchange room.

Next to him, Harley, Gabby and Karissa leaned against the counter, packed shoulder to shoulder.

As the client exited the room, Karissa tilted her head and whispered to Harley, "So, one more time, what's the problem again with starting today?"

"What's holding us back is we don't have the proper components in place, mainly someone to provide medical care in the event of an overdose. I know we all want to forge ahead, but it's not a small detail we can overlook."

Another client entered the room and started dropping needles into the Bio Bin.

"But more importantly," Harley continued, "I wanted to do one last check with you all to see if everyone's still on board."

Gabby bumped Harley with her elbow. "You already know where I stand."

"And you couldn't pay me enough to get rid of me," Karissa added.

Harley held her hands up to slow them down. "I appreciate you both always having my back, but it's important to know what you're walking into before committing to a decision.

Remember, one reason there hasn't been a legal SCS in our country yet is because of the Anti-Drug Abuse Act of 1986, aka the 'crack house' statute. I even Googled it so I wouldn't butcher it for you all." She pulled out her phone and cleared her throat. "Section A of the 'crack house statute' makes it unlawful to 'knowingly open, lease, rent, use, or maintain any place for the purpose of manufacturing, distributing, or using any controlled substance'." She cocked an eyebrow. "And 'any person who violates this section shall be sentenced to a term of imprisonment of not more than 20 years, a fine of no more than $500,000 . . . or both'."

"Up to twenty years?" Karissa asked. "Why am I not surprised? Good thing *More-ass* offered his discretion."

Gabby chuckled. "Sooo reassuring. What do you think, Mateo? Any chance you have half a mill tucked away under the mattress in your dorm?"

Distracted by counting out a handful of needles, Mateo didn't respond.

"You can still count me in," Gabby said.

"Me too," Karissa said. "Let's stick it to the man."

Harley grinned and waited for the client to leave. She motioned for the next person to hold on. "Mateo, I know you were busy, but did you catch what we were talking about? The SCS won't be legally sanctioned, so I think it's probably best for you to sit this one out."

He stared into the Bio Bin and didn't look up. "I want to help, but you're right. If I get arrested, I can lose my Student Visa and be forced to leave the country. I'm sorry. I don't want to let you all down."

"Don't be sorry," Gabby said. "You're not letting anyone down."

Karissa agreed. "I second that. You should never apologize for doing what you have to, and you can't base your decision on ours. The thing is, contrary to popular opinion, I don't have a life outside of here and school. If I get tossed in jail, the only thing I need to worry about is making up some midterms and finding someone to feed Axl."

"Axl?" Mateo looked up. "Is that your perro?"

"Does 'perro' mean dog?" Karissa asked.

He nodded.

"Then in that case, no."

Gabby shuddered. "Mateo, how does one say 'tarantula' in Spanish?"

He chuckled. "That's a little harder. Watch my lips. '*Tarántula*'."

"Excuse me, she's not any old tarántula," Karissa said. "She's a Chilean *Rose-Haired* tarántula."

"Whatever her name is," Gabby said, "it's the reason I stopped coming over to your place."

"Well, the good news is you don't need to be a stranger anymore," Karissa said, "because I finally found out where she's been hiding." She turned to Harley. "It's fascinating, really. I mean, what other animal can live under the lid of a toilet seat for weeks on end?"

Gabby shot her hands in the air. "Fuck it. I'm out!" A pack of cigarettes materialized in her hand as she headed for the lobby.

"They're amazing creatures," Karissa said to Harley. "Did you know the female can produce an egg sac with roughly five-hundred spiderlings? Maybe after this all blows over, I'll bring her in for show and tell."

"That's a joke, right?" Harley asked. "Though I'm with you—she is a little cutie. Now if you don't mind, I think Gabby desperately needs a friend right about now . . . one with two arms instead of eight."

She patted Mateo on the shoulder and left the exchange room when her cell phone rang.

"Hey, Sid. Thanks for calling, and sorry for not getting back to you sooner. I've been meaning to—"

"There's no reason to be sorry. I just wanted to check in on you after seeing the news about a bump in overdoses or something. Is everything okay? Do you need anything?"

As Harley passed her office, she closed the door and hustled toward the exit. "Not at the moment, but I appreciate the offer." She squeezed past the choke point of clients and exited the building.

"You sound busy at the moment, so I won't keep you any longer," Sidney said. "Take care of yourself and let me know if we can do anything to help."

"I will, and thanks for checking in. I'll be in touch once things calm down a bit."

Harley said goodbye, hung up and stared down the street. She knew Gabby always trudged the same path, hooking right at the door and walking the block clockwise. But in case she got pulled off course by a client in need, Harley turned in place and checked behind her.

A familiar line of clients snaked down the sidewalk. Most individuals kept to themselves, but there were a handful of couples and small cliques huddled in place. She looked past the hordes and squinted. In the distance, near the tail end of the line, was the last client she was expecting to see.

"I'm not going to lie. I missed seeing you around," Harley said, motioning for Sophia to have a seat. "How have you been?"

Sophia placed a hand on the chair and avoided eye contact as Harley walked around her desk. "Not well."

"Is everything okay? Do you mind if I ask what's going on?"

"Isn't it obvious? I left detox," Sophia said, sinking into the chair.

"Yes, but how?" Harley remained mindful of her body language and what she was signaling. With few exceptions, she knew the only time a patient ever left detox without completing the program was by asking to leave or by being asked to leave.

Sophia shrugged.

"Sophia, you should be proud of yourself for trying since many people never make it that far. You should also understand that addiction is a chronic relapsing disorder and multiple attempts at detox are the norm. It's a process, and I'm here to help you work through it if you'll let me."

"Thanks for understanding, Harley. I left AMA."

Harley smiled, but knew that a discharge against medical advice triggered certain restrictions if and when a former client wished to return to the detox program. Beyond starting from scratch with the triage process, there was the added hurdle of a fourteen-day waiting period before they were eligible to reapply for admission. She knew that even if she wanted to, Sophia couldn't turn around and head back the way she came.

"When did you leave? This morning?" Harley asked.

"Yeah, right after breakfast. It took longer than I expected to get discharged, but I came straight here after they cut me loose."

"Can I ask why?"

"Why I left detox?"

Harley nodded. "Was there a particular reason you walked out?"

Sophia thought for a moment. "I won't lie to you. I think I left for the same reason everyone else does. I'm not ready."

"And what about Jack? Any idea if he's still there?"

"I hope so, but I have no idea. I tried to ask about him as I was leaving, but they wouldn't tell me anything because of HIPAA—whatever that is."

"It's the Health Insurance Portability and Accountability Act. It protects his privacy and means that unless he signed a release, they won't disclose anything about him."

"So there's no way to tell if he's still in detox?" Sophia asked, sinking deeper into her chair.

"Not really, no. I'm also required to follow HIPAA, but that won't stop us from asking around. Everyone knows Jack, so the second he's out, I'm sure we'll hear about it. In the meantime, did you two talk about what to do if either of you left early?"

Sophia cringed at the question. "No. We just promised each other to stay the whole week, no matter what." She let out a troubled sigh and closed her eyes.

"It's okay, Sophia. These things happen all the time and there's no use in beating yourself up over it. Instead, let's focus our energy on figuring out a safety plan to protect you until Jack finishes detox . . . assuming he's still there."

"What about your friend who runs the program? Can't you call her and pass on a message?"

"You know how it is inside there. There's no communication with patients since they're quarantined from the outside world. But we can leave a message for Jack and he should get it on his way out. That way, we won't interfere with his detox attempt, but if he splits early he knows to find you."

Sophia dropped her head and clutched her hair. "I knew this was going to happen! I knew I shouldn't have left!"

Harley jumped out of her chair and rushed to Sophia's aid, squatting down at her side. "Take a deep breath and calm down. Everything is going to be okay."

"You don't know that," Sophia cried. "What if Jack gets clean and I can't? What if he moves on without me and I'm stuck here all alone?"

"Oh sweetie, you know how much Jack loves you. What makes you think he would ever turn his back on you?"

"I don't know. People change when they get clean. It's one of the first things they do." Sophia pulled her arm away and wiped her nose with her cuff. She ran through some numbers on her fingertips before giving up. "Shit, Harley. By the time I'm even allowed back into detox, he'll already have been out for over ten days."

"Why do you make that sound like a bad thing?" Harley asked. She stood up and sat on the edge of her desk. "We all have different paths in this life and you're not a failure for leaving. Just keep pushing forward and you'll get to where you want to be. That also means having an honest discussion of where we go from here because we can't change the past."

Sophia stared into space with pained and puffy eyes.

"Blink twice if you can hear me," Harley instructed.

Sophia cracked a smile.

"There we go. Now when was your last dose of Suboxone."

"This morning."

"And you understand how the medication works, right? It does more than bind to your opiate receptors—it prevents other opioids from attaching to them for at least twenty-four hours."

Sophia shifted in her seat.

"Can I ask when you used last?"

"The morning of triage," Sophia said.

"So that's what? Three days ago?"

"Something like that."

"Okay, good." Harley gripped the edge of her desk and leaned forward. "Now I'm going to ask a question, and I would appreciate an honest answer, since it's for your own sake. Did you leave detox intending to use again and if so, are you planning to use sometime today?"

Sophia breathed in through her nose. "Yes."

"Even with your blocked receptors?"

Sophia paused. "Yes. I'm sorry."

"Sorry has nothing to do with it." Harley pushed off her desk and returned to her seat. "I think we should run through a safety plan and get you set up with what you need. You've missed out on a lot in a few days, but we're opening a safer consumption space here tomorrow. As for today, if you are going to use, I don't want you using alone. Do you have any drugs on you?"

Sophia shook her head. "No, but that's my next stop."

"Do you have money?"

"Not on me, but we have an emergency stash spot down by the jail for times like these."

"Way to think ahead. What about a trusted dealer? Is there someone you know who—to the best of your knowledge—has fentanyl-free dope?"

"I'm not sure. Jack always took care of that for us, but you know how that played out last time."

"Yeah, let's not go down that route again. What about Gully? Do you know her?"

"Gully?" Sophia asked. "Of course, but Gully doesn't sell black."

"Like I said, you've missed out on a lot in a few days."

"You really think she's the best messenger for the cause?" Mateo asked.

"Maybe not the best, but she can't hurt." Harley looked around the exchange room and scratched her shoulder. "But just like Lurch, Sadie travels far and wide, or at least I imagine she does. And for anyone who doesn't believe her, they can always pop in tomorrow and find out for themselves what the deal is. Plus we need all the help we can get in getting the word out."

"You don't think it'll backfire?" Mateo asked as he counted out a handful of needles.

"Backfire how?"

Mateo turned around to face her. "I feel like the people Sadie talks to won't believe her. Or worse, what if they dismiss her and don't bother to check us out?"

Harley rubbed her temples. "That is one possibility."

Karissa pointed toward the lobby. "Do you want me to run after her? I can ask her not to mention it to anyone."

"No, I think it'll be fine," Harley said, looking around the exchange room. "Word travels fast out there and I think the idea of an SCS will intrigue most people to check it out."

"I have an idea," Gabby said. "Mateo, Harley's right that you shouldn't be here tomorrow, but what about leading a street team to send people our way? That way, you can stay in the fight and have a huge impact, all without putting yourself at risk."

Mateo handed over a health kit to a client. "I think that's a great idea."

The client smiled and agreed. "I can tell everyone I know, too. And if they tell everyone they know, and on and on, it can grow expo...?"

"Exponentially?" Karissa whispered.

"Exactly. It'll be like that old parable where the emperor got tricked into paying a man in rice as a reward for inventing chess. He started with one grain on the first square, then doubled it on the next. This continued on and on until he landed on the sixty-fourth square and there wasn't enough rice in the entire kingdom to pay him. In the end, the Emperor was royally fucked."

"I'm trying to remember if Ethan has a parable about that one," Gabby said.

"Not that I recall, but the last thing we want to be is fucked—royally or any other way," Harley said. "However, if you don't mind doing your part to pass the message along, I think I speak for all of us when I say that we would be eternally grateful."

eighteen
the years burn

Harley paced in her office and considered any last-minute details she wanted to address before the rest of the day was lost. She started with a rundown of any remaining supplies she needed to procure, but soon found herself distracted and started over. After her fourth attempt, Harley sensed frustration building up and decided to reach out for help.

Beep.

"Hi Wayne, it's me. I wanted to check in with you to see how things are going. It's not urgent, but if you can call me back when you can, I'd appreciate it."

Harley placed her phone in the cradle and leaned back in her chair. She thought of why she always struggled to visualize the successful execution of a plan and wondered whether the block was placed there by a fear of failure. As she picked at her fingernails and considered how self care was never her strong suit, her landline rang and snapped her out of self doubt.

"Wayne, your timing is impeccable."

"Now that's a first. So, to what do I owe the pleasure?"

"No pleasure out here, unfortunately. Just another long grind. Tomorrow can't come fast enough."

"Tell me about it. I can't believe how horrible these past few days have been. We've lost more people than I think I'm able to process, but one in particular has been really hard on me."

"I'm so sorry, Wayne. Can I ask who?"

"You can, but I'm not sure you want to know."

Harley pulled the phone away from her ear and squeezed the receiver. "Please don't tell me it was Philly Joe?"

"I'm sorry to have to be the one to tell you."

"I don't even know what to say other than I'm devastated. I know you and PJ go way back."

"We do. PJ was one of my first clients and has been a constant around here since long before you started. In many ways, he served as a patient advocate and helped me design our program to fit the needs of our clients. Things won't be the same without him, but he will always be with us. I'm going to leave it there because if I keep talking, I'll break down and right now I just don't have the heart to grieve."

Harley rubbed her palm against her forehead. "Unfortunately this gives me resolve that I didn't know I needed. As you know, a lot can happen in a few days. It sounds like you've been hit hard up there just like we've been slammed down here."

"I know. It's been devastating, but at least this will all be over soon."

Harley paused. "You sound so confident, Wayne. What are you seeing that I'm not?"

"I believe the streets have no choice but to correct themselves, and the dealers are probably scrambling to fix this as we speak."

"I hope you're right."

"I've been doing this a long time, Harley. If I'm not right, then everything I know is wrong and I should hang up my boots and head on home. Now, back to your news. The suspense is killing me."

Harley scratched at her throat. "I don't want to wait for the dealers to get their shit together. We're doing it, Wayne. We're opening a safer consumption space."

He went quiet for a moment. "You mean, an *unsanctioned* SCS, right?"

"If you want to get technical."

"No shit? When?"

"Tomorrow. It'll be right here at Bridgeworks."

Wayne paused. "How in the—"

"I got a blind eye from the Health Department and a nod from the DA's office, so April supported the idea."

"Wait. Are we talking about the *DA* DA, or one of his cronies?"

"I met with Deputy DA Chief Morris this morning. He runs Division Four."

"Oh I know exactly who he is, unfortunately. Promise me you'll be careful, Harley. When you've been around as long as I have, you see people's true colors. From what I've seen, he's only ever cared about two things: himself and his shoddy career."

"I'm with you, but it's not like I have any other choice."

"Well, whatever happens, know that I'm proud of you and I always have been. I'm also impressed you got the go ahead. I'm not going to lie, I'm a little jealous right now."

Harley rocked back in her chair. "Wait, why would you be jealous?" She thought for a moment and smiled. "Are you jealous because you're also opening a—"

There was a loud ruffle on the other end of the phone. "Hello?" Wayne called out. "Harley, are you still there?"

She leaned forward. "I'm still here, Wayne. Can you hear me?"

"Shit, Harley. I think you're breaking up."

"Wayne, are you there? I can hear you just fine."

". . . Hellooo? Sorry Harley, but I think I've lost you. Call me when you can, okay? And as always, keep your head up."

"Be safe out there," Gabby said as the last client left the exchange. She snapped the deadbolt, turned around and slumped against the glass. "So you say Wayne's doing the same thing up in Tacoma?"

"That's what it sounded like to me," Harley said, "especially with how our call ended. It's hard for me to imagine that our landlines could have such poor reception."

"Is that even a thing?" Mateo asked.

"It is if you want it to be. More importantly though, Wayne's never been one to let the threat of jail or a little civil disobedience stand in his way. So if he believes in his heart something is the right thing to do, he's doing it."

"Right, but he didn't come out and say he was opening an injection site?" Karissa asked.

"No, but don't read into that too much. Wayne's mindful of what he says, especially on the phone. Part of it is paranoia, but most of it comes from a long history of bad blood between his exchange and the police." Harley shrugged. "I honestly would be surprised if someone wasn't listening in."

"I only ask because if he is, I have friends in Seattle that would want to know."

"I would tell them to reach out, but knowing Wayne, I bet he has an outreach strategy in place with a backup plan for his backup plan."

Harley leaned against the wall while she considered the politicization of public health. Admittedly, substantial gains had been carved out over the years, but people from Wayne's era often struggled to move past a toxic history with law enforcement. This created an impasse, one where opposing ideas refused to budge and required a leap of faith from either side to cross the vast divide. It was also at this impasse—in the darkest depths of the canyon below—where those who had already suffered enough continued to suffer the most.

The thought hounded her last night as she wondered if her plan had the potential to unravel years of work by others. She would hate to hinder any advancement in the US that proved so critical for Canadians to ultimately garner governmental support, not only for their sanctioned programs but for their pop-up injection sites as well. But with Wayne proceeding with his own game plan to facilitate an SCS—having arrived at a similar determination on his own—it comforted her to know that they weren't alone in heading down that path.

"I don't know about the three of you," Harley said, "but I think we're about to do something meaningful here. Thank you for standing with me and for supporting our clients."

"You don't have to thank us," Gabby said. "This is what we do."

Mateo shuffled his foot back and forth on the floor, refusing to look at Gabby or Karissa. "I'm sorry I can't do more to help."

"Please don't say that," Harley said, taking a step in his direction. "Remember what we're doing in here won't make a difference if we can't get the word out there, and every person you send our way could be a life you helped save."

Mateo stood up a little taller.

"And I made some flyers for you to pass out," Harley said. "Please don't forget to take them when you leave. They're similar to the drug alert flyers but they also include signs of an overdose and a quick breakdown of the Good Sam Law. There's no mention of the SCS though, since it's probably best to communicate that verbally."

"I can hand them out tonight. Is there somewhere in particular you want me to start?" he asked.

"Alcoves. Doorways. Under bridges. Anywhere that's dry and warm."

"I'm happy to tag along," Gabby said. "It'll be like our own little walking tour. We can start at the Square, make our way to the Waterfront and take that down to the rescue shelters in Old Town."

"And while you two do that," Karissa said, "I'll scour the MAX lines since a lot of people ride them to stay dry."

"I love it," Harley said, smiling. "While you all divide and conquer, I'll work the phone and reach out to my network of first responders and emergency departments. Hopefully, if they discharge anyone, they can send them our way."

"Speaking of discharge, what about the jails?" Mateo asked.

"Didn't you say the odds of overdosing skyrockets even after a brief stint in jail?"

"I did, and that's a good point," Harley said, "but the problem is there's no way to get a message inside."

"What about Ethan?" Gabby asked. "Can't he spread the word?"

"I doubt it, because even if he's not already transferred to Inverness, he would have to reach out to me, not the other way around." Harley thought about it for a moment. "But that's not to say you can't post up outside of Multnomah County Jail tomorrow."

"I can do that," Mateo said, turning to Gabby. "Any chance you know where they get released?"

Gabby nodded. "Inmates are crammed into a holding tank and booked for dress out before riding an elevator to the main floor. They're funneled into a waiting room and wait for their name to be called out on a speaker. Then they head into a property room to collect their things and have their fingerprints matched against a database. If they have any money on their books, they go to the money room to cash it out, otherwise they're let loose into the jail lobby and are home free, so to speak."

"I'm not even going to ask how you know this," Harley said.

Gabby played along and placed a hand over her heart. "What? You think you're the only one who needs some excitement in their life every now and then?" She turned to Mateo. "Lownsdale Square is right across from the jail and is where most people wait for their loved ones to be released. I would start there."

A loud knock on the door startled Gabby. She turned around to reveal the bridge of Sophia's nose smudged up against the glass. Her eyes were cupped between her hands, peering into the lobby, praying to be let in.

nineteen
rinse. repeat.

"Good morning everyone." Harley locked the front door, stepped around Gabby and Karissa, then took her place next to a thin man in tan khakis. "You both remember John, right? He's been a paramedic here in Portland for what? Eight years now?"

"Almost ten, if you can believe it."

"Wow, time really flies."

"That it does," John said, crouching down and setting a black duffel bag on the floor.

Harley checked the wall clock. "Speaking of time, we should go ahead and get started. People will be knocking down our door any minute now."

"I'm ready when you are," John said, twisting his wedding ring back and forth.

Harley turned to her team. "One more thing before I forget. This morning, the Oregon Health Authority published a press release that confirms what we already know, that the sudden increase in overdoses in the Portland area appears to be driven by the presence of fentanyl in the drug supply."

Karissa rubbed her forehead. "Took them long enough."

"That's one way to look at it, or you can take it as a sign that we're making the right decision here." Harley reached out and placed her hand on John's back. "That's what we did, and in case you're wondering why John is here, it's because he's graciously volunteered to be our own in-house medic. But while we're grateful for his help, let's be sure to respect the fact that he has a career and family to feed and not broadcast who he is or what he does."

"So you're basically a superhero in disguise?" Karissa asked. "Who's your alter ego?"

"Just John is fine, thanks. Harley is being considerate, but I've resuscitated so many people over the years that most of your clients will recognize me."

"Fair enough," she said, "but for those who don't already know you by name, your secret is safe with us."

John smiled, then bent down and unzipped his duffel bag but didn't remove any items from it. Instead, he glanced up to make eye contact with the three women. "I want you all to know I appreciate what you're doing here, and I'm honored to have been asked to help. I've always thought that something like this should have been set up a long time ago, so I respect you all for stepping up and showing initiative."

"Thanks John. The feeling is mutual," Harley said. "Just remember that we wouldn't be able to do this safely without you and your skills."

John stood up, removed his glasses and cleaned them with his shirt. "Speaking of safety, Harley and I have discussed what has to be done to keep this experience as safe as possible and considering there's only four of us, we're going to have to divide and conquer."

"Exactly," Harley said. "We've gone back and forth, but ultimately it makes the most sense to use the testing room as an injection booth and my office as the monitoring room."

"I like it," Gabby said. "Like our own little version of Canada's SCS."

"Except we don't have two floors above us with a detox center and transitional recovery housing."

"Either way, it won't stop us from making a difference," John said, stepping forward. "If I remember correctly, this is your testing room, right?" He knocked on the door before opening it and peeking inside.

"That's where we do drug checking as well as run tests for blood-borne diseases and STIs," Harley said.

"It's pretty tight in there," he said, closing the door. "It definitely makes sense to put me in your office."

Harley nodded. "And while you monitor people there, Gabby can run the exchange room while Karissa works the lobby. I'll stick with clients while they use in the testing room and try to expedite the process, but just so everyone knows I won't be rushing anyone. It may seem counterintuitive, but I think most people underperform when the pressure is on. How's that sound to everyone?"

"It makes no difference to me as long as the clients come in for monitoring immediately after they use," John said. "We can't have anyone lingering in the lobby or heading for the door. By the way, how much Narcan do you have here?"

"Not much," Harley said. "We gave most of it away, but I imagine the clients who received them will return with their vials. I also have a few sprays stashed for emergency use."

"Every bit helps." John reached into his bag and removed a bag of plastic syringes with conical plugs on the tips. "I also brought some Narcan and these atomizers. They'll do the trick, but I honestly prefer the IM injections when given the choice."

Gabby scratched her forehead. "You prefer injectables over nasal sprays? Why? Don't injectables take longer to take effect?"

"They do, but they also last longer for the same reason. Remember, I go to a lot of calls where a patient comes to and would rather walk it off than go to the hospital. When that happens, an IM injection should give them about ninety minutes to make it wherever they're headed. The other thing to mention is that when I respond to an overdose call, I try to hold off on administering any form of Narcan for as long as I can."

"I'm confused," Karissa said. "Isn't time of the essence?"

John turned to Harley. "I'm not sure if we have the time to get into it."

"We're good," she said, crossing her arms. "And now I really want to know."

He mulled over his response for a moment. "The main reason I try to hold off on dosing someone is to prevent sending them into precipitated opioid withdrawal. The reason for this is simple —it's extremely painful for them. But if the situation requires a response, I prefer going intramuscularly because a single IM dose is 0.4 mg, whereas the nasal sprays are ten times that. I understand the sprays require a larger dose because of how they're absorbed, but my issue with the sprays—specifically the ones you have—is that they're all or nothing. With the injectables, even these atomizers, I can scale my dose approximately and if I'm careful enough, hopefully avoid precipitated withdrawal."

John removed his hat and ran his fingers through his hair before continuing. "Lastly, remember that overdoses are different for each person. If the person is still conscious and breathing adequately, you'd be surprised at how much progress can be made, not with medicine, but by showing a little interest and humanity. Do what you can to keep someone talking and engaged. I know some of my colleagues—especially the newer medics—will rush to dose patients, but sometimes a little compassion is all the push anyone ever needs."

"I really love hearing that's how you approach these situations," Harley said. "It gives me hope, even though we teach our clients to always go with a full dose. They just don't have the proper training if things escalate."

"And that's the right call." John reached into his duffel bag and pulled out some items. "Very few people have the luxury of carrying a bag-valve mask and an endotracheal tube with them everywhere they go."

"Is that to intubate someone?" Karissa turned her head to the side, inspected the bagged tube and gagged. "Actually, forget it. I don't even want to know."

"Don't worry. If you're at a point where you need this, you

wouldn't, or *shouldn't*, remember it." He shook the tube and let it flop back into his bag. "Mostly, this is the last straw for unconscious patients, but again, if the person is breathing, there are other things to try." He raked his knuckles up and down his sternum. "You can do a sternal rub right here, or press the soft spot behind their ear lobes to initiate a painful response. Another trick is to dig your thumbs under their jaw and press up on this spot right here." He craned his neck to show everyone. "If that fails, then my last trick is to take a pen and push down on their fingernail bed." John pinched his own fingernail for a moment and winced.

"Looks painful," Gabby said.

"It is, but that's the point. We're shooting to elicit a response, remember? But all of this depends on whether or not the patient is breathing. If there's no chest rise, or if they're gasping from agonal breathing, it's time to act fast because cardiac arrest is coming."

Mateo held up a finger. "What's that?"

"Agonal breathing? It's when the heart is no longer pumping fully oxygenated blood and a person's lung activity is decimated. It sometimes sounds like moaning or groaning, but really it's the sound of someone dying." John looked at the rest of the team. "Just so we're all on the same page, if something like that happens today I'll be the first one to dial 911. No one's dying on my watch here today."

"We're with you, John." Harley took a deep breath and focused on the crowd forming outside of the front door. "And since you're our guest here today, would you like to do the honors?"

"Seriously, Clay?" Harley asked.

"Hey, weren't you the one who authorized me jumping to the front of the line each day?" He leaned his guitar against the back of the door and took a seat at the table. "Besides, I wouldn't miss this for the world. It's not everyday I get to shoot up at Bridge-works. And to be the first is . . . well, it's *historic.*"

Harley scoffed. "We're not trying to make history here. This is about desperate times calling for desperate measures, and I have to ask, are you really desperate? I know you don't shoot heroin, and every time we've tested your meth it came back clean. If you want us to test it again, that's fine, but the whole idea here was to make it safer for anyone with fentanyl in their dope."

"That's not what Karissa is saying. She said anyone can use here and no one gets turned away."

"And she's right. We won't turn anyone away, but if you came for the sheer pleasure of saying you shot up here, I would ask you to be considerate of people waiting for that seat."

"I promise I'll be quick. How's that for being considerate?"

Harley reached out and sanitized the table with a disinfectant wipe. "It's fine, Clay. Go right ahead."

He smiled and slapped a bag of meth on the table. His eyes narrowed, then widened as he pulled the plunger out of a syringe.

"Oh, shoot. There's one last thing before you start," Harley said. "Did Karissa explain to you how this all works?"

"How *what* works?"

"Our SCS. Did she tell you what to expect?"

"Not really. She sort of has her hands full out there. But it's not like shooting up is rocket science. I've done it a million times."

"No, I'm not talking about that." Harley closed the lid to the roll of wipes. "Did she mention that after you use here, you're required to stick around for medical monitoring?"

"No, she mentioned nothing about that. And what do you mean by 'monitoring'? For how long?"

"Twenty minutes."

"*Twenty min*—? Do I look like I have twenty minutes to spare? Do you have any idea how long that is?"

Harley shrugged. "I could take a wild guess, but it'll go by fast. I'm sure it'll be over before you know it."

"That's not the point. It'll kill my high," he said, leaning back in his chair. "I think you're only saying this because you know I'm always in a rush."

"It's the same rules for everyone and no one's singling you out. I just wanted to make sure you understood how this works. Now if you don't mind, we have to keep this going."

Clay picked up his syringe and started tapping it on the table. "On second thought, I think I'll let the next guy go. He probably needs this more than I do."

"Sounds like a great idea. Want me to test your meth before you leave?"

"Don't worry about it, we've already tested it." Clay snatched his guitar and slipped into the hallway.

Harley cleared her throat. "Next!"

A bloated client in a leather jacket entered the room. He sheepishly smiled and peeked behind the door.

"Looking for something?" Harley asked. "Or someone? Because it's only me in here."

The man closed the door and inspected the drop ceiling panels. He spun in place, gripped the chair and looked under the table.

Harley leaned over to meet him on his level. "Is . . . everything okay?"

The man stood up. "No cameras, right?" He leaned forward and squinted at her chest. "And no wires, right?"

Harley covered her chest and leaned back. "I'm going to forget you just asked that." She watched as he reached down and tilted his chair forward, inspecting the underside. "Actually, you know what? I'm not going to forget you asked that. *What* makes you think that I, of all people, would be wearing a wire? Don't you know that we're the ones putting it all on the line right now?"

He placed a hand on the back of the chair. "Do you promise?"

"Promise that this isn't a setup?" Harley disinfected the table again and motioned to the chair. "I promise."

The client nodded and sat down.

"Did Karissa tell you about the monitoring afterward? Twenty minutes in my office?"

"Yes, and that's fine. I want to be as safe as the next guy."

"Perfect." Harley picked up a pen and slid a clipboard in front of her. "Before we begin, please confirm your client code and any other drugs you may have used today."

"Does pot count?"

"As a drug? It depends who you ask but I'll still put it down." Harley took the rest of his information and placed her pen on the table.

After removing his jacket, the client rolled up his sleeves, smiled at Harley, then promptly appeared to forget she was in the room. She watched with interest as his OCD came over him. Item after item was removed from his health kit and laid out in the open. He aligned the needle perpendicular to the edge of the table, then spaced his cooker, water container and bag of cottons into a straight line. With everything in place, he thumped his chest and regurgitated a balloon coated in gastric juices from some dark corner of his esophagus.

"Wicked trick," Harley said. She uncrossed her legs and stretched them out beneath the table.

Her comment flew over his head as he cracked off a chunk of heroin, set it into the cooker and filled his syringe halfway with clean water. He sprayed it into the cooker, picked it up with his fingers and reached for his lighter.

"Want to use a twist tie as a holder?" Harley asked, reaching for his bag. "So you don't burn your fingers?"

"Don't worry about me. I won't feel any more pain here in a second."

Harley watched as he snapped a flame beneath the cooker and angled it so the flame danced away from the edge he was holding. Within seconds, the mixture sizzled to life before dying off. The silver cooker, now blackened, was placed on the table and a small cotton ball was plopped into the liquid like a life preserver.

Harley held up a fentanyl test strip. "May I?" she asked. "After you draw your shot?"

"You want me to give you my rinse?" he asked. "This is all I have."

"It's up to you, but the strip barely absorbs any fluid. And you can always save the rest for later by either loading a rig or soaking it up with cotton."

He thought about it briefly, then filled his syringe and placed the cooker in front of her.

Harley added a few drops of water, mixed it with the strip and hummed the Happy Birthday song. "It'll take a few more seconds to give us a result," she said. "I forgot to suggest considering a test shot, but that's up to you."

"I'd rather not, if you don't mind. I'll barely feel this as it is."

"Again, it's your decision to make, but it's strongly suggested."

"In that case, yeah, I'd rather not. And what about the strip?" he asked. "Can I keep it when you're done? To rinse later when I end up feeling desperate."

Harley had never been asked that before. Clearing her throat, she said, "You want to rinse the strip?"

"I mean, it has dope on it, right?"

"Not enough to do anything for anyone. Besides, this strip is probably loaded with all sorts of chemicals."

"So? It's not like I know what's in my dope, either." He held up his loaded needle. "This could be cut with dirt, shoe polish, shit . . . even rat poison for all I know." He tilted the syringe sideways and held it up to the light. The fluid inside the chamber had the viscosity of buttery molasses.

While his attention was elsewhere, Harley picked up the strip, read the results and held it over the trash. "The test is negative. Do you mind?"

He shrugged and turned his attention to his hand, wrapped a tourniquet around his wrist and started poking at the veins with his thumb. Once he settled on a spongy vessel with bounce back, he reached for his needle.

"Can I suggest cleaning your injection site first?" Harley asked. "You should have alcohol pads in your health kit."

"Oh, is that what those are for? I never use them, but would it make you feel better if I did?"

"I mean, it's about your safety, not mine."

The client set his needle down, tore open the package and rubbed the top of his hand with the prep pad.

"Looks good," Harley said. "Now all I ask is that you pack up now before you take your shot. That way you can head directly into my office for monitoring and we can keep this train moving."

"Come on, you son of a bitch! Show me somethin'," he pleaded.

The old man with the DNR tattoo partially removed the needle from his arm and changed the angle of attack. He slipped the syringe back into his upper bicep and fished around for a vein, hoping to spot a flashback of blood in the chamber. After each failed attempt, he repeated the process, pulling the rig halfway out before poking through scar tissue again. As frustration set in, he grew more and more agitated until he finally caved, removed the syringe and laid it flat across his cooker.

"I swear it fuckin' worked last time," he seethed. "I wonder if I need to drink more water?"

"Water helps," Harley said, "but it takes time to rehydrate yourself."

"Motherfucker." He peeled off his bandana and wiped beads of sweat from his brow with a paper towel spotted with blood, then applied steady pressure to a fresh hole in his arm. "How much longer do I got left before I'm kicked to the curb?"

"No one's kicking anyone anywhere," Harley promised. "As long as you're actively trying to inject, you have as long as you need."

"That's awfully kind of you, but I'm not one to overstay my welcome." He tossed the crumpled paper towel into the trash, rolled down his sleeve and stared at the ground. "Mind if I try my foot?"

"Be my guest," Harley said.

The old man peeled off a weathered sock, rolled up his cuff and placed a marred foot on the table. His legs were pasty, puckered and scarred from several abscesses that had left their mark over the years. In certain spots, chunks of flesh looked to have been removed with an ice cream scooper, leaving deep divots that did their best to heal over. Time, it appeared, could not heal all wounds, nor would it prevent him from cinching a tourniquet around his ankle in hopes of summoning some ancient and collapsed vein to the surface.

Someone tapped lightly on the door.

"Who is it?" Harley called out.

"It's me. Sorry to interrupt, but can I talk to you for a second?" Karissa asked.

Harley looked at the client. "Do you mind if my coworker sticks her head in here?"

"No, not at all."

Harley got up and cracked the door open. A raucous commotion bled out of the lobby and invaded the small space. "Karissa, what's going on?"

"Sorry to bother you," she whispered. "I wanted to check and see if everything was okay. It's been over fifteen minutes and we're getting a little cramped out here." Karissa glanced over Harley's shoulder and though his back was to her, she immediately recognized the old man sitting at the table. "I was going to offer to help, but on second thought, maybe you don't need it."

Harley turned around and watched as he wiped his foot. "I think we'll be done when we're done. If people are getting antsy, please remind them they won't be rushed either."

"You got it," Karissa said, pulling the door closed.

Harley sat back down and watched the old man take another stab at his vein.

"I don't know what's wrong with me," he said. "Maybe I'm nervous about having someone around watchin' me."

"Unfortunately I can't leave the room, but if you think it'll help, I'm happy to turn around and face the corner."

He clenched his teeth and withdrew the needle from his foot. "It probably wouldn't make a difference anyway."

Harley stared down at his feet. "You know there are other routes of administration if you can't find a vein, right? Have you considered maybe smoking or snorting again and giving your veins time to heal?"

"Never." The man slipped the needle into his skin and was mindful not to scrape bone. "Do you have any clue how high my tolerance is?"

"Probably through the roof, but I guess you can't smoke it anyway since it's already diluted." She paused and looked at his loaded rig. "What about boofing?"

"*Boofin*?"

"Yes, boofing." Harley scooted her chair forward. "Or booty-bumping or whatever names the kids are calling it these days."

He pulled the needle out of his foot and held it out in front of him. "You're talkin' about me shovin' this shit up my ass?"

"Technically, you would squirt it up there since it's already dissolved. If you want a needleless syringe, we have them in the other room."

"No, I don't want anything like that." Despite having walked in pale, he looked like he'd seen a ghost. "You've got to be shittin' me. In all my years, that's a fuckin' first."

"I'm not shitting you, though it is recommended you shit first, if you can." Harley removed a paper towel from the roll and handed it to the man. "Honestly, I'm surprised that in all your travels you've never considered going down this road, especially when it's comparable to the delivery rate of injecting."

"And you people wonder why I never ask for help."

"All jokes aside, I swear I'm being serious, especially as I sit here and watch you struggling to get off. But there are other benefits too besides a rapid delivery. For example, you don't have the same risks of collapsed veins or blood-borne infections to deal with. Sure, overdosing and anal abscesses are possible, but as long as you dissolve your drugs first and don't cram them like suppositories, you should be good to go."

"Again, no one's stuffin' nothin'." He stood up, dropped his pants halfway and jammed the needle into what little muscle he had left in his butt cheek. Harley watched as he depressed the plunger, took a deep breath and flipped his syringe into the sharps container.

"Just think about it," Harley said. "It's a good trick to keep in your back pocket."

The man sneered as he reached for his walking stick. "When will you kids ever learn that you can't teach an old dog new tricks?"

twenty
safer drug use

Harley turned the knob to open her office door and pushed it open, but it didn't budge. She smiled at the crowd of clients in the lobby and tried again, this time leaning into it with her shoulder. The door bumped open an inch, then slammed shut.

"Need some help?" someone from the crowd asked.

Harley waved him off, jiggled the doorknob again and pressed her ear against the door, but she could only hear a growing chatter echo out from behind her.

The morning rush was like nothing she had ever seen before. Added to the usual line of regulars was an eager crowd waiting to put the injection room to use. Harley could feel their warmth radiating in the small space, along with a spat of confusion in the air as clients negotiated with one another over who was next for what.

With Karissa relieving her for a quick break, Harley made a note to mention the issue to her. It made sense to establish two clear lines, where clients exiting the exchange room needed to wait their turn in the injection room line like everyone else. She turned her attention back to the door and threw her weight into it one last time and stumbled into her office as the door flew open.

A tall client with droopy eyes reached out to catch her. "Sorry," he mumbled as she pressed off of him. "I guess it's probably not the . . . uh . . . not the—"

"Not the best idea to block the only way in or out?" Harley smiled and stepped around him.

She looked around her office and couldn't remember the last time she had so many clients packed into such small quarters. Six clients were scattered around with their baggage strewn about. They were all seated on the floor, leaning against walls, shelves, filing cabinets and each other. John waved to her from behind her desk, then placed his pen down on a notepad. In front of the desk was his black duffel bag, armed and ready.

"How's it going?" Harley asked. She waved to the clients and approached the desk.

"Better than expected. I did have one guy attempt to sneak another shot in here, but I stopped him in his tracks and sent him packing. Other than that, so far, so good." John spun his notepad around to show off his chicken scratch. "There's been three over-doses so far, but they all responded well with no complications. Also, during the second and third OD, I asked if anyone wanted to practice administering naloxone, but everyone already seemed to be experienced."

"Sounds about right," Harley said. "Our last survey reported that over three quarters of all clients have responded to at least one overdose before."

"In that case, I'll keep offering because one in four is still a decent-sized number. And where else do you get to see Narcan in action? Even in Paramedic school, all we had to practice on were rubber dummies until we finally started our internship."

"I think it's a brilliant idea, John. *Teach a man to fish.*"

"Exactly." His cell phone timer went off and John pointed around Harley to the guy standing by the door. "Hey, blue shirt. You're free to go. Everyone else, switch!"

Harley watched as clients rotated clockwise around her, grumbling as they shuffled their butts across the floor. A man roused his buddy and helped guide him to his new location, then moved his friend's belongings for him. The rotation created an opening near the door, just in time for the new client who entered the room.

John pointed at the open spot and reset his timer. "Having them rotate not only helps me stay on top of their time, but it also keeps them alert and moving."

Harley smiled and sensed her client's appreciation for being somewhere safe for once. It was as if they were offered a respite from the endless pressure of an existence known to demand constant movement. Whether being roused by the police in the middle of the night or being escorted out of a hospital waiting room, society loved to sweep these men and women out of sight and mind. But in her office, despite the looming threat to their very existence, her clients could relax in a safe location where everyone around them wanted nothing but the best for them.

She stepped over a pair of legs and headed for the door. The legs belonged to a familiar client who—like the other men and women in the room and lobby—might otherwise be shooting up alone in a park or in a public bathroom. Harley sensed such relief to see him resting there in good hands with John, knowing that John wasn't there to judge or pressure anyone either way, only to ensure proper medical attention was provided as needed.

Harley took a step into the lobby and did a double-take. In the few minutes she'd been in her office, the crowd had nearly doubled. Bobbing back and forth to get a glimpse of the front door, she was curious if the line outside had moved inside, but her line of sight was blocked. She debated the best way to return to the injection room before skirting the wall and tapping someone on the back to let her squeeze by. The man didn't respond to the first tap, but after a second attempt, he slowly turned around and leaned into the wall.

His face, miserably haggard, was drained of color and life. Two sunken eyes flickered, and with the back of his hand, he reached up and pinched his nostrils to prevent any more mucus from seeping out.

"Harley," Sonny muttered, "I thought you were in there?" He glanced at the injection room.

"I am. I just needed to make my rounds." She followed the drips of snot that ran down his shirt and noticed his missing shoelaces. "I take it you just got released from jail?"

Sonny nodded and slapped some papers against his thigh. "Mateo sent me up here, but I had no idea it would be this busy."

"I know. I'm sorry. How long were you in jail?"

"Less than a day. I was booked and released, but went in sick." He raised his voice to speak over the crowd. "Any chance I can get a pass to the front of the line? I feel like I'm about to shit myself."

Harley rubbed her face. "If it were up to me, you know I would, but—"

"Please," he begged. "I don't want to use outside and get arrested again." He transferred his weight back onto the wall.

She cleared her throat and waved a hand in the air. "Can I have everyone's attention for a sec?" Waving her hand from side to side, she waited patiently for the crowd to settle down. Several clients continued on with their conversations as others tapped their shoulders and pointed at Harley. "I know that everyone's been waiting for their turn and I want to thank you all for your patience. I also know that Sonny here was recently released from jail and appears to be in a world of hurt. Does anyone mind if we let him jump to the front?"

The response was minimal, except for a handful of clients who shrugged indifferently and some distant voice that suggested they were all equally sick.

"I'll be quick," Sonny promised.

Harley bounced on her tiptoes and scanned the room. "No one minds?" She did a final take when a hand in the far corner reached for the sky.

She glanced at Sonny and shook her head as the man weaved through the crowd like a rat in a cupboard. His shoes clicked sharply on the linoleum and when he popped out of the crowd, Harley realized the sound was coming from his cleated cycling shoes.

"You said your name's Sonny?" the cyclist asked. He dropped

his hand and gripped the shoulder strap of his roll-top bag.

Sonny nodded and slumped against the wall.

"I've seen you around. Do you know who I am?"

Sonny stared at the cyclist and nodded.

"Good, and do you have what you need?"

"An old friend gifted me a rinse on the way up here, but you know that's always hit or miss."

"Do yourself a favor and toss that shit in the trash where it belongs. I'll set you right as long as you get me back when you can."

Sonny formed a steeple with his hands. "Are you serious? You'd really do that for me?"

"I'll do it for anyone as long as they can back up their story with some paperwork." The cyclist held out his hand.

Sonny reached out and handed his papers over. "I'll even pay you back double."

The cyclist examined the papers and turned to Harley. "Is it still considered dealing in your mind if he's not paying for it? Or would you rather we take a walk?"

"The only way we're taking a walk is if you're carrying me," Sonny said.

Harley looked around at the room and refused to respond.

"In that case, here you go." The cyclist returned Sonny's paperwork and held out a small balloon. "If you're ever in Old Town, hit me up."

"Yo!" someone from the crowd called out. "I also just got released from jail, but didn't think to keep my paperwork. Any chance I can get a front?"

The cyclist waved him off and worked his way back into the crowd while Harley took Sonny by the arm and guided him into the injection room. People stepped aside to make way and someone patted Sonny on the back, assuring him he would be okay.

Despite his weakness, Sonny took a seat and cooked up his shot within seconds. By the time he was tied off at his forearm and fiddling for a vein, Harley imagined it would have been a world record if people tracked and rewarded such things. She wondered if his proficiency was honed over years of rushing to get high in places where he was unwanted, like how he used the back of his thumb to draw the shot to keep his other hand free or how he coughed when he snapped his lighter. Harley had seen the habit before and knew it as a crude attempt aimed to cover the sound and not draw attention when fixing in public bathroom stalls.

"I have to say I'm sick of this shit," Sonny said. "It's all one big clusterfuck of a rollercoaster ride. It always starts out with a rush, but eventually I find myself stuck in a loop, dangling upside down and unable to get off." A flash of dark red blood rushed into the barrel of Sonny's syringe. He popped his tourniquet, depressed the plunger and dumped the shot into his bloodstream, never to be seen or heard from again.

Harley gave him a second to get a few deep breaths under his belt. "How are you feeling now?"

He rolled his head from side to side and smiled grimly. "Like a new man."

Harley leaned forward in her chair. "You know, I couldn't really tell if you were just asking for help or venting, but if you ever want or need help, all you have to do is ask."

Sonny nodded and took his time getting up. "I think I'm good for now, but if anything changes, you'll be the first to know." He picked up his paperwork and tossed it in the trash.

"Twenty minutes in the monitoring room and you're out of here. Be safe and take your time getting there."

Sonny gave her a thumbs up and swung the door open, but he didn't make an effort to leave. Instead, he took a step back to let a woman enter the room, courteous even in his influenced state.

"Sophia?" Harley popped out of her chair as Sonny slipped out of the room and closed the door behind him. "How's everything going?"

"Hi, Harley. I tried to see if they'd let me back into detox this morning but they weren't having it."

"I was worried about that. I know they're pretty strict about their waiting period. Hopefully the women's shelter wasn't too shabby?"

Sophia shrugged. "It was fine, but I miss Jack and feel lost without him. I wish I hadn't left."

Harley gave her a hug and directed her into the chair. "He should be out in a few days. I know it's not how you wanted it all to play out, but you have to hang in there and not beat yourself up over the decision you made. All you can do is own it and move on."

"Trust me I'm trying, but I don't even know where to start," Sophia said, scraping her foot back and forth on the floor.

"What do you mean?"

"Well, Jack used to take care of everything for us. He was the one who would always meet our dealers, fix our shots and inject for me."

Harley looked down at the health kit Sophia was holding. "Did you just get that from Karissa?"

"This? No. Jack likes to keep a backup kit in our stash spot just in case."

"So you're here to fix?"

"That's the plan."

"What about your dope? Did it come from Gully?"

"Yeah, I caught her last night but sat on it. I did snort a little at the shelter but you were right, my receptors must've still been blocked." Sophia pulled out a twisted circle of plastic and placed it on the table. "I bought a half gram from her, but the problem is even though I've seen Jack prep our shots a million times, I don't know where to start."

"And the same goes for injecting?"

Sophia nodded. "I've only had to do it once when Jack was in jail, but I was terrified. I tried this morning, but I missed miserably."

"Can I see?"

"Sure." Sophia pulled her sweater over her head and placed her arm on the table. "I'm not sure if I hit an artery or not, but blood coagulated inside the needle before I could find a vein."

Harley examined Sophia's arm and felt her pain. "How many times did you try to hit?"

"A lot? I'm not sure. I was frustrated and scared."

"I can tell," Harley said, leaning back in her chair. "You can tell me if it's none of my business, but I have to ask: was there a reason Jack never let you fix your own shots or inject yourself?"

"It's not so much that he wouldn't let me. I'm afraid of needles."

"Oh, okay. Just checking, because it's something we see all the time in abusive relationships, where one partner controls the drugs and the other partner becomes trapped."

Sophia shook her head. "It's not like that with Jack, I promise. If anything, it's a burden for him and he's tried to teach me, but I never wanted to learn."

"Totally makes sense. Just checking."

Sophia turned her attention back to the dope on the table. "Do you think you could do it for me?"

"Do what? Fix your shot for you?"

"Not only that, but I was thinking maybe, well . . . you know."

"I'm sorry, but I can't."

"It was a stupid question, I know."

"Actually, it's not," Harley said. "In fact, this has been a heated debate within the harm reduction community since forever, mainly because the laws won't protect professionals from culpability if they doctor a shot and someone gets injured."

Sophia stared at Harley and acknowledged that she understood her position.

"It's also why we put so much focus on teaching safer drug use, especially since most drug users learn how to inject from another drug user who wasn't trained on the best practices. And when you have someone like yourself who is physically dependent, it's even more important to learn how to do it because otherwise you find yourself in a vulnerable spot."

"So you'll at least teach me?" Sophia asked, clutching her belly.

Harley leaned forward. "I'll teach you how to fish, so to speak, but you should know that this isn't the only way. There are alternatives to mainlining, such as snorting or smoking, both of which can hold you over until you get back into detox. We're only talking about less than two weeks, if that. It's not that long."

"Maybe not to you," Sophia said, rubbing her cheeks. "I used to smoke, but now with my tolerance being what it is, I feel like I'm past the point of no return."

"There's no such thing, but you need to remember that even after a few days in detox, your tolerance may have dropped dramatically. However, I'll walk you through the steps, especially if I can prevent you from hurting yourself further, but this is one of those 'I can only show you the door' type moments."

"I understand," Sophia said as she looked toward the door. "And we have time?"

"All the time in the world. Remember, people make mistakes when they're rushed and we're not going to do that today."

Sophia turned back to Harley and smiled. "Thank you."

Harley watched as Sophia arranged her supplies on the table and then peeled the dope off of the plastic. She broke off a small piece and added it to her cooker along with a splash of water.

"It's good to have more water than less since it's better for the valves in your veins," Harley advised, "but next time you may want to use your syringe to measure the water. That way, you won't accidentally prepare too large of a shot and end up injecting yourself twice. As for the dope, is that your normal dose?"

Sophia nodded.

"Okay, good. Now to start, everything you have here is clean, but it's always good to think 'one needle, one shot' and to never share any equipment with anyone."

"Right," Sophia said. "I mean, except for Jack, of course. Whatever he has, I already have and vice versa."

"So that may or may not be true, but if either of you catches something in the future, you could avoid sharing it with the other if you get into the habit of using your own supplies."

"But I don't see how he could get something that I don't have. He doesn't use or sleep with anyone else."

"These are all just suggestions," Harley said. "Feel free to take or leave what you like."

Sophia smiled and held up her cooker by the makeshift twist tie handle and fumbled for her lighter. The fluid roared to life and once the dope was dissolved, she added a cotton ball and stabbed the heart of it with her syringe, careful not to dull the needle by scraping metal on metal. "Okay. I think I'm ready," she said as she placed her loaded rig on the table.

Harley scooted her chair around the table to be by Sophia's side. "Where does Jack usually inject you? Arms? Hands? Legs? Feet?"

"Arms, but he never goes in the same spot twice. That's one thing he taught me."

Harley smiled. "Good. It's important to give your veins a rest so they're less likely to scar over and collapse on you down the road. And I can see you already did a number on your right arm, which means you're probably a leftie, correct? Normally I'd suggest giving your arm a rest, but I think it's better to use your dominant hand for better needle control. Does that work for you?"

Sophia wiped her forehead with the back of her left hand. "I think so. I know I have a good vein there somewhere."

"Perfect. Then why don't you clean the site with an alcohol pad while I toss on some gloves? Be sure to get rid of all of this dried blood and wipe in one direction so you don't just smear bacteria around."

With her back to Sophia, Harley snapped on latex gloves and examined them for holes. "Do you know how to properly tie a tourniquet?"

"I think so," Sophia said, reaching for the elastic band. "I wrap it like this, right? And leave this end tucked so I can pop it right before I inject."

"Exactly. That way you're less likely to disturb your arm with the needle in it and avoid damaging the vein. Why don't you pop it for now while we go through the angle of attack."

Sophia undid the tourniquet while Harley reached for a pen and a piece of paper.

Harley drew two lines. "This one is your vein and this one is your needle. Notice this angle? It's important to shoot for somewhere between fifteen and thirty-five degrees . . . not too deep . . . not too shallow." She circled the tip of the needle on her drawing. "I know it's hard to make out, but notice how the bevel is facing up? This helps the blood flow in and out easily."

Sophia stared at the needle on the table. "It's a lot to take in."

"Hang in there, okay? We're almost done." Harley picked her pen up and drew an arrow on the paper. "The needle should always point toward your heart, regardless of where on your body you choose to inject. That way, it's in the same direction as your blood flow so that once you register, you'll know you're in a vein. You can also tell by the color of the blood in your syringe, but that's more nuanced. One trick is to pay attention to the color of your blood. If it's bright red, stop. Do not pass go. You're in an artery and you don't want that world of hurt."

Sophia scrunched up her face. "I think that's what happened earlier. I stopped when it burned like hell."

"It doesn't just hurt—it's also dangerous if you blow out the other side and can't stop the bleeding. If that ever happens, remove the needle, apply pressure and raise your limb above your heart."

Sophia smiled and tried to ignore the rising commotion in the lobby.

"Sophia, listen to me. I need you to forget about them out there. There's no pressure from them and there's no pressure from me. The only thing you should be focused on right now is taking your time and staying calm. We'll get through this together."

"Okay. I think I'm ready. I think I can do this," Sophia said.

Harley scooted her seat forward. "Trust me, I know you can."

twenty-one
pressure cooker

Harley stood at the door to the injection room and watched Sophia as she felt her way through the grumbling crowd. It took longer than expected for her to reach the monitoring room, but when the door closed behind her, Harley took her hand off Karissa's shoulder and allowed her to continue.

"Sorry to cut you off like that," Harley said. "I had to make sure she made it to John."

"It's fine and I'm glad she's in good hands, but I think that went on way longer than what anyone expected."

"What am I supposed to do? You know I can't rush her through her shot or turn her away."

Karissa shrugged. "Do you think we can talk for a second? Privately?"

Harley scanned the lobby again and turned to the next client. "Give us a sec, okay? We won't be long."

Karissa followed Harley into the injection room and closed the door behind her. "I'll make it fast because as you just saw we have a growing problem out there. More people are showing up than I think we can deal with, and because there's no time limit or urgency with how long people can take in here, we're not the ones in control."

"I'm well aware that some clients are taking longer than expected, but don't forget that some are moving quickly, too. And with clients like Sophia, we both know that if I didn't show her how to inject safely, she was going to continue butchering herself." Harley sat down and placed her hands on the table. "But you're right, our setup here is not sustainable."

"Not only is it unsustainable, but what you see out there is only half of the picture. A lot of clients have been turned away from how long the wait is."

"You know, it's not like I didn't see it coming, but I'll admit I didn't expect to see it right off the bat." Harley tore off a wipe and began disinfecting the table. "Our problem is this space wasn't designed to manage a surge of clients. Think of the SCS in Canada—they have a wall lined with injection booths and we have what? A glorified closet and two succulents that need to be watered." Harley pushed off the table and scooted her chair back. "Let's start by doubling down and sending in two clients at a time. As long as John can monitor them, I think we can get this back on track."

Karissa rocked her head from side to side. "That'll help, but what about the clients who come back for seconds? Or thirds?"

"What about them?"

"Why not cut them off after they leave? That would help thin the line, because I've seen a number of people who leave the monitoring room and circle right back into the queue."

"I don't have a problem with people doing that as long as they wait their turn like everybody else."

"Just had to ask," Karissa said. "I had another thought too. If you're okay with clients using multiple times, would you also reconsider adding a maximum time limit?"

"Again, my hope is for clients to be considerate of one another and for the most part, they are. But I still say no on the time limit as long as the client is actively trying to hit. And as soon as they do, I send them to the monitoring room. It's not like we're in here shooting the sh—"

A dog barked in the distance.

Karissa smiled. "Was that Count?"

"Sounded like him, though I wasn't expecting to see Lurch today. He said, or rather implied, that he wouldn't be gracing us with his presence today."

The dog's barking continued and grew louder, which sparked a commotion out in the lobby.

"*Help!*" a muffled voice shouted. "We need some help here!"

Harley launched out of her chair and beat Karissa to the door.

"Move!" Harley yelled as she cleared the way, splitting the sea of clients with her hands. A small opening had formed in the crowd and clients held their arms out, holding one another back to make space.

Karissa slipped past Harley and into the void. Lurch was crouched on the floor and using his hands to support the head of an unconscious teenager. The teen's face was blue and as he laid on his side in the recovery position, Count let out another bark and spun in a circle, further entangling his leash around his legs.

Lurch looked up at Harley as Count whimpered beside him.

Harley dropped to her knees and tried for a pulse on the teen's stiff neck. "Karissa, we need John out here now." She dropped an ear to the teen's mouth, hoping to hear a breath escape.

As Count pawed Harley, someone from the crowd took his leash and coaxed him outside.

"What happened here?" Harley asked.

Lurch looked around at everyone surrounding him.

Harley leaned forward. "Lurch, look at me. I need to know what happened."

As Lurch opened his mouth, a heavy duffel bag dropped next to the teen's body. John dropped to his knees and reached for a pulse.

"I couldn't find one," Harley said, "and I don't think he's breathing."

"Let's get him off his side and onto his back," John said, tapping Lurch on his shoulder.

Harley reached for the teen's arm and noticed it was stiff. She shot a look at John.

John felt for a pulse, then snapped a disposable mouthpiece onto his Ambu Bag resuscitator. "Karissa, call 911. Harley, work the compressions while I man the bag. Your thirty compressions to my two breaths. And you"—he tapped Lurch's shoulder—"switch places with me."

Harley clasped one hand on top of the other, locked her elbows and drove the heel of her palm into the teen's chest. "One . . . two . . . three . . ." she counted, letting his chest rebound fully between each compression.

While she worked up a sweat, John lifted the teen's chin and maneuvered his head into the sniffing position to open his airway. He carefully secured the mouthpiece over the teen's nose and mouth and waited.

Lurch looked down at the teen. "I was making my way up here and Count lunged into a bush. I looked inside and he was facedown in the dirt. I didn't know what to do, so I dragged him out and brought him here."

Harley glanced up and nodded. "Twenty-eight . . . twenty-nine . . . and . . . thirty."

John pumped the self-inflating bag against his thigh and watched the teen's chest inflate artificially.

"You did the right thing," Harley said, huffing as she dove back into compressions.

"What are you guys doing?" A client stepped into the circle and leaned over the teen.

"Give us space," John demanded without looking up.

"Why don't you hit him with some Narcan already. Can't you see he's dying?"

Karissa switched her phone to her other ear and grabbed the client with her free hand.

He tore away from her grip and held her back with a stiff arm. "What the fuck are you waiting for?! Are you out of Narcan? Here, take mine!"

Lurch started to stand, but John grabbed his pants and held

him back. "We have Narcan," John said, turning to the client. "But Narcan would only help to restore his respiratory drive, and in case you can't see"—John smashed his Ambu Bag and inflated the teen's chest—"it won't help him right now. The only way he's going to make it is if we can get his heart working, and you distracting us isn't helping."

Harley remained focused and started the count over.

"Can't you hit him with Epi or some shit?" the client asked. His eyes bounced back and forth on the surrounding people. "Or meth? Or coke? Someone here has to have something!"

"Buddy! You need to do us all a favor and calm down so we can concentrate," John demanded. He crushed the Ambu Bag two more times and studied the teen's falling chest. He leaned forward and whispered into Harley's ear, "We need to clear these people out of here now."

Harley closed her eyes and drove her palms into the teen's chest. "I need everybody out of here," she called out. "Now."

A number of clients started a slow exodus, but Lurch knew they could do better. He jumped up and started tugging on sleeves and collars. "You heard the woman," he bellowed. "Everybody out!" He pushed shoulders and tugged collars as he corralled clients toward the door. "Move! Move! *Move!*"

A change came over the crowd, and though Harley felt the life force being sucked out of the lobby, she kept her eyes trained on the back of her hands and counted thirty compressions to the tune of *Stayin' Alive*. She wiped her face and noticed a drop in temperature as bodies vacated the eerily quiet space.

Gabby entered the lobby and placed a hand on Harley's back. "I'm right here if you need a break."

"I'm good for now," Harley said, flexing her hands and wrists.

"Which room did he OD in?" Gabby asked.

"Neither. Lurch found him nearby," Harley said, huffing. She turned to Karissa. "Did you see him earlier?"

Karissa shook her head as Harley resumed compressions.

"Do we know if he'll be okay?" Gabby asked as she locked the front door.

"I can't make that call," John said, "but it's hard for me to see him as recoverable at this point. I'm sorry. I didn't want to say it in front of everyone."

Lurch sat back on his heels as Harley finished another round of compressions.

"How long until the EMTs arrive?" Harley asked.

"They should be here any second," John said.

Harley turned to Gabby. "Can you make sure my office is cleared of clients?"

"Of course," Gabby said, nodding.

"And Karissa, can you flag down the paramedics?" Harley tapped Lurch's shoulder and fought to catch her breath. "Even though you were the one to find him, don't feel obligated to stick around and give a statement to the police."

Lurch nodded.

She looked down at the teen's face, which rocked slightly back and forth with each compression. There were fresh scrapes on his forehead caked with dirt and fresh blood.

The front door popped open and flashing red lights flooded inside. "They're here," Karissa said, holding the door open for the paramedics while Lurch slipped past her.

"John? What the hell are you doing here?" a medic asked Gabby as he entered the lobby, maneuvering a gurney through the door.

John puffed the Ambu Bag for the last time and pressed off his knees to stand up. He threw his resuscitator into his open duffel bag and kicked the bag toward the wall. "Just trying to make a difference."

Harley pulled her office door closed and clutched her twisted stomach. The sickness first came over her when the paramedics phoned the hospital instead of continuing John's resuscitation efforts. She understood what that meant, as John had once explained their policy to her. There were some exemptions to the rule—decapitation, incineration, rigor mortis or separation of the heart, lungs or brain from their body—but unless the victim was obviously deceased, EMTs were required to request approval from a physician at the hospital prior to making a declaration of death.

Everything that followed upturned Bridgeworks like a vengeful tornado. The police, tailed by detectives, poked and prodded their way through the requisite questions, all while trying to read into events that never happened. In stark contrast, the medical examiner was centered, courteous and professional, though uncharacteristically distant.

Harley squeezed her eyes shut and tried to piece it all together. The photos. The statements. The angered confusion and how the detectives attempted to pit each team member against one another. The way they didn't believe Lurch's story and kept rephrasing the same questions as if he was covering his tracks, only to translate his selective mutism as a crude attempt to hide his guilt.

Harley shuffled toward her desk, slumped in her chair and made the one phone call she could no longer put off.

"April," Harley said. "I don't even know where to start. I would have called you sooner, but I didn't have time to break away until now. We had an incident here today that you need to know about." She pulled the phone away from her mouth. "Well, not here exactly, but it's about as bad as it gets."

Harley heard her boss maneuver toward a quiet place. "How bad are we talking about? A fight? A hospitalization? A—"

"An overdose," Harley muttered. "Someone died here today." She hoped for a response where there was none. "April? Are you still there?"

"I'm here. Sorry, but can you repeat what you just said?"

"April, a young man overdosed and died in our lobby. A client found him nearby and brought him to us for help. We tried to save him but it was too late." Harley pinched her lips together and fought back tears.

"I don't even have words right now," April said, then she went quiet for a moment. "Who was there when this happened?"

Harley leaned back in her chair. "We had an off-duty paramedic helping, but he took off after the first responders arrived. Gabby and Karissa were here too, along with a room full of clients."

"And did the young man pass away in front of everyone?"

"Yes and no, because everyone saw what happened, but the exchange was emptied by the time the medics made their determination of death."

"I can't even imagine how hard that must have been." April paused. "I'll make plans to ensure that trauma counseling is available to help deal with the emotional aftermath of this incident. That goes for not only staff, but for clients as well and anyone else who needs it. In the meantime, don't move. I'm on my way."

"Thanks, but I'm not sure you need to come down here. We're all exhausted from dealing with this all afternoon and I think we all just want to go home."

"What do you mean 'all afternoon'? When did this happen?"

"A few hours ago."

April's voice grew heavy. "Harley, why in the world am I just finding out about this now?"

"I meant to call you earlier but I didn't have a chance. Everything happened so fast with the EMTs and the police and the ME."

"Is the medical examiner still there?"

"No. It's just us here and we're decompressing and getting ready to shut down."

"Okay, good. That was going to be my next question. Go ahead and lock it up and get some rest. While you file your incident report, I'll attempt to figure out what this means for me, you, Bridgeworks or BBB. The SCS is obviously done, but I'll do what I can to keep the syringe exchange open for now."

"Why do we have to shut down the SCS and be punished us for something that happened outside of our walls?"

"It's not that I'm punishing you, Harley, but think of the liability—let alone the optics—if something else were to happen. I see negligence and potentially criminal charges for not just you and me, but for all involved. I know you're hurting right now, but you have to trust me on this. We took our shot and the game's over."

Harley squeezed the receiver in her hand. "If we saved multiple lives today, we can save more tomorrow."

"I wish it were that simple, but you know as well as I do that this isn't a decision left up to me. We need to follow procedure here which starts with your critical incident report. Once I have that in hand, I can take it to the Board and request a special meeting to determine *if* and *how* to proceed, but I wouldn't count on it. Regardless, that's the only way forward and until they make their determination, there's no other hand to play."

"I don't understand why you're talking about giving up time that we don't have and leaving this up to people who don't get it."

"And I don't understand why you, of all people, are talking like I have any other choice."

"I knew she would pull something like this," Gabby said, unlocking her bike from the bike rack. "Every time there's even a whisper of pushback, April's the first to bend."

Harley locked the door to the exchange, dropped her keys into her pocket and turned around to face the street. Except for Karissa and Gabby, the sidewalk was clear. "I don't have the energy to argue right now, but April's right. It's the Board's responsibility to decide how to proceed from here. And maybe we should give her a little more credit since she's balancing a much larger house of cards than us. I hate to say it, but if I put myself in her shoes, I can see where she's coming from."

"So that's it?" Karissa asked, forcing herself into the conversation. "One day and it's all over?"

"Not even a day," Gabby added, leaning on the handlebars of

her bike. "I swear to God this world is so impossible. How does anyone stand a chance when there's so few options out there? The detox centers keep turning people away because they're at maximum operational capacity and even if they weren't, not everyone wants to stop using. So they only have two options: either use out in the open and hope that if they overdose, someone will see them and care enough to do something about it, or slip into the shadows and use in places like a bush where they're hidden from view and help."

Harley winced at the thought. "It breaks my heart because overdoses are so preventable."

"Did you tell that to April?" Gabby asked. "Because to me that sounds like the only motivation I need to keep going."

"Who said we're not going to keep going?"

Karissa stopped pacing and faced Harley.

"You did," Gabby said. "Right? Unless I misheard you." She turned to Karissa. "Didn't she just say—"

Harley held her hand up. "I said April's shutting down the SCS, but that doesn't mean we're throwing in the towel."

"But what will April say when she discovers we defied her?" Gabby asked.

"Nothing, because we're not going to. April said not to run an SCS at the exchange, so we won't. But this isn't the end of the road."

Karissa lifted her chin. "Does that mean we're taking it to the streets?"

Harley shrugged. "If they can't come to us, then what other choice do we have but to go to them?"

"I'm in," Karissa said. "With both feet. Tell me what to do."

"Hold on," Gabby said. "I agree it's total bullshit that we're being shut down, but is this really the best option? Do we have any idea how long it will take the Board to convene? Because once we're in jail, we're *done* done."

Harley rubbed her chin. "Forget the Board for now since there's no guarantee they'll vote in our favor if and when they get around to discussing this. As for being arrested, I'm willing to cross that bridge when it comes, but I won't put you two in that position. The best way for you both to help is to keep Bridgeworks running and let me and John take it from here."

"Oh, hell no," Karissa said. "I'm coming with you."

"I appreciate that," Harley said, "but keeping Bridgeworks open is equally as important, and Gabs will need your help."

"What about Mateo?" Karissa asked.

"Mateo's out, remember?"

"But that was only because of the SCS. If there's no SCS, there's no problem."

Harley thought for a moment. "I guess one of us needs to call him anyway so he stops sending clients up here."

"I'm on it." Karissa whipped out her cell phone and started walking down the sidewalk.

Gabby watched her for a moment before nudging Harley. "You know I'll always have your back, but can't we try to talk some sense into April?"

"We could, but the more I think about it, the more I think it's best to leave it alone. Remember, it's ultimately her call to make and she's taking into account things like possible civil forfeiture and the jobs of everyone we work with. But that doesn't mean our hands are tied. We can do this if we work together because ultimately, reversing an overdose isn't rocket science. All it takes is having someone around who knows how to respond."

"Alright. Let's do this." Gabby looked down the road and smiled. "I have your back and always will."

"Perfect," Harley said, "because a lot of people will show up tomorrow looking for a safe place to use. I need you to send them our way, wherever we turn out to be."

"Hey!" Karissa called out as she hustled up the sidewalk. "Mateo's in."

"Perfect," Harley said. "So now that the dream team is lined up, all we need is an actual plan."

"As long as I'm coming with you, I'm happy." Karissa craned

her neck back and studied the sky. "And it looks like we still have a few hours of sunlight left if you want to start now."

Harley looked up. "No, not without John, but I've been texting him since he left. Though he's done for the day, he said he's good to go in the morning. All he needs from us is a time and a place."

"Which is probably half the battle," Gabby said.

Harley shrugged. "We should start at first light since most folks begin their day with a wake up hit."

"Which actually works out since B-SAP doesn't open until late morning."

"Exactly," Harley said, agreeing with Karissa. "As for locations, if either of you have any ideas, now would be a great time to toss them out there."

"The Park Blocks would be great," Gabby said. "Not too far from here with lots of places to sit, but it's a bit too exposed."

"Not only that, but there are too many bike cops." Karissa thought for a moment and placed a finger to her lips. "The Square would be perfect since it's centrally located, but it's so exposed you'd need a giant circus tent and a secret password to pull it off."

Harley snapped her fingers. "Karissa, if I haven't said this lately, you, my friend, are a fucking genius."

Karissa deadpanned. "Harley, I wasn't being serious."

Gabby fiddled with her keys. "I'm with Karissa on this one. The *Square*? There's no way that would fly unless you're going on a suicide mission. In which case, I'm happy to hang back."

Harley smiled. "I'm not literally suggesting the Square, but if we're going to pull this off, why not set up shop out in the open where no one would expect it?"

Gabby cocked her head. "I'm not following you."

"Look, our organization is Building Better Bridges, right? Let's start by doing just that." She held her hand up and started counting on her fingers. "There's Broadway Bridge. The Steel Bridge. Burnside. Morrison. Hawthorne. The list goes on and on and on. What if we set up a couple of Coleman tents and blended in with the backdrop?"

"Like urban camping?" Karissa asked. "I like the sound of that."

Gabby shrugged. "I don't know. To me, it sounds like a nice way to get trapped."

"True, but you know as well as I do that most people turn a blind eye to the world around them. I can't believe I'm saying this, but maybe, *just maybe*, that can benefit us for once."

twenty-two
under the bridge

Harley sat cross-legged and stretched her beanie over her ears, hoping it might drown out the endless rumble of the traffic overhead as the walls of her tent swayed back and forth in the lofty breeze. Her cozy and portable shelter provided a semblance of protection from the wetness of the morning, but it stopped short of blocking out the biting cold. A swirl of muddy footprints painted the floor as if Van Gogh's tortured spirit lived on and as much as Harley appreciated street art, she made a mental note to bring a welcome mat with her next time.

She had staked her claim under Burnside Bridge not only for the growing number of tents in the area, but because its location made access a breeze. Portland had long been divided into four major quadrants—northwest, northeast, southwest and so on—with Burnside selected as the major thoroughfare to bisect the north and south sides of the city. The lazy Willamette River naturally separated east from west and the MAX connected them all.

"I'm almost ready," the man sitting across from Harley said, dressed from head to toe in black. Harley guessed he was in his mid to late forties—give or take a decade—though she knew it was hard to get an accurate read once life took a toll.

She watched as he used the back of a fingernail to flick his syringe a few times to remove any lingering bubbles. He then squeezed out the smallest amount of dope from the needle tip to ensure no air was left and to avoid an air embolism. With a cracked tongue, he lapped up the last inky drop and took a deep breath as his raspy lungs crackled. Harley watched him plunge a thumb into his mouth and curl his lips around his knuckle to make a seal so that when he blew, the built-up pressure forced a rush of blood to his head. His eyes bulged slightly as the hidden veins in his neck swelled before diving back beneath the surface like terrestrial earthworms.

The man reached up and tapped his neck with his fingers. "Almost there." He coughed with his mouth closed and inhaled once more, then closed his eyes and groaned while clenching his diaphragm. Streams of air hissed around his knuckle, but a quick adjustment of his thumb helped seal the deal.

When he opened his eyes, he wobbled where he sat and pressed a palm against the polyester wall to steady himself. The tent wall caved, and his hand slid down the flimsy fabric that buckled beneath his pressure. He took the tent with him as he toppled over, sinking the upper canopy into Harley's head.

"Cheap-ass tent!" he cursed as he rushed back into his sitting position. He looked around for his needle and noticed his cooker had tipped over. Reaching for his cottons, he stuffed them back into the cooker and folded the sides over to save them for a rainy day.

Harley leaned back and readjusted her beanie. "I don't know how you would sanitize that, but it wouldn't hurt to hit it with an alcohol wipe. A lot of boots have blessed this floor."

He breathed through his nose and reached for an alcohol prep pad.

"While you do that, you might want to swab your neck too. I understand that if you made it this far, you may not have other options available, but the neck is one of the riskier spots to inject so abscess prevention is really critical."

The man looked at her with a raised eyebrow. "I don't know what that means."

"It means clean hands, clean gear and a clean injection site when possible. Deep neck infections can develop into abscesses which can be dangerous, especially being so close to your throat, tongue and trachea. I know you say you've been lucky so far, but remember that it only takes one deep infection which a doctor can't localize and you're potentially set up for breathing, eating or speaking issues for the rest of your life."

The man tore open a prep pad and began wiping his neck and hands.

Unlocking her cell phone, Harley pulled up her camera app, switched it to the front-facing camera and turned her phone around. She scooted forward, braced her elbows on her knees and held the screen to his face like a mirror.

"A little up," he said as he stared at himself on the screen. "Right there. Don't move."

He raised his chin to spot a vein, then isolated it with two fingers to prevent it from rolling. Holding his breath, he slid the needle into his flesh and once the rig flagged with blood, he gently depressed the plunger.

Harley flipped her phone around and called Karissa. "I'm ready when you are," she said. "Is the coast clear outside?"

The man's eyelids flickered before shutting down.

"Just a second," Karissa said.

Harley put the phone on speaker and set it down. She grabbed his knee and shook it. "You doing okay?"

The man snorted and sat up. "I'm good," he mumbled.

"I need you to stay awake until we get the all-clear, then you're going to pop into the other tent like we talked about. Hang out with John and help yourself to some water and snacks."

"Okay. Coast is clear," Karissa said over the phone. "Heads up. Sadie's next."

Harley stood up and helped the man rise to his feet. With her other hand, she tugged on the zipper and a sharp breeze rushed into the tent while the man made his escape. Seconds later, a petite hand jutted through the slit.

"So, is it true?" Sadie asked, darting into the tent. She zipped the door shut and made herself comfortable. Her bright eyes danced back and forth as she reached into her bra and reverted to old habits. "SAFR-F—"

"We're not doing client codes today," Harley said. "As data-driven as I am, this is one of those rare instances where it's best not to have a record."

"If you say so," Sadie said, unwrapping a sticky blob from a piece of plastic.

"Did you want to test that?"

Sadie declined. "I already checked it and it's fine." She dropped a piece of black tar heroin into her cooker. "You know, this almost reminds me of a time when I was at a shooting gallery in San Fran, except it was more of a spruced-up crack house and run by a cartel. I'm guessing you don't have any gang ties, do you?"

"None that I know of, but that may all change once Ethan gets released—assuming he cliqued up during his recent bid," Harley said, failing to keep a straight face.

"I don't see why anyone would go through all the trouble of getting jumped into a gang, only to get bailed out the same week. Seems a bit fishy."

Harley sat up straight. "What do you mean bailed out?"

"You didn't hear? Ethan got released last night."

Harley scrambled for her phone. "No. Where did you hear that from?"

"Sorry, but a good street reporter never reveals her sources."

Harley texted Ethan and placed her phone in front of her. "Alright Sadie, let's keep it moving."

Sadie lit a fire under her cooker. "Anyway, that spot in San Fran was a lot like this. Not only could you buy your dope and use there, but they had workers hanging around to Narcan anyone who overdosed. The only difference though is I'm not worried about falling unconscious and being taken advantage of here."

Harley dragged her fingers through her hair. "I hate to say it, but there are a lot of places like that and I always have mixed feelings about them. Sure, we encourage everyone to look out for one another, but a big concern with those operations is that you never know if the person watching your back has your best interests at heart. I imagine more often than not they're users themselves who are working for a fix and the other concern is if a criminal enterprise is involved or there's other illegal activity going down, no one will call for help."

Sadie nodded along. She peeled off a sock and inspected her foot, which was bruised and spotted with track marks. "But isn't that what the Good Sam Law is for?" she asked, wrapping a tourniquet around her ankle.

"On paper, sure," Harley said, "but just because you get a pass for a day doesn't mean you won't be on their radar tomorrow." She looked down at her phone and texted a pin of her location to Ethan.

A trickle of blood bloomed inside Sadie's syringe.

"That's true unless they're on your payroll," Sadie said. "Which reminds me of another crazy story . . ." She popped her tourniquet and depressed the plunger. She opened her mouth to continue, but her chin crashed into her chest before she could get a word out.

Harley leaned forward, shoved her hands under Sadie's armpits and caught her. "Sadie!" she called out, patting her cheek. She fumbled for a Narcan packet on the floor of the tent, peeled the lid back with her teeth and inserted the nozzle into Sadie's left nostril. But before she could depress the plunger, Sadie jerked her head back.

"Sadie, are you with me?" Harley asked, shaking her by the shoulder.

"I'm fine . . ." Sadie mumbled. She lifted a weak hand to brush the nasal spray away but her arm went limp.

Harley laid Sadie down and watched her eyes flutter shut. She slipped the nozzle back into her nose and administered the dose, then caressed her head as she called Karissa.

"Karissa, I need your help. I just dosed Sadie and need your help with transferring her to John's tent."

"Can it wait a few minutes?" Karissa asked. "The Yellow Line is pulling up and there's about to be a ton of foot traffic."

Harley looked down at Sadie who was moaning on the floor. "She's coming around so she'll be okay, but please get in here as soon as it's safe." Her phone beeped and she glanced at the screen and cursed.

"Knock, knock." Karissa scratched the tent door with her finger and waited for a response.

"Hey April, I hope you don't mind but I have to put you on hold," Harley said. She put her phone down, reached for the zipper and scooted away from the entrance.

"Sorry that took longer than planned," Karissa said, entering the tent. "Fare inspectors and transit police were on the last train and I didn't want to make a scene."

"No, it's best you waited." Harley motioned toward Sadie who was supporting herself on the floor, clutching her knees to her chest. Despite her drooping shoulders, she seemed to be back to her old self.

"Hey there, girl. You feeling better?" Karissa asked.

Sadie looked up and nodded. "I'm fine. This isn't my first rodeo," she said as she rose to her knees. "Though as far as rodeos go, nothing tops the one in Kalamazoo."

"Is that so? Why don't you come with me and tell me all about it." Karissa tapped Harley's knee and waited for her to scooch back before placing a hand on Sadie's back. "But take it easy, okay? We're in no rush." Karissa gripped Sadie's wrist and helped her up.

Harley smiled and took April off hold. "Sorry about that. You still there?"

"I'm here, but unfortunately we have a problem. I just got off the phone with the District Attorney and he's asking me to shut you down."

Harley made eye contact with Karissa as she slipped out of the tent and zipped the door shut from outside. "Did you tell him we've already shut down?"

"He wasn't talking about the SCS, Harley. He wants to shut down Bridgeworks."

Harley covered her eyes. "You're not serious, right? Did you tell him there's no fucking way?"

"If we don't at least try to meet him halfway, we could risk—"

"*Halfway?*" Harley yelled, dropping her hand. "April, there is no halfway here and we both know what our clients are facing if we shut down. One would think it would be self-explanatory, but did you explain to him what happens when we stop giving out life-saving supplies?"

"I think we should start this conversation over."

"So we get a second chance here but our clients don't? Don't you think they have enough to worry about right now besides catching or passing on Hep C and HIV? What about contracting sepsis or endocarditis? Or necrotizing fasciitis? I know flesh-eating diseases are rare, but they still turn up from time to time, so let's not rule those out either."

"I'm being serious here," April said sternly.

"So am I!" Harley snapped. "Doesn't he know what we're up against? What more could he want from us? Or maybe I have him all wrong and he wants nothing at all, and this is retaliation for not giving him the heads of three dealers on a silver platter? Or—and I wouldn't put this past him—maybe this is some sort of perverted punishment for trying to save that kid's life because deep down he wants all of our clients to suffer the same fate."

"Or maybe he thinks that by shutting us down he'll prevent more deaths? Or maybe he knows something we don't? Or maybe it's none of that and it's all one big petty response for not being kept in the loop."

"What the hell are you talking about?"

"Harley, I want to know why you told me you met with the DA."

"Because I did! I met with Chief Morris *in person*. Do you have any idea how hard that was for me?"

April didn't immediately respond. "Did you just say Chief Morris?"

"Yeah . . . why?"

April let out a light chuckle. "Well, that explains it."

"Explains *what*? Is something funny?"

"You were supposed to meet with Harry Dalton, the *Elected* District Attorney . . . not one of his lackeys. It sounds to me like Chief Morris not only overstepped his bounds, but he kept his boss in the dark on this one, which makes perfect sense now."

"Not to me it doesn't. Didn't you read the email I sent you?"

"Which one?"

"The one where I recapped my entire conversation with Chief Morris?"

"If it's sitting in my inbox, then no, I don't think so. You know how backed up I've been."

Harley sensed a tightness in her chest and crouched forward. "I knew I couldn't trust that asshole. I felt it in my bones when he refused to put our discussion in writing." She buried her face in her palm as brakes squealed on the bridge above.

"I wouldn't go so far as to call him an asshole."

"Well I would, because that *asshole* set me up."

"And you know this how?"

Harley dropped her hand. "If only you could see my face right now."

"Take a deep breath, Harley. I know you're upset, but remember that I've known Chief Morris for years. You're right, I don't buy that he gives two shits about our clients, but I know he supports the police and their safety. That means he supports what we do because we reduce the amount of used needles on the streets that turn up during pat-downs and personal property searches. It's self-serving, but as long as it serves our cause, do his motivations matter? I honestly believe in a roundabout way he's an ally."

"An *ally*? That's a new one." Harley pulled the phone away from her head and held the mic to her lips. "His boss is now retaliating against us because Chief Morris didn't do his job or keep his word."

"But what if he didn't go to his boss because he knew damn well what Dalton would say?"

"I think you're giving him too much credit here."

"Am I? Have you never done something like that before?"

Harley was unmoved. "The problem with that idea is that I don't believe Dalton would have said no. He's gone to bat for us before. Something about this doesn't make sense."

"Dalton may have our back, but he has a public image to maintain and knows this is a battle for the courts on a federal level. Now with this recent overdose, I think he has no choice but to distance himself."

Harley heard a scratching on the tent door and spun in place as someone from outside jiggled the zipper. Ethan slipped into the tent, tossed a pile of paperwork on the ground and gave Harley a hug.

When she pushed him away, she pressed a finger to her lips and placed April on speaker. "So just to be clear April, you're asking me to shut down Bridgeworks?"

Ethan mouthed the last three words of her sentence.

"Harley, we can't go to war with the DA. He has the power to shape policing priorities, decide when to charge someone or not, and frankly, make our lives and the lives of the people we serve a living hell."

"You didn't answer my question. Are you asking me to shut down Bridgeworks?"

April took a deep breath. "Actually, Bridgeworks is already

closed. Right before I called, I tried you at your office, figuring you'd be in early. You know I never want to undermine your authority, but Gabriella answered and said she was getting ready for the day, so I had to tell her."

"Oh, really? And how'd that conversation go?"

"It didn't sit well and she had some choice words, which I understand, because this isn't the outcome any of us had hoped for. But I think she understood that sometimes in this world you have to bend before you break."

Harley stared down at her bouncing heels and struggled to process it all. "April, I have to run. Let's leave it at that." She hung up and glared at Ethan. "Why didn't you call me as soon as you bailed out?"

"My phone was dead and I must be getting old, but I don't seem to know anyone's number from memory anymore."

"And you didn't think to call when you got home?"

"By then it was so late, I figured you needed all the sleep you can get. But at least I'm here now."

"And not a moment too soon. I need to get to Bridgeworks. What are your plans for today?"

"I wanted to grab some cash to get your car out of limbo before the bill gets out of hand."

"Don't worry about the car for now." Harley removed his bike key and handed it over, then filled him in on an abbreviated version of the past few days.

"So that explains why there's so many familiar faces milling about outside."

"Exactly, and they're all looking for a safe place to use. John is in the monitoring tent next door and Karissa is organizing the flow of people in and out. Can you take over from here? Feel free to say no since you're in recovery, or maybe you want to switch with—"

Ethan raised his palm to cut her off and unzipped the door. "Don't worry about us. Go do what you have to do and we'll take it from here."

"I knew I could count on you," Harley said as she grabbed her things and reached for the zipper.

"One last thing," Ethan said, grabbing her wrist. "I know April said not to go to war with the DA, but never forget . . . *'It's better to be a warrior in a garden than a gardener in a war.'*"

twenty-three
red line

As a shrill bell rang out, Harley tilted forward in her seat and felt a vibration course through her as steel sharpened steel on the MAX tracks below. Air brakes hissed outside and a programmed voice from a speaker clicked on.

"Oak, Southwest First Avenue. Doors to my right."

A scatter of riders swapped places with newcomers who quietly claimed the closest seat as their own before burying their face in a screen or newspaper. Two young men bumped shoulders as they squeezed past one another, though neither apologized or took offense. Leaning back, Harley wondered how public transit could connect yet distance so many people at the same time.

She pulled out her phone, typed a name into her browser and made the call she dreaded, then listened carefully as an answering machine clicked on.

"You've reached the Multnomah County District Attorney's office. If you know your party's extension, please press one now. If you would like to dial by name, please press two. If you would—"

Harley tapped her keypad.

"Using the keys on your touchtone phone, please enter the name of the party you wish to reach, last name first. Press star at any time to return—"

She was patched through to a soft-spoken voice. "Thank you

for contacting District Attorney Harry Dalton's office. This is Jillian. How may I help you?"

"Good morning. This is Harley Hammond from Building Better Bridges. Is DA Dalton available to speak?"

"May I ask what this is regarding?"

"He'll know."

"Oh. In that case, please hold."

The daisy-chained speaker boxes running the length of the train blasted, "*Mall, Southwest Third Avenue.*"

"I'm transferring you now. Have a nice day."

"Thank you."

"*Doors closing. In the priority seating area, you are required to move for seniors and people with disabilities. En el área de asientos prioritarios, debe moverse—*"

"Ms. Hammond? I was wondering if I'd be hearing from you this morning. I take it you spoke with Mrs. Cartini?"

"I did, and trust me, with everything else going on right now, this is *not* the conversation I was expecting to have today." Harley gazed out the window and caught her muddled reflection in a passing storefront.

"What can I do for you?"

Harley's phone beeped, and she declined a call from Gabby. "Maybe start by not closing us down during the middle of a hot batch crisis?"

"For clarification, I am not the one closing the exchange. Your own organization is. I simply requested that Mrs. Cartini not compound the situation further. Trust me, this is not something I set out to do, but we now have a situation that leaves me with little choice moving forward. I'm sure you understand."

"No, Harry, I don't understand. What's this really about?"

"*Mall, Southwest Third Avenue.*"

"There are several concerning accusations which require us to—"

"If this is about the teenager—"

"*The doors are closing. Train departing. Please hold on.*"

Harley paused and recomposed. "If this is about the teenager who overdosed at our exchange, you need to know he was brought to us on death's door."

"Unfortunately, I can't get into the specifics of our investigation at this point."

"What investigation? The teen didn't overdose at our exchange. A client discovered him nearby and brought him to us for help." Harley took a moment to remember some of the faces who had been delivered to her on the brink of death over the years and took in a deep breath. "All we did was try to save him. We did what we are trained to do."

"And you expect me to believe this was all one big coincidence? It just so happens that on the same day you converted your exchange into an illegal shooting gallery, someone dies under your watch?"

"But he didn't use with us! Though, to be honest, I wish he had, because he'd probably still be alive. Look, the entire purpose of yesterday was to be proactive and prevent as many deaths as possible. Yes, I facilitated a safer consumption space, and yes, we had a handful of overdoses, but every single one was averted because we were right there when it happened."

"That doesn't justify breaking the law, especially when we both know the syringe exchange has always operated in a legal gray area."

"What in the world are you talking about?"

"*Proof of payment and validated fare is required on MAX. Se requiere comprobante de pago—*"

"Come on, Harley. You know as well as I do that every used needle your exchange accepts contains traceable drug residue. I've turned a blind eye to felony drug possession and paraphernalia charges for how many years now?"

"You're shitting me. We have decades of precedent and support from both the CDC and the Oregon Health Authority," Harley said, her voice hardening. "I don't know where this is coming from, but it's ridiculous."

"As ridiculous as you not keeping me in the loop about your recent stunt?"

"To even call it a stunt boggles my mind. And just so you know, I'm passing the same Starbucks where I discussed this with Chief Morris two days ago. He ended our conversation by giving us two days to work with and left me with the impression you'd be okay with it."

"Kip may work for me, but he doesn't speak for me. Also, I don't know the details of what you two discussed and therefore have no comment."

Harley swallowed. "Why are you doing this to us?"

"As far as I'm concerned, you did this to yourself when a young man died on your floor. And unless you have proof he didn't use there, this conversation is over."

"I've told you the truth, but if that's not enough for you, would you like to review my records from yesterday? I have a detailed list of codes for each client that used in our exchange, plus the room was packed with witnesses. I'm sure they would all be happy to corroborate what happened."

"If the records are yours, then what's to stop you from doctoring them? And as far as your witnesses, they aren't reliable in my eyes since they were all engaged in illegal activity. But the good news is nowadays everyone has a phone on them. If what you say is true, find me a video to corroborate your story, prove this young man wasn't a victim, and we can back it up and start the conversation over."

"Pioneer Courthouse Square. TriMet ticket office. Doors to my left."

Harley looked across the plaza at a group of street kids. As the doors opened, chatter from the busy platform bled into the far corners of the train.

"Harry, not everyone has a phone on them, and we don't have cameras so I can't help you there, even if I wanted to. All I can say is if you won't believe me, at least let me appeal to your senses and explain why it's so important Bridgeworks remains open. As you know, beyond offering sterile supplies, we provide a range of services to our clients, including drug checking and crisis counseling. We reduce HCV and HIV infections along with a host of other blood-borne infections. Every week, we—"

"Harl—"

"*Every week* we refer several clients to both treatment and detox, and teach new and old clients about safer injection practices. Imagine how many needles we recover and where they would end up *if* we were shut down. We provide overdose medication and training to save lives. I could go on and on about the facts of what we do, but again you know all of this because I've personally briefed you on what we do."

Harry cleared his throat. "I know what you do and recognize its importance, which is why I'm so baffled that you didn't consider this before risking it all."

"*Galleria, Southwest Tenth. Transfer to the Portland Streetcar on Tenth and Eleventh Avenue. Doors to my left.*"

Harley stood up, took hold of a hanging hand loop, then turned in place and froze. "This is where I get off, Harry. But before I go, I want you to know that like you, I have work to do and people counting on me to do it."

"I would think long and hard before going rogue out there. It's not a battle you will win."

Harley let him have the last word and ended the call. Swiping through her contacts, she fired off a text and looked down the train aisle as Armando reached into his back pocket and pulled out his phone.

Armando gripped the straps of his backpack and stepped off the train. He looked in both directions before heading toward Tenth Street and was swarmed by a small crowd of customers within seconds. They circled him like sharks in a feeding frenzy, each vying for his attention and hoping to score their next fix before he ran out.

"One at a time! One at a time," he hissed, checking over his shoulder in case he was being followed.

Harley hung back but was close enough to watch the scene unfold without getting caught up in the fray. She noticed Pogue in the mix and watched him bully his way to the front of the pack and slip Armando a folded-up bill. He pocketed the money without counting it, coughed into his palm and clapped Pogue's hand, sealing the deal. Having got what he came for, Pogue turned around and spotted Harley, then immediately looked away. His smile faded as he popped the balloons into his mouth and took off in the opposite direction.

"What the fuck am I supposed to do with these?" Armando asked.

Harley turned back and saw him inspecting a pair of shoes. He flipped the tongue back and shoved the tag in a young woman's face. "Can't you read? These aren't my size." He flipped the shoes over and studied the soles. "And these ain't even fucking new!" He chucked the shoes back at her and kept walking.

"I only wore them out of the store!" She scrambled to pick them up and started chasing him, begging him to accept her trade. As he turned down Tenth Street, a client at the rear of the pack spun around to stop her from following.

"He said he didn't want them. Now quit drawing heat!"

Refusing to quit, she pressed past him and followed the group down the sidewalk. The huddled mass took a few more steps and a frantic exchange of cash and dope ensued. One by one, people peeled away until Armando was left alone with the desperate woman.

"I said I don't want them. Go away!" he shouted. He turned his back on her and started to take off.

"Please!" she shouted in an effort to draw attention their way. She pulled a handful of change from her pocket to sweeten the deal.

"Get out of here," Armando demanded. He did a one-eighty and headed back the way he came as she continued to tail him.

After a short chase that led nowhere, Armando finally caved. He turned around, plucked a white balloon from his mouth and lobbed it over her head.

"*Meth*? Meth won't help, you asshole! I'm *dope sick!*" She grabbed him by the hand and as he pulled away, she stumbled backward and hit the sidewalk with a scream. Spotting his escape, Armando spun around and booked it directly toward Harley.

Harley looked past him as the young woman scrambled after the white balloon. Instinctively, she stepped out in front of him to cut him off.

It took a moment for him to register her. "And what do you want? We're nowhere close to your exchange."

"That's not why I'm here. Did you get my text?" Harley asked.

"That was you?" Armando asked, checking over his shoulder. "Who gave you my number?"

"An old friend who thought you might help me out since many of my clients are also your customers." Silence fell between them as she chose her next words carefully, not wanting to spook him. "Can you please follow me to my office? I don't carry much cash on me."

Armando brushed past her and started walking away. "I don't know what you're talking about."

"I'll pay you double," Harley pleaded.

"You think I'm stupid? I know you're not a fiend." Armando turned and looked her up and down. "So you're either the police or trying to set me up to get robbed again."

Harley shook her head. "Neither of those are true."

"So you're buying to use? I don't think so."

"No, I'm buying to check them."

Armando rubbed his nose. "What do you mean?"

"I want to see if the drugs you are selling have fentanyl in them."

"You can do that? How? Do you have someone who tests it for you?"

It took Harley a moment to put the thought out of her head. "No, we don't test on actual people. I have test kits back at my office where I keep my money. It only takes a few seconds."

Armando thought about it for a moment, then reached up to his mouth and coughed out two slobbery balloons. "How about this? These are yours as long as you show me how to test them."

twenty-four
bridging the gap

"Is this some sort of joke?" Clay pointed at a hand-written note taped to the front door of Bridgeworks that "thanked" the DA for shutting down the exchange. He turned around to face Harley and the group of clients circulating around him. "Or is this because some kid died here yesterday?"

Armando glanced at Harley.

"And where does that leave us?" Clay asked. "Where do we go to get supplies in the meantime?"

"Clay, I need you to calm down and take a deep breath." Harley turned to the small crowd gathered on the sidewalk and spotted Sophia in the mix with Jack at her side. Seeing him with her brought a sense of relief she didn't know she needed.

"It's good to see you, Jack. Welcome back."

"Thanks, but it's not what it looks like." He threw an arm around Sophia and pulled her tight. "A friend of mine just entered detox and told me he saw Soph here yesterday, so I knew I had to leave to support her. But don't worry, we've got a plan in place." He reached into his pocket and pulled out some hexagonal orange tablets. "I cheeked a few of these while I was there that should get me through the rest of my detox. At least that's the plan."

Sophia reached up and hugged his torso.

"If I can help in any way, let me know." Harley motioned for Clay to step aside and stuck her key in the door. On her way into the lobby, she removed the note from the glass and crumpled it up. Propping the door open behind her, she motioned for Armando and the clients to follow suit.

"We're not actually closed, but give us a few minutes to get ready," Harley called out. "Gabs. Mateo. You got a second?"

Clay squeezed through the door and gave Harley a decent love tap with his guitar. A few more stragglers flowed into the exchange before Harley broke away from the entrance and met Gabby and Mateo in the lobby.

Gabby watched as the line piled up and scratched her cheek. "I didn't want to shut it down, but April said we had no choice and you weren't picking up your phone."

"I know. I saw you called and would've answered but I was talking with Harry Dalton." Harley realized she was competing with the chatter in the lobby and motioned to her office.

"Want me to wait out here?" Armando asked.

"If you want, but please don't do any business here."

Harley followed her team into her office and left the door open. "I don't know what April told you, but the reason I'm here is that the DA wants us to shut down while he completes an investigation . . . whatever that means. He couldn't say how long that would take and April wants to oblige because it's fewer problems for everyone down the road." She took a shallow breath and waved the idea off. "But that doesn't work for me, or for our clients. We're not closing Bridgeworks. Not like this."

Mateo rubbed his chin. "Why not go mobile like you did with the injection tent?"

"I thought about that too, but our clients need to know where to find us."

Gabby agreed. "Not everyone has a phone, and while we can always put the word out, word on the street doesn't travel that fast."

"Exactly," Harley said, "but while I refuse to shut down based on principle, I know this can get ugly fast and don't want either of you getting caught up in this mess." Harley looked past Gabby and Mateo to the waiting line of clients. "You both should take off and check in with me later today. I'll run the program and we can—"

"Oh, hell no," Gabby said, flipping her hair back. "You can't get rid of us that easily." She paused and turned to Mateo. "Sorry, I didn't mean to speak for you."

Mateo turned around and studied the line. "Harley, if you don't mind, I'd rather not leave."

Harley shook her head and smiled. "Mateo, I appreciate your enthusiasm, but this isn't something you need to do. You can still lose your visa, remember?"

"Forget the visa. I may be new, but I've been around long enough to know that this isn't a team but a family. And where I'm from, family always comes first. I also saw enough desperation yesterday that I won't let some little small book stand between me and doing what's right. So if it's okay with you, I'd like to get to work."

Harley leaned against her desk. "It's been a long morning so far. Honestly, I don't know if I have the energy to stop the two of you." She stared at them and drummed her fingers on the edge of her desk. "I don't know—as buttery as my heart feels right now— what kind of person would I be to let you two go down with the ship? Remember, long before either of you came on board, I often ran this exchange by myself." Harley studied the floor for a moment, catching herself reminiscing on lighter days. She looked away before she became overwhelmed. "You know what? I appreciate the offer, but it's best that in the event I get arrested, fired . . . or both, I can count on you two to step in for me and take over."

"What about Ethan or Karissa?" Mateo asked. "Why can't they be your backup plan? At least they have the keys to this place."

Gabby smirked. "You know he's got a point. Also, don't we have a policy about no one running the exchange room alone because of safety?"

Harley crossed her arms. "I see where you're going with this."

"Good, and one last thing." Gabby turned to Mateo and gave him a light shove. "How heavy are you? One seventy? One eighty?"

Mateo nodded. "At least."

"Harley, can you imagine how much energy it would take to physically remove the two of us? Wouldn't it be easier on everyone if we put our heads down and got back to work?"

"Fine. You both win, as long as you know what you're getting into. I hope you understand I can't protect you from getting fired."

"Good thing I'm a volunteer," Mateo said.

"I can't protect you from getting arrested or deported, either."

Mateo shrugged. "I'll take my chances."

"No, *we'll* take our chances," Gabby said, "but one last question before we start."

"What's that?"

Gabby leaned forward and dropped her voice. "The person loitering in our lobby—that's not who I think it is, is it?"

"It's about time I got some good news today." Harley spun the test strip around so Armando could see the results. "Your sample tested negative for fentanyl, which is amazing."

"That's it? That little pregnancy test?" Armando leaned over the dipstick and rubbed his chin. "I imagined you having a super-computer or some shit."

Harley rocked back in her chair. "I wish. You're talking about GC-MS, which is an entirely different beast."

"What's that? Sounds like a gang."

"Definitely not a gang, though I might kill to get my hands on one. It's a gas chromatograph-mass spectrometer."

"Huh?"

"It's a machine capable of analyzing almost anything you throw at it. The chromatograph separates the substances on a molecular level, then the spectrometer takes those ionized fragments and—"

"It reads the shit," Armando said.

"Exactly, but it also saves lives, which is how I'll pitch it for funding. The only problem though is with today's current laws, drug checking is still technically illegal because the handling of drugs puts us in possession. And depending where you're at in the country, they still list some drug testing devices as paraphernalia."

Armando nudged the strip on the table with his knuckle. "But why would you need all that anyway when this does the trick?"

"One reason is this test is specific to fentanyl and won't tell us what additives or fillers were used as cut. But there are other benefits from having access to a machine that analyzes drugs, too. For example, once people can check their dope for lethal additives, dealers may stop adding substances like shoe polish or dirt because their customers will find out and word will get around."

Armando waved off the idea. "Somehow I don't believe that."

"And why's that?"

"Because that's not how it works. Yeah, you might get a guy here or there who stomps their shit to stretch it, but in my mind those are users trying to support their habits, not dealers."

Harley crossed her arms. "You think?"

"No, I know." Armando scanned the room and studied the pictures on the wall. "You've been doing this a long time, huh?"

Harley nodded.

"And you're not the police, right? Because you'd have to tell me, right?"

"Not necessarily, but don't worry—if I was law enforcement, you'd have been arrested long ago."

Armando didn't appreciate the joke and looked down at the strip. "Let's talk, *hypothetically*. Where do you think the dope you just tested came from?"

"Hard to say. Could be Afghani or Colombian, but most likely harvested in Guerrero, then ran up through Sinaloa and

Tijuana by the cartels before being funneled across the Southern Border."

Armando whistled. "Not bad. Now do you know how many bags a dealer or runner can push a day?"

Harley shrugged. "A lot?"

"Hundreds, if not more. And by the way, runners don't package or repackage their own product." Armando cocked an eyebrow. "That's just how it goes with most syndicates. It's a job for the baggers, and the runners and the baggers don't talk because a smart organization is compartmentalized."

"So by the time you get your dope delivered to you, it's already prepackaged?" Harley paused. "*Hypothetically*, of course."

"There's a string of safe houses throughout the city where deliveries are sent daily. Runners branch out from there to hit their territories."

"So, are my suspicions correct that since this tested negative for fentanyl, it's likely a new batch and everything else out there should run its course?"

"We can always test the next bag and see, but I'd put my money on it. And let's hope I'm right, otherwise my hands are tied and all we can do is wait."

"Is that really the only option?" Harley asked as she stood up.

He chuckled with a half-clenched smile. "Like I said, I don't control the supply. As for not selling it, what difference would it make? My customers aren't loyal to me. They'll go somewhere else in a heartbeat and get the same exact shit."

Harley heard some laughter in the lobby and looked away. "If you don't mind, I should go and relieve my coworkers."

"Wait. I don't want to leave you with the wrong idea." He reached out and cut her off. "It's not that I don't care. I'm happy to see these results and never intend to hurt anyone who doesn't have it coming to them."

"In that case, why don't you take a few test strips so you can check your dope later on?"

"Sorry, but I can't swallow those if the cops run up on me."

"Well, if you won't take them, at least know you can come by anytime and I'm happy to test your supply." Harley dropped the tests in the open drawer and removed a few bills. "And this is to cover the dope we tested."

Armando waved her off and began repackaging the dope. "Don't worry about it. We used so little dope no one will even notice, plus I owe you for stepping in when . . ."

He trailed off and turned around as police sirens bled through the wall. Gabby threw Harley's door open and stuck her head inside.

"Cops are here," she called out. "I'll lock the front door."

"You motherfucker." Armando popped the balloons in his mouth, cocked his head back and swallowed his stash.

"It's not what you think," Harley said. "I promise they're not here for you."

Of all the clients who burst out the front door and scattered down the sidewalk, only one looked back. Harley was the last to filter out, and as she exited the exchange she motioned for Gabby to lock the door and stay inside. When she turned around, her face was glowing red, lit up by the flashers of a cop car parked out front.

The officer in the driver's seat cut his siren as Harley approached his partner's door. She bent at the hips and kept her distance.

"Names and badge numbers please."

The driver leaned over the center console and tapped his badge. "Atwood, 90192."

Harley looked at his partner. "And yours?"

The officer in the passenger seat chuckled. "Webber. 96321."

"Is there something I can help you with?"

Webber unfurled a McDonald's bag, handed Atwood a burger and peered into the bag. "Since you offered, do you happen to have any ketchup in there?"

Harley stood up and blocked the flashing lights with her hand. "Why are you really here?"

"We're here to find out why you're here," Atwood said.

Harley watched as Officer Webber took a bite of his burger and used his thumb to dab a splotch of sauce off his lip.

"This is where I work," she said, waving her hand at the building.

Webber chuckled again and bit into a handful of fries. "In that case, this is where we work too."

Harley leaned on her knees and stooped to their level. "Don't you two have some real criminals you could be arresting right now?"

Atwood elbowed Webber. "She's right. Maybe we should just cut the shit and arrest her already."

Harley took a step back. "On what grounds?"

"We can start with possession," Atwood said. "Schedule One is a Class B felony, punishable by up to 10 years in prison and $100,000 in fines."

Webber smiled at his burger and took another bite. "I'm sure we can also make a strong case for conspiracy," he said with a mouthful of food. "Maybe even attempt to distribute, along with whatever else we find in there."

"Don't forget, that goes for everyone inside," Atwood said.

Harley crossed her arms. "No one's going inside without a search warrant."

"Do you really think I would go through all this trouble just to see the charges get thrown out? Of course we'll get a warrant . . . if and when we need to."

Harley bit her tongue and looked down the empty sidewalk. "You're trying to scare away our clients, aren't you?"

Atwood looked up and adjusted his rearview mirror. "I don't see any clients." He cut his lights, stepped out of his vehicle and placed his hands on the roof of his squad car. "It was Harley, right?"

"My friends call me Harley. You can call me Ms. Hammond."

"If that's how you want it Ms. Hammond. Here's the deal: we received an anonymous tip and numerous complaints that—"

"I know Harry Dalton sent you here." Harley looked at him coldly.

The officer smiled. "Our chief sent us here after receiving an anonymous tip about illegal activity occurring inside your premises. As you know our job and top priority is to keep the community safe and—"

"When did that change?" Harley asked. "Because everything about this moment says otherwise."

Officer Atwood stood up tall. "I'll remind you that we're in the middle of an ongoing investigation, meaning we'll remain here as long as it takes to get the job done. Makes no difference to me." He paused and waited for Harley to make eye contact with him. "Listen to me, Harley. I don't know who you rubbed the wrong way, but if I have to arrest you, I will. In the meantime, we're going to sit tight and enjoy our lunch."

Atwood put his weight on his car door, sat in his seat and flicked on his patrol lights as Webber rolled up his window.

Gabby unlocked the front door to Bridgeworks as Harley approached. "What the hell is going on?" she asked.

Harley charged through the door and into the lobby. "Nothing I wasn't expecting."

"Isn't this harassment?" Gabby asked, peeking out the window.

Armando appeared from the exchange room. "Is there no back door to this place?"

"No, but there's no need to panic," Harley said. "It's not you they want, and I would puke your dope out while you still can." She turned to face Gabby and Mateo. "And don't worry, they're also not here for either of you." Harley's eyes softened while scanning the empty exchange, devoid of the very people she needed to support. Behind her, the frosted window pulsed an intolerable red.

"What'd they say?" Gabby asked. "Are they planning to sit out there all day?"

"Not if I have anything to say about it." Harley entered her office and closed the door behind her, leaving her team and Armando in the lobby. She picked up her phone and called the DA's office.

"Ms. Hammond? I had a sinking feeling you'd be—"

"*Why?*" she asked. "Why are you coming after our services when you know our clients need them now more than ever?"

"I'm not coming after your services. I'm only ensuring no one else gets hurt down there. You can think of it as . . . oh, what's that term again? *Harm reduction?*"

"If you have a problem with me, take it up with me, but don't punish my clients. Many of them suffer from substance use disorder and physically depend on their drug of choice. Having access to clean supplies and naloxone, especially at a time like now, is vital to their survival."

"Again, Ms. Hammond, this all sounds to me like something you should have thought about before you ventured down this path. Now, let's do ourselves a favor and keep it simple. Did you or did you not open up your exchange to allow drug abusers to inject illegal narcotics inside of an illegal shooting gallery?"

Harley looked up at the ceiling and dropped her voice. "There's so many things wrong with that question that I don't even know where to start. And if you think it's as simple as that, then I have failed to—"

"It's a simple question, Harley. Yes? Or no?"

"Harry, to call it a 'shooting gallery' isn't just offensive—it tells me you really don't understand how and why safer consumption spaces can save lives."

Gabby knocked on the door and helped herself into the room. Harley held a finger to her lips, put her phone on speaker and set the handset on her desk.

"Harley, you can call it a drug injection room, injection site, overdose prevention center or whatever else helps you sleep at night—it doesn't matter to me. The only thing I care about is whether you hosted an illegal 'safer consumption space' there at Bridgeworks?"

"Yes. I did."

"See, now how hard was—"

"And I would do it again because it was the right thing to do."

"I know," the DA said. "I know you would, which is exactly why I can't in good conscience allow you to remain open." Harry paused for a moment. "And even if what you said is true and the young man who lost his life did not use on your property, no one wants to see a repeat of yesterday. The fact that this has been brought to my attention means I can't look the other way."

Harley looked at Gabby. "But what if you didn't have to?"

"I don't see how I couldn't after knowing what I know."

"What if I left so you don't have to look the other way?" Harley asked, her eyes focusing on Gabby.

"We both know that won't make a difference," Harry said. "You being off property won't inhibit you from calling the shots. We see that all the time with gang leaders and shot callers who are moved to seg. Where there's a will, there's a way."

Harley removed a photo from her wall and held it in her hand. It was a picture of her and Taylor in high school, right before their lives would be forever changed. "I didn't mean leave as in I'm going home for the day. I meant leave as in *leave* my position. You win, Harry. I promise to contact April and hand in my resignation, effective immediately."

Gabby took a step forward but Harley reached out to hold her back.

"You're resigning?" Harry asked.

"It was painful enough to say it the first time so I'll only repeat myself once." Harley removed the remaining photos from her wall and stacked them on her desk. They were faces that entrusted her to be there for them when they needed it most, and she fought to honor and fulfill her commitment to them. She wondered if they would understand that part of her commitment to them meant they always came first, no matter what. "I am resigning from my role as the Health Services Program Coordinator at the Bridgeworks syringe access program. And can you hear this?" Harley slapped the picture of her and her brother onto the desk. "I am collecting my personal items as we speak. I'll notify April of my decision as soon as we are done here and you will be cc'd on a notice of resignation email sent within ten minutes."

Harley looked up and locked eyes with Gabby. "And Harry, I need you to understand something—what happened yesterday was my idea and mine alone. I accept full responsibility and ask that you not punish my staff or our clients for my decision. The staff I'll leave behind only want to operate Bridgeworks per protocol and will do so under all laws, archaic as they may be. I will exit here shortly, and it would be very much appreciated to have a personal police escort, preferably Officers Atwood and Webber, if they're not too busy."

Gabby opened her mouth, but no words came out.

The DA took his time responding. "Send me the email. As soon as I receive it, I'll reach out to the Police Chief."

Harley clicked the speaker button to end the call.

"Harley, you don't need to do this," Gabby pleaded. "You can't quit. I won't let you."

Harley blew out a long breath. "You know better than that, Gabs. I only said I was resigning. Not once did I ever mention anything about quitting."

Harley pulled the yellow cord to request a stop and steadied herself as she rose to her feet. While approaching the back door of the bus, she braced herself as the hospital entrance came into view through a scratched-up window. The back doors popped open and with hesitation, she caught her reflection in a murky puddle. Seconds later, the driver engaged the kneeling function of the bus to assist her on her way out. With a quiet leap of faith, she stuck the landing.

About a mile south of Portland sat Marquam Hill, home to two major hospitals and a medical center that competed with one another for priceless views of the city they overlooked. As the bus pulled away, Harley looked down from her vantage point and admired her distant city below. A muted sunset lit up a number of buildings, which cast long cold shadows behind them. Her first thought was of Ethan and how he once explained that "Yin" and "Yang" translated to the "shady" and "sunny place." The iconic symbol, he suggested, depicted the delicate relationship between sunlight hurling itself over a hillside and the darkness that ensued.

Harley turned around and decided to push on. She followed the familiar slick sidewalk and watched her footing until she made it to the ICU entrance. The doors opened to welcome her, but rather than pass through the gates, she turned around and looked back to where she came from.

Alone on the sidewalk, she filled her lungs with crisp air and forced herself to remember that her people under Burnside Bridge were in good hands with Ethan, John and Karissa. She thought about how Gabby and Mateo were holding up and knew that nothing would stop them from finishing the day strongly. Her assurances stockpiled the confidence she needed to enter the hospital so as she crossed the threshold and approached the receptionist, momentum was on her side.

"Good afternoon. I'm here to visit a patient," Harley told the worker.

He finished typing out his train of thought and reached for a clipboard. "Do you have an appointment, miss?"

Harley shook her head. "No, but I've been here before. The patient's name is Olivia. I apologize, but I never caught her last name."

The receptionist set the clipboard down and gave her his full attention. "I'm so sorry, but we're no longer accepting walk-ins."

Harley leaned forward. "I understand, but the last time I was here, the other receptionist paged the unit and Donna, Olivia's

mother, came out to greet me and escorted me to their room."
Harley pointed to the door but kept her eyes trained on his.

He blinked but didn't look away. "Again, I'm afraid I can't do that, miss. Might I suggest contacting the patient's family or power of attorney to see whether or not a visit is possible."

Harley dropped her hand. "I don't understand. Can't you just page Donna for me and tell her Liv has a visitor?"

"Unfortunately, it's not that simple." He removed his glasses and set them next to his keyboard. "Might I suggest contacting—"

"I'm not following you. What is stopping you from picking up that phone and . . ." Harley trailed off and studied the receptionist's bleak face. "You can't call her because she's not here."

The receptionist opened his mouth but was slow to respond. "Miss, if you have a means of contacting Mrs. Simmons, I suggest you reach out to her. I'm sure she could use a friend right now."

Harley instinctively grabbed the counter before her knees buckled. "Liv's gone, isn't she?"

The receptionist glanced at a young couple sitting in the waiting room, staring at their phones. Quietly, he said, "I'm so sorry, but because of HIPAA, I cannot disclose whether—"

Harley held up her hand, either to cut him off or prevent herself from breaking down. "I understand. I wish I didn't, but I do."

"I'm sorry I couldn't have helped you further, but unfortunately my hands are tied."

Harley bit her upper lip, pushed off the counter and pulled her cardigan around her torso. With a faraway look, she started for the exit to make the lonely trip back down the mountain.

twenty-five
black balloon day

"What a day, huh?" John tiredly stepped out of his tent and reached for the moon. "I will say though, it's kind of sad I've had more face time with your friends over these past two days than in all my years on the job. Normally when I roll up on a scene, I'm the only one talking."

"I told you my people are awesome." Harley forced a strained smile and turned to help Karissa to her feet as she exited the tent.

"I never doubted you, but my problem is that I rarely get to talk with my patients. If I'm not actively working on them, I may get a few words in while en route to the hospital—assuming they don't refuse transport—but that only ever seems long enough to ask someone how their day was or where they're from. I often find it hard to dive into a meaningful conversation and get to know someone when a siren is wailing in my ear."

"I can only imagine." Harley caught herself yawning and covered her mouth. "Thanks again for your help. We couldn't have pulled this off without you, and though this setup wasn't ideal, I can't help but feel like we made a difference here today."

"Hell yeah we did," Karissa said, bumping shoulders with John. "Though I have to say, there were a lot fewer overdoses than what I was expecting." She set his bag at his feet and started breaking down the monitoring tent.

Ethan poked his head out of his tent door. "We calling it a day?" he asked, looking around. "Or I guess I should say night?"

"Yeah, it's about time I got home to my family," John said. "My phone died a few hours ago, so they're probably wondering where I'm at."

"I still have some juice left if you want to borrow mine," Harley said as she unlocked her phone and held it out.

"Thanks, but I'll be home soon enough."

Harley turned around to help Ethan up. When he made it to his feet, he brushed her hands away, slumped forward and pulled her in for a hug.

"Again, I'm so sorry to hear about Liv," he whispered. "It doesn't seem real."

"Does it ever?" She lifted her hand from behind his back and wiped away a tear.

"And yet you still believe we're going to allow you to resign."

With a deep breath, she pushed him away. "I told you, it's done."

"I don't care if April has accepted your resignation or not. She has no clue how much work it takes to keep B-SAP afloat."

"She doesn't have to know, because she can count on you and Gabs." Harley nudged Karissa's boot with her shoe. "And she can count on you too. Same goes for Mateo."

Karissa glanced up but said nothing. Instead, she turned her attention back to the tent, rolled it up tightly and began wrestling it into its bag.

"Alright everyone, I'm out of here." John swung his bag over his shoulder and gave both Ethan and Karissa a one-armed hug before turning his attention to Harley. "Thanks again for letting me prove my skills and sharing a part of this world I've only ever read about. If the need arises again, you know who to call. And next time, I'll bring a friend or two if that's okay with you."

"Now that's an offer I can't refuse, but let's hope that next time it won't be in a tent under a bridge downtown." Harley waved goodbye and kneeled down across from Ethan to help him pack up his tent.

"He doesn't know about Liv, does he?" Ethan asked.

Harley shook her head.

"What about Gabs?"

"Not yet. I think it's best to tell her in person."

"I can respect that," Ethan said. "So, have you put any thought into the plan for tomorrow? I have a meeting with my lawyer in the morning but I'm free to join you once I'm done." He motioned toward the middle of the tent and together they flipped their corners inward.

"I don't think we should attempt this without John and he's headed back to work tomorrow," Harley said, then sat on her heels and watched him roll up the tent. "But after testing Armando's dope earlier, I want to say I don't know if it would be necessary."

Ethan looked up. "You think?"

"I really hope so. We were so busy earlier that I forgot to mention I stopped by the Square on my way down here from OHSU. Gully said a couple of street kids bought black from the Hondurans and asked her to test it for them. Both bags came back negative, so she's planning to sell what she has and call it a day. With all things being equal, she says she can't compete with their prices." Harley's eyes lit up as she looked past Ethan. "Took you two long enough."

Ethan rose as Gabby rolled up on her bike with Mateo only a few steps behind.

"Welcome home, jailbird," she said, coasting to a stop. She set her bike on the ground and pinched his belly with her free hand. "I see they fed you well on the inside."

Ethan knocked her hand away. "I would've eaten a lot better if someone remembered to put money on my books. Some ride or die friend you turned out to be."

While they bantered back and forth, Harley snatched the tent from Ethan and pressed it into Mateo's chest. "We won't be needing these again anytime soon. Why don't you and Karissa see if you can make some new friends?"

Mateo scanned his surroundings and everywhere he looked, there was someone calling the streets their home for a night. There was an occasional lone wolf, but most had banded in groups, backed up to the closest wall to keep the rain at bay.

"Any preference for who I give this to?" Mateo asked, holding up the tent.

"No, but if you pressed me for guidance, I might suggest giving it to someone without a tent."

"Of course." He stepped around Gabby's bike and slipped into the shadows with Karissa.

Gabby nestled up to Harley and watched the two disappear.

"You would have been proud, Harley. He really stepped up today after you left and we were slammed with people wanting access to the injection room."

"We heard," Ethan said. "I'd say at least half of the people who showed up here said they went to Bridgeworks first." He stretched from side to side until something in his back popped in place. "I have to say though, there were times today where I felt like a trapped rat. I never enjoy being anywhere with only one way in or out."

Harley nodded. "Same. I kept waiting for the police to show up or sweep the streets, especially after talking to Dalton this morning."

Mateo and Karissa emerged from the shadows near the metal staircase beneath the bridge. He waved his empty hands and started heading back toward the team, but Harley motioned for them to hang tight. She did a quick spin to ensure she wasn't forgetting anything, then started toward the bridge to reunite the crew.

"Unfortunately, I have some news to share," Harley said to Gabby. As she walked slowly next to Ethan, Gabby sat on her bike seat and matched their pace. "It's about Liv."

Gabby squeezed her brakes and hunched over her handlebars.

Harley gazed into the distance. "I haven't officially confirmed it yet, but I think she may be gone."

"Please don't tell me that," Gabby begged. She went quiet for a moment and stared at the ground. "How do you know? Did you see her?"

"I tried—right after leaving Bridgeworks. I needed to check in on her but also didn't want to come straight here, in case I was being tailed."

Gabby's eyes glossed over as she twisted her handlebars from side to side.

"I would have told you earlier, but I knew I had to tell you in person."

"No, I appreciate that." Gabby forced herself to steal a glance at the team. "I take it Mateo doesn't know yet?"

"No, and I'm not sure if I should tell him now or wait until I get confirmation."

"I'll support you either way." Gabby smiled bitterly and gave her bike a small push.

As the two approached the team, Harley cleared her throat and dug deep for strength. "I can't even begin to tell you how grateful I am that everyone stepped up today. Trust me, I appreciate it as much as our clients do." She placed her hand on Ethan's back and looked past Karissa to the bright spotlight of a MAX train headed their way. "I know we're all exhausted, but before we break it off I think we owe it to ourselves to figure out where we go from here."

Electricity zapped in the power lines above the tracks, disturbing a man in a sleeping bag who groaned and rolled over. Harley motioned toward the staircase and lowered her voice. "Let's go somewhere where we won't disturb anyone and figure out our next steps. I think we owe that to ourselves."

Mateo spat over the guardrail and gave up on counting how long it took to disrupt the surface of the peaceful river below. It was a decent trek, but the team had made it to the apex of Burnside Bridge, leaving enough clearance on the sidewalk for joggers or bikers to pass. An occasional bus roared by, but otherwise the twentieth-century bascule bridge felt timeless beneath their feet.

Light pollution from the heart of downtown overpowered the moon's superiority and glimmered on the water's surface. A gentle breeze came and went, tussling hair and muffling echoes of a glam-punk band that wailed somewhere deep within the bowels of Old Town. Harley leaned on the concrete guardrail and watched a train leave the station before turning her attention to the Waterfront Park Trail. In the distance, cyclists made use of the bike path, their white and red lights weaving around dog walkers and couples on a peaceful nighttime stroll.

Harley looked down the sidewalk and ran her fingers through her hair. "I know it's difficult to look to the future when life blindsides you, but that's often the most important time to do so. I also wanted to remind everyone that tomorrow is Black Balloon Day, and though this has been one hell of a week, I'd like to keep with tradition and remember the lives lost to overdoses."

"What is that?" Mateo asked.

"We normally stage a public event to raise awareness and shine a light on the overdose crisis. In the best of times, it's always difficult, but having lost too many good people recently, there's no better opportunity to educate the public on how they can get involved and make a difference."

Karissa pulled out her phone and began swiping through some images. Once she found the one she was after, she flipped her phone around to share it with Mateo. The picture was a sobering sea of black balloons in a park tied to individual paperweights. Each balloon had a name and represented a family member or friend or loved one frozen in time. "This was from last year."

Harley studied Mateo as he absorbed the image. The memorial was many things for many people. For professionals like herself who analyzed the data in their free time, it was a grim reminder that the work was far from over. For others, it was a lot to take in and far too often hit close to home.

As Karissa pocketed her phone, Mateo rubbed his hands together. "Tell me where to be and I'll be there."

Harley thought for a moment and pointed toward the heart of the city. "8 a.m. Lownsdale Square. Let's meet under the Soldier's Monument, across from the Justice Center and District Attorney's office. If we want to raise awareness, I can't think of a better place to start. And this time, I'll bring the donuts."

Karissa scratched her throat and stepped forward. "Donuts sound great, but you can't get off that easy. I know we were too busy to talk about it earlier, but now I have to know: did you really quit? Because I don't believe it."

Harley rubbed her mouth. "I'll tell you what I told Gabs earlier: I didn't quit. I *resigned*. There's a big difference."

"But that doesn't make any sense."

"It doesn't have to make any sense," Harley said. "It only has to make a difference." She looked down the walkway and held her arm out. "Watch out."

The team stepped aside to let two bikers pedal by.

"I want you all to understand where I'm coming from," Harley continued. "When I spoke to DA Dalton this morning, he explained—"

"Fuck the DA," Karissa said. "All he cares about is protecting his ass and how he looks in the public eye. Him not giving two shits about what Morris said proves it."

"Maybe, but that's the world we live in. And you know as well as I do there's a lot we wish we could change, but we can't let that stand in the way of making an impact where we can." Harley glanced at Gabby. "Ultimately, I took a gamble and lost. Or maybe not, because we got the go-ahead that ultimately saved people. As for Dalton, maybe he's reacting the only way he knows how, and if having me out of the picture is what it takes for him to pull back, so be it."

"So be it?" Ethan threw his arm around Harley and nearly

knocked her off balance. "No one wants or expects you to be a bloody martyr. Now that you got that off of your chest, let's figure out how to rescind your resignation and get your job back. We've fixed bigger miscommunications before, right?"

Harley dropped her head and gave his arm the slip. "Imagine how much more difficult Harry could make our lives if he wanted to. He knows how and where to apply pressure and that's the last type of person we want to make an enemy out of."

"But he's being unreasonable," Gabby said, failing to see her logic. "Why not go public tomorrow and explain our side of the story? Maybe we can pull security footage from our neighbors and prove the teen used off property. We can contact the news or we can—"

"We can do a lot of things," Harley said, "but as much as I appreciate the sentiment, I think you're all focusing on me right now. What happens to our clients if we take a moral stand and that leads to a standstill? No one wins that way, at least no one we care about."

"You're talking like this would be the first time our clients have been harassed," Karissa muttered.

"Look, I love you and your passion, but please try to see my point. The last thing I want to do is stand in the way of what needs to be done. And as much as I love what I do, the work isn't about me." Harley faced Ethan. "I know you've turned down this job once before, but you've got seniority and know the exchange in and out. Are you comfortable taking over?"

Ethan reached into his pocket and pulled out his papers. "If you want me to, I can, but my concern is this open case. Who knows how this will play out, especially if Morris is going back and forth on his word," he said, leaning against the edge of the guardrail.

"I can do it," Gabby said. "If you need me to. I still don't agree this is the best option, but if you need someone to count on, you can count on me."

"And I'll support you every step of the way," Ethan said.

"Unless you accidentally get arrested and need money on your books—then you're on your own."

Gabby pretended to give him a smack.

Harley asked Mateo, "You're awfully quiet tonight. Are you still on board . . . assuming we haven't scared you away."

Mateo sighed. "Not at all, but being so new, I feel like it's not my place to interject."

"No, that's not going to fly," Harley assured him. "You're part of the team now. You proved that today."

Mateo smiled. "In that case I'm still ready to get to work. I know I have a lot to learn, but I'll support whoever I can. You can count on me."

Karissa turned around and wiped her mouth as she walked in a tight circle. "This isn't how this is supposed to end. You can't just fall on your sword and quit on us. What kind of message does that send? If Dalton sees you do that, what's to stop him from coming after Gabby next? Or Ethan? Or me? People depend on you, Harley. *We* depend on you."

"Karissa, listen to me. *We* depend on each other. I resigned from my position, but I would never quit on you, our team or our people. I'm still a member of our organization, and though I don't have an immediate role to fulfill, I can think of a number of places where I can make an impact. I can dive into advocacy, justice reform, public benefits access, housing rights, counseling—shit—even education or employment services. The options are limitless." Harley looked to the horizon and stood tall. "Who knows? Maybe I'll even go back to school and get my master's degree while I'm at it? But whatever the direction is, the plan is to never give up because the fight's not over. Trust me on this."

Mateo buried his hands in his pockets and sat on the guardrail next to Ethan. It took Karissa a moment longer to stop pacing, but once she was ready to stand still, Gabby threw an arm around her.

"I want you all to know something else." Harley turned to face her team. "I would never go down this route if I didn't think the four of you couldn't handle it, and I would never step away from my role unless I knew you could step in and fill it." She looked down for a moment and scraped her foot on the sidewalk. "You know, when I first started in this field, I didn't know where to begin. All I knew was I wanted to make a difference and was fortunate to have a mentor like Wayne show me how to channel my anger and pain. He taught me a lot about keeping an open-door policy and my ears to the streets. He made me promise not to accept the world for what it is, but for what it could be. But the biggest lesson he passed on was that our clients are our teachers. You don't need me to keep the doors open. You need our clients to keep the doors open. Everything else is processes and policies—stuff you'll pick up along the way—but if you want to learn how to help someone, start by listening to their needs and trust me, everything else will fall into place."

Ethan wrapped his arm around Mateo and pointed down the length of Burnside Bridge. "*If you want to find out about the road ahead, then ask about it from those coming back.*'"

Harley leaned in close to Gabby. "I'll always be a phone call away if you need me, but to be honest, you already know where to go from here. Plus, I know how you are with our clients and the people who depend on you are in good hands." She smiled and took a step back. "The same goes for all of you—there is no doubt in my mind that the four of you will take this further than I could have ever dreamed of. My hope is that you continue to support one another the same way you did me because if that happens, you will find you can do anything together. Just promise me to make it a point to train the next generation so they can carry the torch and pass the light on to others." Harley looked to her team, starting with Ethan and ending with Mateo. Another bus roared by and when the rumble faded, she reached out and pointed at their city. "And above all else, never forget who the work is really for. Keep sight of that, and I promise you all this: your work will matter, more than you'll ever know."

the end

afterword

This book is roughly
93,000
words.

In 2020,
an estimated
93,000
people lost their lives
to overdoses.[1]

In 2021,
an estimated
100,000
people lost their lives
to overdoses
during a 12-month period
ending in April 2021.[2]

Visit your local harm reduction organization
& learn how to be part of the solution.

1. Products - Vital Statistics Rapid Release - Provisional Drug Overdose Data. (2021). Retrieved 23 December 2021, from https://www.cdc.gov/nchs/nvss/vsrr/drug-overdose-data.htm
2. Drug Overdose Deaths in the U.S. Top 100,000 Annually. (2021). Retrieved 30 November 2021, from https://www.cdc.gov/nchs/pressroom/nchs_press_releases/2021/20211117.htm

nyc opens nation's first overdose prevention center

In November of 2021—during the final production of *Bridgetown: A Harm Reduction Novel*—Mayor Bill de Blasio of New York authorized the opening of the nation's first Overdose Prevention Centers. The two locations in upper Manhattan will exist as part of two previously established syringe service providers[1], and Mayor de Blasio has committed publicly and *in writing* "not to take enforcement action" against their operation:

> ". . . After exhaustive study, we know the right path forward to protect the most vulnerable people in our city. And we will not hesitate to take it. Overdose Prevention Centers are a safe and effective way to address the opioid crisis. I'm proud to show cities in this country that after decades of failure, a smarter approach is possible."[2]

Trained staff reversed two potentially fatal overdoses on their very first day in operation.[3]

---

1. Taylor Romine, C. (2021). First US overdose prevention centers open in New York City in an effort to combat overdose deaths. Retrieved 3 December 2021, from https://www.cnn.com/2021/11/30/us/new-york-city-overdose-prevention-centers/index.html

2. Mayor de Blasio Announces Nation's First Overdose Prevention Center Services to Open in New York Cit. (2021). Retrieved 23 December 2021, from https://www1.nyc.gov/office-of-the-mayor/news/793-21/mayor-de-blasio-nation-s-first-overdose-prevention-center-services-open-new-york

3. Nation's First Supervised Drug-Injection Sites Open in New York. (2021). Retrieved 3 December 2021, from https://www.nytimes.com/2021/11/30/nyregion/supervised-injection-sites-nyc.html

mahalo nui loa

Thank You!

If you enjoyed this book, and feel inspired to share, please help spread the word by leaving an honest review on the book's page at Amazon.com and/or Goodreads.com.

Not only do reviews keep me going, but as a full-time *independent* author, reviews often translate to more exposure. This affords me more time to write and promote this book, which also helps to put this message into more hands.

Mahalo for your continued support!

acknowledgments

Mahalo Ke Akua.

To Haven Wheelock, MPH—your work matters, more than you'll ever know.

To the First Responders, Health Care Professionals, Policy Reformers and Harm Reduction Advocates who dig deep to give the most and best of yourselves—mahalo nui loa for meeting us where we're at and for not leaving us behind.

To Jen Cutting, Morgan Godvin, Ryan & Coral, Rick Graves, John Zogas, Sara Wong, KC Lewis, Lucia "Looskrilla" Blake, Erik Robinson, Amy Hebenstreit, MBA, BS, RN, CCRN and P. Todd Korthuis, MD, MPH, FASAM—what started off as a vision became a reality because of your pivotal and professional input.

To Uncle Steve & Aunt Crystal, Sparkle Barnes, Sara Warner, Kourtney Wytko, Donovan Climie, Karen Hermann, Cullen & Cheryl Chong, Ian Nash, Glen Dahlgren, Tutu & Goong Goong and Jordan Jeck—mahalo to everyone for your precious gift of time and support, from beta reading to proofing and offering invaluable feedback to this project that challenged me to constantly improve.

The lion share of this book was written during writing sprints with other fantastic authors on Clubhouse. Writing clubs such as Author Arena Writing, Author Conference Room, Beta Readers Club, Diverse Shelves, Epigraphs, LitBuzz, Indie Author's Club, YA all the Way, Writers: Craft + Career and Writers on the Storm have proven invaluable for both accountability and productivity. Mahalo, for many and varied reasons, to: AJ Oakes, Amanda Spell, Anjali Sinha, Aubrey Spivey, Bart Baker, Damyanti Biswas,

Deanna Roy, Ellie Masters, Elizabeth Reed, Fatima Fayez, Hyunjin Jo, Jade Greenberg, Jatin Bajaj, Jennifer Bailey, Julie Kenner, Joe Crawford, Kian Ardalan, Marlayna James, Melanie G., Merri Maywether, Rachel Lithgow, R.J. Gray, Rosie Meleady, Sean Dustin, Shannon Humphrey, Suzi Katz, Tamara H., Vanessa Hollis, Vivian Rolfe, Wendy Ross, Yvonne Nicolas and the rest of the gang who educated, inspired and motivated me along the way.

To Alex Wittwer—mahalo for being involved with this project and sharing the gift of such a moving photo.

To my editor Jessey Mills—your edits that previously unveiled a world of confidence in my craft have now led to a staggering sense of purpose in my life. Thank you for being in my corner and for all you have taught and continue to teach me. I am so proud of the work we have accomplished together.

To Savannah Gilmore—mahalo for lending your voice to this project.

And to my wife Chelsea and son Logan, who supported me and this project from start to finish, at much sacrifice and understanding—I love you both with everything I have.

RULES
TO DIE BY
A HEROIN ADDICT'S TAKE ON LIFE IN LONG-TERM RECOVERY

download your free copy:
jordanpbarnes.com/rulestodieby

about the author

Jordan P. Barnes is a grateful alcoholic & addict in recovery and Sand Island Treatment Center is his home group. When he's not sharing his experience, strength and hope through writing or talking story, he enjoys bodysurfing and gardening.
Residing in beautiful Kailua, Hawai'i with his lovely wife Chelsea and son Logan (soon to be a big brother!), Jordan has been sober from all mind and mood-altering substances since August 29th, 2011.
Jordan is a member of the Hawai'i Writers' Guild and his debut book, One Hit Away: A Memoir of Recovery won 2020's "Best Book of the Year" award from www.IndiesToday.com, was a B.R.A.G. Medallion Honoree as well as a finalist in both the 15th Annual National Indie Excellence Awards and the 2021 Independent Author Network Book of the Year Awards.

Learn more at:
www.JordanPBarnes.com

Subscribe to my YouTube channel:
www.youtube.com/OneHitAway

Follow me on Goodreads: www.goodreads.com/jordan_p_barnes

Get the latest deals and new release alerts by following me on BookBub: www.bookbub.com/authors/jordan-barnes

Correspondence:

info@jordanpbarnes.com

Let's join forces:

[f] facebook.com/jordanbarnesauthor

[▶] youtube.com/onehitaway

[O] instagram.com/jordan_p_barnes

[y] twitter.com/jordan_p_barnes

[g] goodreads.com/jordan_p_barnes

[BB] bookbub.com/authors/jordan-barnes

[in] linkedin.com/in/jordanpbarnes

[d] tiktok.com/@author.jordanpbarnes

interview - haven wheelock, mph

Photo Cred: Nigel Brunsdon

On an overcast Tuesday morning during the heights of the Covid-19 Pandemic, I took a longer than normal lunch break and tuned in to an online Zoom panel called Undoing the War on Drugs: Hope, Healing, & Measure 110. Hosted by Partnership for Safety & Justice, the stacked panel consisted of Andy Ko (PSJ), Talia Gad (PSJ), Deborah Small (Break the Chains) and Haven Wheelock (Outside In).

In his opening remarks, Andy Ko, Executive Director of Partnership for Safety & Justice, referred to Haven as the "Goddess and Heroine of harm reduction."

I couldn't agree more.

I am fortunate to call Haven my friend for many reasons, the least of which is that I am alive today from the naloxone program she fought to create at Outside In, the parent organization to her Syringe Services Program in Portland, Oregon. I received clean supplies, testing, referrals and have reversed many overdoses with naloxone I received from Haven personally. I have also been saved myself with naloxone from my own pocket, but that's another story.

It's also important to note that Harley Hammond's character is not based on Haven or her life. However, I aspired to create a character that honored Haven's life work to oversee the continual improvement and well-being of people who use drugs. With that said, please remember this book is fictitious and my imagination wild.

As a contributor to this novel, I interviewed Haven multiple times and continuously reached out to her to ask for input, and the plot would often pivot based on our discussions. Haven's perspectives were inspiring and invaluable, and it's not an over-statement to say that this book wouldn't exist without her input.

I had the opportunity to sit down with Haven and interview her for you. Here's a small glimpse into her soul:

What books have affected you the most and why?

I read a lot and mostly fall in love with every book I read while reading it. However, my favorite book on drugs is Unbroken Brain: A Revolutionary New Way of Understanding Addiction by Maia Szalavitz. It has one of the best chapters on harm reduction that I have ever read.

That said, it is not my favorite "drugs 101" book. That would be Johann Hari's Chasing the Scream—the way he escalates the history of the War on Drugs is great. To understand the war on people who use drugs, The New Jim Crow by Michelle Alexander is a must-read, because let's be real—we can't talk about the War on Drugs without talking about mass incarceration and white supremacy.

If I can move away from just books on drugs, I would also say I loved The Wisdom of Whores: Bureaucrats, Brothels, and the

Business of AIDS by Elizabeth Pisani, which pulls in my love of all things HIV, though I will warn you, some of her language around gender is cringe. Anything Paul Farmer has written has changed my life, but because his books are kind of boring to read, I usually suggest reading Mountains Beyond Mountains: The Quest of Dr. Paul Farmer, a Man Who Would Cure the World by Tracy Kidder to learn more, unless you like the nerdy stuff, in which case I would suggest Social Inequalities and Emerging Infectious Diseases or Pathologies of Power: Health, Human Rights, and the New War on the Poor, both by Paul Farmer. (Full disclosure: I have two more of his books sitting on my stack of books to read that I haven't gotten to yet.)

I also have to shout out Medical Apartheid: The Dark History of Medical Experimentation on Black Americans from Colonial Times to the Present by Harriet A. Washington for helping me put our reality into a historical context. If you haven't figured it out yet, I read a lot of nonfiction, and not all of it is this heavy. I think Mary Roach can do no wrong. All her books are amazing, although I think Stiff: The Curious Lives of Human Cadavers is my favorite. I recently read a book about beavers that blew my mind called Eager: The Surprising, Secret Life of Beavers and Why They Matter by Ben Goldfarb.

I have pre-ordered Peter Staley's book Never Silent: ACT UP and My Life in Activism, and I can't wait to read it. Also, Maia Szalavitz's new book on harm reduction called Undoing Drugs: The Untold Story of Harm Reduction and the Future of Addiction is going to be so exciting. If you want my favorite drug user memoir, I should say One Hit Away: A Memoir of Recovery is so real and kind of golden.

As for why these are my favorite . . . I love learning. Although now I have fancy letters after my name, I am a high-school dropout, I am dyslexic, I am not the typical learner. I always felt like I had to prove I was smart, so reading anything I could get my hands on was something I could do, even when I was dirt poor and living in my car. I read slowly, but I read a lot. Books have a powerful way of leveling the playing field and opening up the world. All these books have inspired me in so many ways.

What does harm reduction mean to you?

This question is really hard, to be honest; the term is used in so many ways. I mean, harm reduction means just what it says; it's about reducing harm in all kinds of ways. But for me, harm reduction will always be centered on preventing harms of drug use, as that is the first time these concepts were really used.

To me, the heart of harm reduction is all about promoting health, hope and dignity for people who use drugs. We do this by providing tools to prevent disease and death, increase humanization by showing up for people without judgment or agenda and push for policies centered around health and human rights. People often say that "harm reduction is about meeting people where they are at," and that is true, but I also think it is essential that harm reduction is not only about meeting people where they are, but not leaving people where they are. It is about meeting people and helping them move forward, or if people are not interested in changing, it is about standing with them and not leaving them alone.

At the end of the day, harm reduction is all about unconditional love for people. It is about showing up for people and helping them stay happy and healthy and not dead. It is about making sure people have the things they need to do that. It is about honoring people's dignity and autonomy and modeling that they have a voice in their care.

My favorite part of my job is that I get to love on people who are often at a point in their lives where they feel less than worthy of love. I get to help people feel safe, so they can both stay alive and have space to get their questions answered. I get to provide unbiased and factual information to people about topics related to using drugs and translate health information to people into a language they can understand. I am kind of the luckiest person in the world that I get to do this work.

Are there any annoying misconceptions about harm reduction?

Oh, there are so many things. It really depends on who is putting forth the misconceptions and what their intention is that changes how annoying I find their misconceptions or misinformation. As a culture, we've been taught that people who use drugs are bad, less moral and are less human, so if people are just starting their learning, I get less annoyed compared to people who are buying into the shaming of people for their drug use, or who are trying to promote a specific way of healing from substance use disorder.

That said, I think the idea that harm reduction is a passive intervention annoys me the most. I guess that gets back to the whole idea about not only meeting people where they are but also not leaving them there. We are constantly working to engage with people along with increasing access to good, solid information. It is about building therapeutic relationships with people and listening to them about what they want or need to feel happy and healthy, then helping them get there. Harm reduction is not only an active partnership with people but a modality of treatment and not just a thing we do until some other "treatment" steps in.

I also get annoyed when harm reduction is thought of as different from other treatments. Harm reduction is an integral part of the continuum of care for people who use drugs, not just about keeping people alive "until they get ready for treatment" or as a safety net for people who might start using again. I use quotes around that blip about people being ready for treatment because I do not believe that people need to be "ready for treatment," or that people need to stop using at all to deserve care and health care. I just really get annoyed when harm reduction somehow falls outside both healthcare and drug treatment.

What is the biggest obstacle you are currently facing in your line of work?

To be honest, I think our biggest threat right now is the overwhelming amount of heartbreak, trauma and grief all of us doing this work are living through. Just this week, the CDC put out new numbers for overdose deaths in 2020—we topped last year's record losses *by nearly 30%*. 93,000 people lost their lives to overdose, which is more than twice the number of deaths from AIDS at the peak of the HIV epidemic and three times the number of people who died in car accidents in 2020. There were several weeks where I confirmed the deaths of 3 or 4 people I knew. I have lost countless people I consider mentors and friends to overdose.

There are times when my heart hurts so much. I've had days when I learned someone I cared about died and I cried in my office, smoked a cigarette and then put on my game face so when the next client asked, "How I was?" I could muster, "I'm getting by."

I know that the work we do needs to happen or more people will die. I don't know many in this field who are not pretty fried and who don't keep showing up because we know we are a lifeline to people. It just doesn't feel sustainable or fair. I don't want that to come off like harm reduction is all heartbreak—it's not that at all—we are just experiencing the worst overdose crisis we have ever seen, and my friends doing this work are all hurting, which makes me worry.

I also think the politicization of science is a real concern. Harm reduction programs are founded on solid science. These programs lower HIV and Hep C rates, overdose death rates, and increase recovery rates, yet there are places fighting to close programs all over the country. West Virginia is fighting to stay open after the state legislature voted to close them despite having an HIV outbreak happening, and the CDC saying that syringe access is one of the pillars of HIV prevention. I think the more our society is willing to brush off science, the harder programs like ours are going to have to fight to do the work.

If you could author one bill for the POTUS to sign into law, what would that be and why?

If I only get one, then I would say universal health care for all. The fact that our systems are so disjointed and inequitable is something that really does harm to all of us. People with means should not get access to better care than people without. I've had to navigate how to help people with out-of-state insurance get into treatment (they mostly can't), and I have struggled with navigating what insurance programs and medicines are covered. Any barriers that stand between getting people help when they need it most can be life or death, PLUS—because I am a public health nerd—if everything was in one central data set, we would have a much fuller understanding of the scope of any health problems, which gives us a more complete idea of how to address it.

If I was in front of the President, I wouldn't leave without making the argument that it's finally time to end "the War on Drugs." We have spent trillions of dollars trying to control the supply of drugs, and frankly, it has not worked. If anything, it has made the drugs more dangerous. It is time to admit that we will not be able to punish our way out of this crisis and start investing in solutions that can really improve the lives of people who are using now, which will prevent this dangerous cycle from moving forward to another generation.

Can you give me one random statistic off the top of your head?

Just one? *93,000 people died of overdose in 2020.* 64% of people who inject drugs in Oregon are living with Hepatitis. Our harm reduction program gave out 2.2 million syringes last year and we hit our 3,000th overdose reversal report this month. I got lots of random stats in my brain. I'm kind of known for being a data nerd.

What was the most beautiful moment you've seen at your program?

After all that doom and gloom, I am really glad you asked me this. When most people who've never been in a syringe access program think about what our spaces are like, they envision something very different from what the spaces are actually like. People often talk about how hard it must be to spend so much time with people who use drugs or how depressing my job must be, and they couldn't be more wrong. Harm reduction programs are often just full of joy and gratitude. Hell, I get way more "thank yous" in the exchange every day than I ever did back when I was bartending or waiting tables. As for what the BEST moments are . . . that is super hard to pin down because part of using a harm reduction lens is seeing all the wins as beautiful. Every day, I pretty much get to celebrate with someone about something.

Today, the last person I talked to in my office was a tough guy asking about medication for addiction. He was really just done and had so much misinformation that when I told him he was brave for talking to me, he just started crying. We got to talk about all the medications, the pros and cons to all of them and we made a plan for his next steps. Now, whether or not he takes them, the fact he got to have a conversation about what options are out there and what his concerns were was a win.

Literally once a week, I hear how the space we provide is the only place people feel safe. I've had people come in to clean out their backpacks because if you are using and you are scared, you will drop a syringe on the floor. The options for safe places you can do things like that are so much less than what we would like to see.

That said, I have some memories I'll never forget. Many years ago, I worked with a young woman who was using heroin, and she found out she was pregnant. It took a lot of love and support to get her to a point where she was ready to deal with her pregnancy, but we got her the support she needed. One day, when the baby was about two years old, she brought him by. As she handed me this baby to hold, she said to him, "Without this woman, neither of us would be here today." My heart just exploded since I hadn't seen her since I went with her to her doctor's appointment.

I also love the time when a former client and I had a "dance party" on the street because he dropped his first non-reactive UA. PS: What other diseases do we spend so much time thinking about pee with outside of urology?

I also have to say getting the email from you, Jordan, years ago, that started with "I don't know if you remember me, but I am writing a book" was a highlight. You were someone who just vanished. You were someone I shared a really hard and rare event with but who had no obligation to inform me about what was happening in your life. It is common that people I care about vanish without me knowing where they land. I always wonder about them.

I think the joy of this work is so often missed, so I don't feel bad for long. I find so much joy in the work I do every day, and so many people I call friends and mentors are people who use or have used substances. It is pretty magic.

What keeps you up at night?

Hmmmmm. Other than my crushing sense of self-doubt and concern that I am not doing enough? I think the things I find scariest right now are how quickly our drug supply has changed and that we are seeing more and more novel substances in our drug supply and our drug market. People not knowing what they're using is much more dangerous, and these changes really worry me. For example, as we're seeing more fentanyl in our drug supply, I worry about the overdose risk people are dealing with.

What makes you sleep easy?

I'm guessing wine is not the answer you are looking for. Mostly kidding . . . but really, I am actually hopeful about the path we are on. I have been in this game long enough to see how far we've come. I remember having to fight my way into state HIV prevention meetings and even have a letter from the Oregon Health Authority saying that they would never support syringe access. Now they pay us to advise other places across the state to implement harm reduction services. I remember going to budget meetings alone to plead my case to not cut funding for our program, and the last time we had to have that fight, there were nearly 30 people who all testified alongside me.

I have seen our bench grow, and I have seen policies to improve the lives of people who use drugs become accepted. There are thousands of people across the country doing amazing and inspiring work. I have the honor of calling many of them my friends. I sleep easy knowing there is a new generation of warriors coming up with fresh passion and ideas for doing better than what we have in the past. There is still so much work to do, and the work is life and death as it always has been, but harm reductionists of my generation learned from the greats like Dan Bigg, David Purchase, Kathy Oliver and Edith Springer. We stand on the shoulders of giants. Hopefully, folks in my cohort can be stepping stones and mentors to people who are now coming into our work.

Most notable accomplishments?

To be honest, my favorite wins are the little guys. An example of this was when I was able to get someone into housing by tracking down his jail ID from an arrest 20 years before in Florida. I have people tell me that if I'd not talked to them about medicine for their addiction, they wouldn't be off heroin today. Other wins are when I see people start medication for their hepatitis infections or anytime people report overdose reversals back to us. I love the moments when someone tells me about something that's life-changing for them, and I get to know it was only possible because of the advocacy I've been a part of. We fought for YEARS to get naloxone in the hands of people who use drugs. I don't know how many times I drove to the capital to fight to get Oregon's Medicaid to cover the cost of HCV medications for people who were actively using. And we are still pushing to make it easier for people to get medication for their addiction.

I do think the passage of Measure 110, which made Oregon the first state in the nation to decriminalize small amounts of all drugs, will be one of the most monumental and historic wins I will get to be a part of. I still can't believe that is a thing I can say I was a part of, and I still haven't wrapped my head around what this will mean in the future.

A more personal accomplishment has to be getting my Masters of Public Health from Hopkins in 2020. "Kids like me" who didn't finish high school, who come from a family that doesn't value education, who struggled in school because of a learning disability, who were homeless; people like me don't graduate from the top public health school in the nation. So to be a part of the inaugural class of Fellows was such an honor. Who would have ever thought I could go from homeless to Hopkins?

A quote that hit home for you?

There are two quotes that get me through on the regs. The first was from Dave Purchase, who started the first legal syringe exchange in the country. I'd been doing this work for about 5 years, and at the time, I was at a conference presentation called "Ask the old-timers." After being intimidated for so long, I asked how I could be like them and what advice they had for someone like me who'd been doing the work for a few years but wanted to make it to 20 years in the field.

Dave said, "See both the forest and the trees, and know how to switch between both." He explained that sometimes when the whole issue hurts too much, you need to zoom in and focus on the individuals in front of you. AND when that hurts too much, you need to be able to pull back and work on the "big picture" and alter the systems-level change that might be needed. That quote has been written on my whiteboard in my office for 15 years. And to this day, it might be the best advice I have ever gotten about how to keep coming back even when it hurts. I really miss Dave.

Another quote I really think shook my world was for Cortney Lovell in the film Everywhere But Safe. She said, "A little taste of dignity can grow into an entire appetite for self care." This sentence is so much at the heart of what we do in the harm reduction world. Our whole job is to show people that they can be healthy, that they deserve care and respect, that they have the power to decide what is best for them. We are here to share information and compassion and kindness, so people can choose how to be the healthiest versions of themselves that they want to be today.

There are many classic things said by harm reductionists, but these are the two who live on my whiteboard to remind me every day why I do what I do and how to keep doing it.

What would you tell budding public health aficionados who are looking to enter the world of harm reduction?

I love new people coming into the world of harm reduction and public health. I think the first thing I would say is, "Welcome to the team!" Harm reduction is a weird and wild world full of amazing people with incredible hearts. We are feisty for the rights and health of people who use drugs and those affected by the war on drug users. We are passionate about creating a world together where people can be safe and treated with dignity.

I would remind them that at the end of the day, it is all about people. Our funding sources and how our public health systems are set up are often focused on specific diseases or particular outcomes. Still, one of the beautiful things about harm reduction is that it is not just about HIV or overdose or treatment for substance use disorders. It is about all of that. It is about making sure people have the tools to do all of that depending on what the priority of the person in front of you thinks is most important. It is about seeing people as people and not as someone who is at an increased risk of hepatitis or who somehow needs to be fixed in any way. There will be plenty of reports you'll have to write that want you to narrow your work down to health outcomes, but don't lose humanity and the radical love that brings us to harm reduction.

I would also say that the people who use drugs are the experts in their lives. They know so much, and there is always so much to learn from the people you work with. Listen to them and learn from them. I've been doing this work for nearly 20 years, and I still learn new things all the time. The way things were in this world 5 years ago differs from what they are today. So much of what I know I learned by talking to the people we serve and their generosity with my stupid—and often—very personal questions.

Lastly, I would say this work is really hard sometimes. Hell, it's sometimes downright heartbreaking. You will lose people you care about. You will sit with people who have been harmed. You will have days that just hurt, and it is imperative to set strong boundaries to make sure you are taking care of yourself. It is hard to forget that this work is literally life and death because there is so much death in this, so your impulse will be to work tirelessly, but that is not sustainable. Having boundaries and engaging in self-care is really important, and truth be told, I am terrible at it, but I want to be better.

What people or organizations do we need to know about, past and present?

This is another hard question to answer because there are so many amazing people and organizations that I've had the honor of learning from. I think the most important harm reduction organization any of your readers need to know about is the one operating near them. Your local harm reduction organization needs your love and support. I say that with the utmost confidence without knowing where anyone who is reading this lives. If you are in the US and are interested in finding your local harm reduction program, I suggest checking out the North American Syringe Exchange Network (NASEN) www.nasen.org. They have a syringe exchange locator that's pretty cool.

I really believe that we stand on the shoulders of giants in this work, so in addition to Dave Purchase, who I talked a bit about earlier, I would say no one in the US would have access to naloxone if it were not for a man named Dan Bigg. He was probably the person who taught me to do the right thing even if others were telling me it was wrong. I remember one time he and I were plotting about getting Medicaid to pay for the cure of Hep C, so we got talking about how I was running low on naloxone due to an issue with my standing order. A few days later, 1,000 doses of naloxone landed on my doorstep with no note or return address. I don't know for sure that it was Dan, but I know that a strong batch of heroin came through a couple of weeks later. Had I not had that naloxone, many people might have died. Every time I feel frustrated by the work we are doing these days, I wish I could call Dan. The whole harm reduction community lost a great heart when Dan died because of our poisoned drug supply in 2018.

I am also super inspired by the giants who fought to get HIV to where it is today. AIDS Coalition To Unleash Power, aka ACT UP, might have been one of the most influential protest movements in modern history. If you have heard the phrase "nothing about us, without us," that is ACT UP. The fact we were able to use emergency authorizations to roll out the vaccine for COVID-

19 was also because of ACT UP. They brought HIV/AIDS and the fight for treatment to Main Street, the FDA, and the White House Lawn. They might have also wrapped Jesse Helms' house in a giant condom, which is really cool. If you want to learn more, there is an excellent documentary called How to Survive a Plague. www.surviveaplague.com.

When I'm looking forward instead of back, I am really excited to see all the things happening across the country around drug user organizing. As we saw with ACT UP, we are seeing people who use drugs come together to advocate for drug users' rights. Probably the most famous Drug Users Union is the Vancouver Area Network of Drug Users (VANDU) www.vandureplace.-wordpress.com, but there are groups forming around the globe. www.inpud.net/en/links.

I could go on and on about all the fantastic work that's happening around harm reduction, but I might get fired if I don't call out the amazing work we do at Outside In as well. We are doing our best to fight the fight every day, and it is an honor to be part of such an amazing organization. www.outsidein.org

Any last words?

I mean, I feel like you should have lowered the curtain on me a while ago. I get really excited about this stuff, if you can't tell. I guess my final thoughts are just thoughts of gratitude. Thank you, Jordan, for giving me the space to get on my soapbox and for caring so much about bringing harm reduction to people who may not fully understand it. We have known each other for a long time, and I am grateful to call you my friend. I am thankful for all who are working to bring health and human rights to people who use drugs and for all the teachers who keep us moving forward. Be safe and kind out there, everyone.

harm reduction
resources

American Addiction Centers
www.AmericanAddictionCenters.org

Centers for Disease Control & Prevention
www.CDC.gov

Drug Policy Alliance
www.DrugPolicy.org

Free Harm Reduction Supplies in Your Locale
www.Facebook.com/FreeNarcanResourcesNationwide

Harm Reduction Therapy Center
www.HarmReductionTherapy.org

Hooper Detox
Portland, Oregon
www.CentralCityConcern.org

International Network of People Who Use Drugs
www.INPUD.net

Lines for Life

www.LinesforLife.org

National Harm Reduction Coalition
www.HarmReduction.org

NEXT Distro: Stay Alive, Stay Safe
www.NextDistro.org
&
Free Naloxone and Training, Mailed to your Door
www.NaloxoneForAll.org

Nigel Brunsdon
Photography of Harm Reduction
www.NigelBrunsdon.com

North American Syringe Exchange Network (NASEN)
www.Nasen.org

Outside-In
Portland, Oregon
www.OutsideIn.org
503-535-3826

Partnership for Safety and Justice
Harm reduction policy advocacy in Oregon
www.SafetyandJustice.org

Safe + Strong Helpline
1-800-923-4357 (800-923-HELP)

Toward the Heart
www.TowardTheHeart.com

narcan® nasal spray instructions for use

In opioid overdose emergencies, recognizing symptoms and taking prompt action is critical. NARCAN® Nasal Spray can be administered by a bystander (non-health care professional) before emergency medical assistance becomes available, but it is not intended to be a substitute for professional medical care. Emergency medical assistance (calling 911) should be requested immediately when an opioid overdose is suspected, before administering naloxone.

You and your family members or caregivers should read the Instructions for Use that comes with NARCAN Nasal Spray before using it. Talk to your healthcare provider if you and your family members or caregivers have any questions about the use of NARCAN Nasal Spray.

Use NARCAN Nasal Spray for known or suspected opioid overdose in adults and children.

- Important: For use in the nose only.
- Do not remove or test the NARCAN Nasal Spray until ready to use.
- Each NARCAN Nasal Spray has 1 dose and cannot be reused
- You do not need to prime NARCAN Nasal Spray.

How to use NARCAN Nasal Spray:

Step 1. Peel back the package to remove the device. Hold the device with your thumb on the bottom of the plunger and two fingers on the nozzle.

Step 2. Place and hold the tip of the nozzle in either nostril until your fingers touch the bottom of the patient's nose.

Step 3. Press the plunger firmly to release the dose into the patient's nose.

Additional Steps :

- Move the person on their side (recovery position) after giving NARCAN Nasal Spray.
- Watch the person closely.
- If the person does not respond by waking up, to voice or touch, or breathing normally another dose may be given. NARCAN Nasal Spray may be dosed every 2 to 3 minutes, if available.
- Repeat Steps 1 through 3 using a new NARCAN Nasal Spray to give another dose in the other nostril. If additional NARCAN Nasal Sprays are available, Steps 1 through 3 may be repeated every 2 to 3 minutes until the person responds or emergency medical help is received.

Contraindications:

- Patients who are hypersensitive to this drug or to any ingredient in the formulation or component of the container.

Most Serious Warnings & Precautions:

- Emergency medical assistance (calling 911) should be requested immediately when an opioid overdose is suspected, before using naloxone.
- Individuals with a satisfactory response to an initial dose of naloxone should be kept under continued surveillance.
- Caregivers administering naloxone should be prepared to act in response to or assist the patient in cases of potential adverse reactions such as aggressive reactions, convulsions and vomiting. Special attention

is warranted if naloxone is administered to a neonate or a pregnant woman.

Other Relevant Warnings and Precautions:

- In opioid dependent people, naloxone may trigger an acute opioid withdrawal syndrome
- Rebound opioid toxicity, including respiratory depression, following the temporary reversal of the opioid overdose
- Not effective against respiratory depression due to non-opioid drugs
- Rare cases of cardiac arrest, tachycardia and ventricular fibrillation
- Post-operative consideration: instances of hypotension, hypertension, ventricular tachycardia and fibrillation, dyspnea, pulmonary edema and rare cases of cardiac arrest have been reported. Death, coma, and encephalopathy have been reported as sequelae of these events
- Rare cases of convulsions or seizures
- Irritability and aggressive behavior
- Gastrointestinal reactions including diarrhea, nausea, vomiting and abdominal cramps
- Use in nursing women has not been established

Not a Substitute for Emergency Medical Care.

Before administering NARCAN® Nasal Spray, call 911 for emergency medical help. Do this immediately if you suspect or are aware of an opioid overdose.

Do this even if the person wakes up. Keep the patient under surveillance or close watch. If breathing does not return to normal or if breathing difficulty resumes, after 2-3 minutes, give an additional dose of NARCAN® Nasal Spray using a new device in the alternate nostril.

Keep NARCAN Nasal Spray and all medicines out of the reach of children.

This Instructions for Use has been approved by the U.S. Food and Drug Administration. Distributed by Adapt Pharma, Inc. Plymouth Meeting, PA 19462 USA.

For more information, go to www.narcannasalspray.com or call 1-844-4NARCAN (1-844- 462-7226).

never use alone

1-800-484-3731

No Judgment. No Shaming. No Preaching. Just Love!

CALL US IF YOU ARE GOING TO USE ALONE!
One of our operators will stay on the line with you while you use,
to try and ensure that you don't die from fentanyl poisoning!

HOW IT WORKS

When you call **1-800-484-3731**, one of our volunteer operators
will answer your call. You will be asked for your first name, exact
location (down to the exact room you're in) and the phone
number you're calling from.

After you've given us the required information, you can go
ahead and use your substance. We ask that you let us know when
you're done. If you stop responding afterward, we will notify
emergency services of a possible fentanyl poisoning at the location
you've given us! If you call, and cannot connect with an operator,
please call our backup number (931) 304-9452.

CONFIDENTIAL

We don't share your personal info with anyone other than EMS, if we have to call them. We are NOT affiliated with any law enforcement agency or treatment center.

TREATMENT RESOURCES

If you are interested in getting help, we have a large list of free/low cost, and state-funded facilities throughout the country. We will never push this on you though.

HARM REDUCTION RESOURCES

If you need Narcan, or access to safe supplies, we can assist you with locating resources within your state.

No Judgment. No Shaming. No Preaching. Just Love!

1-800-484-3731
www.NeverUseAlone.com
www.Facebook.com/NeverUseAlone

jen cutting

"We recover loudly so those
behind us do not suffer in silence."

Jen Cutting is a friend and woman in long-term recovery. Hailing
from NY, she is a CARC (Certified Addiction Recovery Coach),
a CRPA (Certified Recovery Peer Advocate), a Rape Crisis
Counselor, a Narcan Trainer, a Prison-Reform Activist and a
Harm Reduction YouTuber.
As you can see, Jen does a lot, but I most admire how she pairs an
amazing online community with an ever-evolving Amazon.com
wishlist. Jen uses these donations to create "Go Bags," providing
food, clothing, supplies and *hope* to those who need it most.
Connect with Jen and Supplies for Life below.

facebook.com/jen.cutting.75

instagram.com/jlcutting

youtube.com/jencutting

tiktok.com/@jencutting1

morgan godvin

www.MorganGodvin.com

Morgan Godvin was sentenced to five years in federal prison for
her best friend's overdose. Now, she fights for overdose
prevention, drug and justice policy reform, and safer, healthier
communities.
She is the founder of a first-of-it's-kind hip hop harm reduction
program, Beats Overdose. She took overdose prevention on tour
with Atmosphere and Cypress Hill and is expanding to other
venues and artists. Music can save lives.

Learn more at MorganGodvin.com

f facebook.com/drugpolicymorgan

instagram.com/morgangodvin

youtube.com/morgangodvinpdx

twitter.com/morgangodvin

glossary

Acronyms:

AMA: Against Medical Advice
DNR: Do Not Resuscitate
HAT: Heroin-Assisted Treatment
HCV: Hepatitis C Virus
HIPAA: Health Insurance Portability & Accountability Act
HITDA: High-Intensity Drug Trafficking Areas (Program)
HIV: Human Immunodeficiency Virus
IMF: Illicitly-Manufactured Fentanyl
MAT: Medication-Assisted Treatment
MET: Motivation Enhancement Therapy
NAS: Neonatal Abstinence Syndrome
NIMBY: Not In My BackYard
OCD: Obsessive-Compulsive Disorder
OHSU: Oregon Health & Science University
OPC: Overdose Prevention Center
OPS: Overdose Prevention Site
OUD: Opioid Use Disorder
PPB: Portland Police Bureau
PWID/PWUD: People or Person(s) Who Inject/Use Drugs
SCS: Safe Consumption Site/Space
SEP: Syringe Exchange Program
SUD: Substance Use Disorder

Key Terms:

Abstinence: Not using drugs or alcohol.

Addiction: A chronic, relapsing disorder characterized by compulsive (or difficult to control) drug seeking and use despite harmful consequences, as well as long-lasting changes in the brain. In the past, people who used drugs were called "addicts." Current appropriate terms are people who use drugs and drug users.

Agonist: A chemical substance that binds to and activates certain receptors on cells, causing a biological response. Oxycodone, morphine, heroin, fentanyl, methadone, and endorphins are all examples of opioid receptor agonists.

Antagonist: A chemical substance that binds to and blocks the activation of certain receptors on cells, preventing a biological response. Naloxone is an example of an opioid receptor antagonist.

Buprenorphine: An opioid partial agonist medication prescribed for the treatment of opioid addiction that relieves drug cravings without producing the high or dangerous side effects of other opioids.

Comorbidity: When two disorders or illnesses occur in the same person. Drug addiction and other mental illnesses or viral infections (HIV, hepatitis) are often comorbid. Also referred to as co-occurring disorders.

Contingency management: A treatment approach based on providing incentives to support positive behavior change.

Craving: A powerful, often overwhelming desire to use drugs.

Dependence: A condition that can occur with the regular use of illicit or some prescription drugs, even if taken as prescribed. Dependence is characterized by withdrawal symptoms when drug use is stopped. A person can be dependent on a substance without being addicted, but dependence sometimes leads to addiction.

Detoxification: A process in which the body rids itself of a drug, or its metabolites. Medically-assisted detoxification may be needed to help manage a person's withdrawal symptoms. Detoxification alone is not a treatment for substance use disorders, but this is often the first step in a drug treatment program.

Drug abuse: An older diagnostic term that defines use that is unsafe, use that leads a person to fail to fulfill responsibilities or gets them in legal trouble, or use that continues despite causing persistent interpersonal problems. This term is increasingly avoided by professionals because it can perpetuate stigma. Current appropriate terms include: drug use (in the case of illicit substances), drug misuse (in the case of problematic use of legal drugs or prescription medications) and addiction (in the case of substance use disorder).

Fentanyl: A powerful synthetic opioid analgesic that is similar to morphine but is 50 to 100 times more potent. It is a Schedule II prescription drug, and it is typically used to treat patients with severe pain or to manage pain after surgery. It is also sometimes used to treat patients with chronic pain who are physically tolerant to other opioids. In its prescription form, fentanyl is known by such names as Actiq®, Duragesic®, and Sublimaze®.

Harm reduction: A range of public health policies designed to lessen the negative social and/or physical consequences associated with various human behaviors, both legal and illegal. [1]

Heroin-Assisted Treatment: The prescription of pharmaceutical-grade heroin (diacetylmorphine) to people with severe heroin use disorders who have not responded well to more traditional forms of treatment like methadone or buprenorphine. Typically, clients are provided injectable or inhalable heroin 2-3 times per day by prescription, and they consume it on-site in a medically-supervised clinic setting. [2]

HIV, Human Immunodeficiency Virus: A virus that attacks the body's immune system. If HIV is not treated, it can lead to AIDS (acquired immunodeficiency syndrome). [3]

HIPAA, Health Insurance Portability and Accountability Act: A federal law that required the creation of national standards to protect sensitive patient health information from being disclosed without the patient's consent or knowledge.[4]

HVC, Hepatitis C Virus/Hep C: Hepatitis C is a viral infection that causes liver inflammation, sometimes leading to serious liver damage. The hepatitis C virus (HCV) spreads through contaminated blood. [5]

IDU, Injection drug use: The act of administering drugs by injection. Blood-borne viruses, like HIV and hepatitis, can be transmitted via shared needles or other drug injection equipment.

Illicit: Illegal or forbidden by law.

Intranasal: Taken through the nose.

MAT, Medication Assisted Treatment: The use of medications, in combination with counseling and behavioral therapies, to provide a "whole-patient" approach to the treatment of substance use disorders. Medications used in MAT are approved by the Food and Drug Administration (FDA) and MAT programs are clinically driven and tailored to meet each patient's needs.[6]

Mental disorder: A mental condition marked primarily by disorganization of personality, mind, and emotions that seriously impairs the psychological or behavioral functioning of the individual. This is sometimes referred to as a *mental health condition*. Addiction is a mental disorder.

Methadone: A long-acting opioid agonist medication used for the treatment of opioid addiction and pain. Methadone used for opioid addiction can only be dispensed by opioid treatment programs certified by SAMHSA and approved by the designated state authority.

Motivational Enhancement Therapy: A counseling approach that uses motivational interviewing techniques to help individuals resolve any uncertainties they have about stopping their substance use. The therapy helps the person strengthen their own plan for change and engagement in treatment.

Naloxone: An opioid antagonist medication approved by the FDA to reverse an opioid overdose. It displaces opioid drugs (such as morphine or heroin) from their receptor and prevents further opioid receptor activation.

NARCAN ®: A potent narcotic antagonist (trade name Narcan) especially effective with morphine.[7]

Neonatal abstinence syndrome (NAS): A condition of withdrawal that occurs when certain drugs pass from the mother through the placenta into the fetus' bloodstream during pregnancy causing the baby to become drug dependent and experience withdrawal after birth. The type and severity of a baby's withdrawal symptoms depend on the drug(s) used, how long and how often the mother used, how her body broke down the drug, and if the baby was born full term or prematurely. NAS can require hospitalization and treatment with medication to relieve symptoms.

Opioid receptors: Proteins on the surface of neurons, or other cells, that are activated by endogenous opioids, such as endorphins, and opioid drugs, such as heroin. Opioid receptor subtypes include mu, kappa, and delta.

Overdose: An overdose occurs when a person uses enough of a drug to produce a life-threatening reaction or death.

Recovery: Individuals may have differing definitions for what recovery from substance use disorder means for them. For some, this term is used to describe the voluntary process of improving health and quality of life by pursuing treatment for substance use disorder and/or controlling problematic substance use (See also definitions of recovery from Substance Abuse and Mental Health Services Administration and American Society of Addiction Medicine).

Relapse: In drug addiction, relapse is the return to drug use after an attempt to stop. Relapse is a common occurrence in many chronic health disorders, including addiction, that requires frequent behavioral and/or pharmacologic adjustments to be treated effectively.

Reward system (or brain reward system): A brain circuit

that includes the ventral tegmental area, the nucleus accumbens, and the prefrontal cortex.

Risk factors: Factors that increase the likelihood of beginning substance use, of regular and harmful use, and of other behavioral health problems associated with use.

Route of administration: The way a drug is taken into the body. Drugs are most commonly taken by eating, drinking, inhaling, injecting, snorting, or smoking.

Safer Consumption Space, or SIF (Supervised Injection Facility), or SIS (Supervised Injection Site): Indoor environments in which people can use drugs with trained personnel on site to provide overdose reversal and risk reduction services. SCS have been shown to reduce fatal overdoses, decrease public syringe disposal, and reduce public drug consumption.[8]

Self-medication: The use of a substance to lessen the negative effects of stress, anxiety, or other mental disorders (or side effects of their pharmacotherapy) without the guidance of a health care provider. Self-medication may lead to addiction and other drug- or alcohol-related problems.

Sexually Transmitted Diseases (STDs), or Sexually Transmitted Infections (STIs): Infections that are passed from one person to another through sexual contact. The contact is usually vaginal, oral, and anal sex. But sometimes they can spread through other intimate physical contact. This is because some STDs, like herpes and HPV, are spread by skin-to-skin contact.[9]

Stigma: A set of negative attitudes and beliefs that motivate people to fear and discriminate against other people. Many people do not understand that addiction is a disorder just like other chronic disorders. For these reasons, they frequently attach more stigma to it. Stigma, whether perceived or real, often fuels myths and misconceptions, and can influence choices. It can impact attitudes about seeking treatment, reactions from family and friends, behavioral health education and awareness, and the likelihood that someone will not seek or remain in treatment.

Substance use disorder (SUD): A medical illness caused by disordered use of a substance or substances. According to the Fifth Edition of the Diagnostic and Statistical Manual of Mental Disorders (DSM-5), SUDs are characterized by clinically significant impairments in health, social function, and impaired control over substance use and are diagnosed through assessing cognitive, behavioral, and psychological symptoms. An SUD can range from mild to severe.

Tolerance: A condition in which higher doses of a drug are required to achieve the desired effect.

Withdrawal: Symptoms that can occur after long-term use of a drug is reduced or stopped; these symptoms occur if tolerance to a substance has occurred, and vary according to substance. Withdrawal symptoms can include negative emotions such as stress, anxiety, or depression, as well as physical effects such as nausea, vomiting, muscle aches, and cramping, among others. Withdrawal symptoms often lead a person to use the substance again.

Note: Unless otherwise noted, all definitions are from NIDA.[10]

1. "Harm Reduction." *Wikipedia*, Wikimedia Foundation, 12 Aug. 2021, https://en.wikipedia.org/wiki/Harm_reduction.
2. "Heroin-Assisted Treatment." *Drug Policy Alliance*, https://drugpolicy.org/issues/HAT.
3. "About HIV/AIDS." *Centers for Disease Control and Prevention*, Centers for Disease Control and Prevention, 1 June 2021, https://www.cdc.gov/hiv/basics/whatishiv.html.
4. "Health Insurance Portability and Accountability Act of 1996 (HIPAA)." *Centers for Disease Control and Prevention*, Centers for Disease Control and Prevention, 14 Sept. 2018, https://www.cdc.gov/phlp/publications/topic/hipaa.html.
5. "Hepatitis C." *Mayo Clinic*, Mayo Foundation for Medical Education and Research, 31 Aug. 2021, https://www.mayoclinic.org/diseases-conditions/hepatitis-c/symptoms-causes/syc-20354278.
6. "Medication-Assisted Treatment (MAT)." *SAMHSA*, https://www.samhsa.gov/medication-assisted-treatment.
7. "Narcan." WordNet 3.0, Farlex clipart collection. 2003-2008. Princeton University, Clipart.com, Farlex Inc. 29 Sep. 2021 https://www.thefreedictionary.com/Narcan

8. O'Rourke, Allison, et al. "Acceptability of Safe Drug Consumption Spaces among People Who Inject Drugs in Rural West Virginia." *Harm Reduction Journal*, vol. 16, no. 1, 2019, https://doi.org/10.1186/s12954-019-0320-8.
9. "Sexually Transmitted Diseases | STD | Venereal Disease." *MedlinePlus*, U.S. National Library of Medicine, 10 Sept. 2021, https://medlineplus.gov/sexuallytransmitteddiseases.html.
10. NIDA. "Glossary." *National Institute on Drug Abuse*, 27 Jul. 2021, https://www.drugabuse.gov/publications/media-guide/glossary Accessed 28 Sep. 2021.

ONE HIT AWAY

"...A gripping,
startling account into
addiction, compassion and
ultimate salvation."

—ANNIE GRACE

This Naked Mind: Control
Alcohol, Find Freedom,
Discover Happiness &
Change Your Life

A MEMOIR OF RECOVERY BY
JORDAN P. BARNES

one hit away

A Memoir of Recovery

At the age of 24, Jordan Barnes woke up next to a lifeless body, rifled through his dead friend's pockets for any remaining heroin and went right back to using.

Strung out and homeless during the supposed best years of his life, there was no clear way out of the Opioid Crisis ravaging the streets of Portland, Oregon. But though Jordan had long accepted his fate, his parents still held out hope, and would do everything in their power to get him the help he so desperately needed.

After a harrowing journey that proves the life of an active addict will always get worse, never better, Jordan found himself at the gates of Sand Island, Hawaii's most notorious two-year inpatient treatment facility. He soon discovers that though his heart was in the right place, the hardest battle of his life was yet to come.

One Hit Away is his arduous and unlikely true story of recovery, rehabilitation and redemption.

one hit away sample

Chapter One: Carried Away

Portland, Oregon.
June 18th, 2011.

Sprawled across the side entryway to Beth Israel Congregation, I roll onto my side and wipe a palmful of dew off my clammy face. Everything about this morning is brittle, cold and still. Suspended in limbo, I'm drained from squirming all night on the slick ground like a caterpillar in a cocoon. As first light swirls around me and creeps into the shadows, I'm in no rush to greet it— there's no point jump-starting the engines until the street dealers kick off their rounds. Having suffered through too many of Portland's sunrises in recent years, the art on the horizon has either lost its beauty or I'm too jaded to see in color anymore.

Peeling my head away from an uncomfortable makeshift pillow made of rolled-up sweatpants, I see that both Simon and the surrounding streets are sleeping in. We're nestled in darkness, lit only by the headlights of an occasional car that turns down Flanders Street. My sleeping bag is bunched under my hip to help relieve the pressure from the cold stone beneath me, but it's not the only reason I had a hard time sleeping last night.

A few hours ago, I woke up to the alarm of Simon snoring and rattling away in his sleep—it was an eerie and guttural sound like an empty spray-paint can being shaken. I was still fighting to fall back asleep, long after his sputtering faded and drifted away with the breeze. So, while he put another day behind him, I was reminded that long nights take a toll and this life never pays.

We both went to sleep with full bellies and a shot, so we're fortunate that neither one of us will be dope sick. It's nice to catch a break now and then and wake up without wishing I would die already. But it's never enough—I'm still skeptical about how hard Simon crashed out and wonder if he's holding out on me. Though if I were in his shoes, there's no doubt I'd do the same. Riding high comes naturally in a free-for-all where everyone looks out for themselves. We all have it—a grizzly survival instinct to take what we can, when we can and figure tomorrow out if it comes.

This isn't our land, but we periodically come here to stake a claim in the covered alcove guarding the ornate entryway. If unoccupied, I prefer this location because it's a reasonably safe place to hang my boots. Not only is there protection overhead from the frequent rain that tends to ruin a good night's sleep, but it's also set back from the street enough that being noticed, roused and moved by the police is a rarity.

The groundskeeper here is a man of quiet compassion. It isn't in him to run us off outside of business hours, and he refuses to call the police on us. For the most part, we are often gone before he would have to step over our bodies to open the temple doors. Scattering like roaches, we are sent packing by an internal alarm that forces us to get up at first light and attend to our bad habits.

Simon is still asleep. He's had it easy after spending all day yesterday collecting free doses from every street dealer he could pin down. This is common for any junkie recently released from a stint in jail. Any time after I've been arrested, all I have to do is show one of my dealers my booking paperwork and they'll set me right. A freebie from them is a cheap investment in their own job security, reigniting the habit that was broken by an unpleasant jailhouse detox. Our dealers also need us back up and running again, racking up goods and on our best game. It's no secret that a dope sick junkie is unprofitable.

I pull myself together and pack with purpose, grabbing the dope kit I stashed in a tree nearby and then my shredded shoes that I left out to dry. I often struggle to tell whether my insoles are wet or merely cold, but when water oozes out of my shoelaces as I double-knot them, I take note that at some point today I need to steal fresh socks.

"Time to go," I call out.

Simon, in one of the few ways that he is needy, often depends on me rousing him. He's never been a morning person and is still sound asleep, his face buried in his sleeping bag.

"Come on, get up." I spin in place and scan the ground to make sure I'm not forgetting anything. Eager to start the day, I nudge him with my toe a bit harder than I intended to.

When that doesn't wake him, I reach down to shake his shoulder and feel an unnatural resistance. Something, everything, is wrong. His whole body feels stiff, and as I pull harder, Simon keels over, his rigid limbs creaking out loud like a weathered deck. There is lividity in his face—his nose is dark purple and filled with puddled blood. A pair of lifeless, open eyes stare through me and into nothingness. Instinctively, my hand snaps back and Simon sinks away.

I stumble back and try to make sense of my surroundings. Nobody is around yet, but soon, the world will rise.

"No, no, no." I lose control of the volume of my voice and squeeze my throat. "Don't be dead, please, don't do this to me," I chant as I drop to my knees, pleading over his corpse.

My hands hover over him as if trying to draw warmth from a smothered fire. I desperately grasp for a way to fix this. My heart is racing as though I just sent a speedball its way, but the surge doesn't stop. A decision needs to be made, and fast, but before I can make sense of anything, a wisp of breath rolls down my collar and an invisible hand clutches my cheeks, forcing me to stare down death.

I snap the clearest picture in my mind and my eyes sting. Even though I know a lot of junkies who walk these streets with no life left in them, this is the first dead body I've ever seen. Looking down at Simon, I finally understand how pathetic this existence is and how lonely this life will always be. I see nothing beyond this moment for Simon, other than being hauled away like trash on the curb. We are forever trapped here, alone and useless, likely remembered only for our crimes, selfishness and former selves. Heaven is out of the picture, and because of that, I am okay with what I have to do next. I know the act is irreversible and unforgivable, but then again, if God has abandoned us, he's not around to judge me.

Dropping my sleeping bag onto the ground, I slide my backpack off my shoulders and let it fall like a hammer. I kneel over Simon's body, steal one last look around and wince as I rummage through the front pocket of his jeans. I know he always keeps a wake-up hit on him. His pocket is tight and fights my hand as I dip into them. My fingers scratch around but keep coming up empty-handed. Time is running out and traffic is increasing.

I reach into his back pocket and soon realize the dope isn't in his wallet either. The longer I search, the more determined I am, but I can't bring myself to roll him over and disturb him further. By the time I give up, I sit back on my heels. I can't believe what I've become.

"I'm so sorry, Simon."

Please stop looking at me. I can't take it. Pulling my sweater cuff over my palm, I reach out with a shaky hand to close his eyes. My hand gets close, then backs off as I turn my head away to exhale. When my hand reaches forward once again, my palm lands on his face but fails to brush his frozen eyelids closed. Backing away, I grab my belongings and shrink into the distance.

My legs give out less than a block away. Hunched over a fire pit of a stomach, I can barely breathe. On the surface, I know this isn't something I should run from—this is not who I am. I have to go back but I don't know what that means. If I turn my back on Simon and keep running, it won't be hard for the police to identify me once they start asking around. Nobody I know will protect me.

All my life, I only seem to make matters worse, but this is bigger than me. I can't leave my friend there alone—he deserves better. Stashing anything potentially incriminating in the nearest bush, I turn toward the synagogue and in the distance, see the groundskeeper making his morning rounds.

"Pierce! Please, *help us!*" My feet scuffle toward him and I cast my hands toward the alcove. I witness his heartbreak when he discovers how we've repaid his compassion. He fumbles for his phone, strikes three numbers and asks for the police. While he talks to the operator, he stares me down until I look away. His kindness doesn't deserve this ultimate betrayal. My eyes chase his words as he describes the scene to the dispatcher. He respectfully approaches and leans over the body to make a clearly hesitant observation.

"Yes, it appears the young man is deceased," he says. "1972 North Flanders Street. Yes. Correct. Seven. Two. Please hurry, and oh my, we have a bat mitzvah scheduled today!"

Both of us stand by the body in silence until an ambulance arrives, followed by police and detectives. Paramedics apologize for our loss and announce the time of death before handing over the scene to the medical examiner. Detectives keep me around throughout the photography process and body bagging, burning the image into my mind. Pacing back and forth, I hold myself together until I am finally questioned.

I tell them everything I know and don't catch my breath until they rule out homicide. I steal a glance at the Investigation Report and wonder how a drug overdose can be classified as a natural death.

As the detectives comb over the body, they recover a small amount of dope folded inside a torn piece of plastic. A lump of coal ignites in my stomach. I need that more than ever. Simon made the fatal mistake of assuming his opioid tolerance was the same as it was before his incarceration.

The bat mitzvah is beginning, and a short procession of young teenagers—accompanied by their parents—walk by the scene. Some look confused and scared while others are talking among themselves, understandably curious. One boy pulls out his phone and lifts it up to take a picture.

"Take a picture of my friend like this and I'll fucking kill you." My warning flashes through gritted teeth.

The cop glances at me, letting my threat pass as the boy smirks. I'm sure they're all judging me and they keep coming. There is nowhere to hide while they surround us. Pierce steps forth to intervene, but his body isn't large enough to block the tragedy behind him. He directs the families toward the main entrance around the corner, begging the parents to lead by example.

"One . . . two . . . *three.*"

I turn around in time to catch Simon's covered body being slid onto a stretcher. Death has always seemed so close but never so set in stone. I picture myself inside the body bag which isn't hard since I've overdosed twice before. That could easily have been me. The only difference between me and where Simon is laying now is that the EMT's reached me in time to reverse my past opioid overdoses with a shot of Narcan.

Narcan. If only I had some on me last night, and that I wasn't so used to tuning out my surroundings while I slept. There once was a time when I wouldn't leave home without the small vial that lived inside my dope kit. That was back when I had a home and before I hawked what remained in my bottle for a meager dime bag of dope. I can only imagine how many lives could be saved were it not such a controversial drug. I think back to a night that I'll never forget, where my ex-fiancée overdosed in my dorm room. I wouldn't be here today had I not had Narcan on me to save her life, which isn't to say that this is a good place to be. It's a painful memory to recall, so I lock it away.

I provide what little contact information I have for his family to the detectives. I think he's from Florida. He once mentioned his parents are separated, but I never caught their names. I am handed a police report number and a card with a name and number to call for a follow-up within a few days. For now, I am free to go, but the medical examiner—having loaded the gurney into his truck—peels off his gloves, closes the door and motions for me to hold on for a second. As he approaches, he looks into my eyes with the care of a father talking to a son.

"Sorry you had to go through that. I'm Deputy Medical Examiner Bellant. You're Jordan, right?"

I nod.

"Jordan what?"

"Barnes."

"Do you have a family, Mr. Barnes?"

I nod again, though I'm not being completely truthful. There was a time when I had a family.

"What about a phone?"

The instant I start to shake my head, he reaches into his pocket and plucks out some loose change.

"Here, take this." A couple of quarters drop into my palm. "Do me a favor and give them a call. Tell them you love them, before it's too late." He takes one last look around at the scene. "Oh, and Jordan. Don't take this the wrong way, but I hope I never see you again. You understand?"

As he pulls away, I'm left with his words ringing in my ears like so many other junkies who must have received a similar warning. Down the road is a pay phone that's calling my name. Holding the quarters on edge, I drop them into the slot and punch a familiar number. He picks up on the first ring, which means he's working.

"Hello? Who's this?" the voice asks.

I pull the receiver off my ear and press it to my forehead. I have to choose my next words carefully.

"Hello?" he asks again.

"Hey, it's Jordan."

"What do you want?"

"I need to meet up with—"

"Nah, man," he says, cutting me off. "It's too early to trade. Call me later—I don't want to be carrying your shit around with me all day."

"Wait! I have money!" It's a lie, but I know that as long as I can get him to meet me, he'll show pity and either help me out or pay me to disappear. This detective's business card will also prove my story. "Hello? You still there? I have forty bucks." I stand straight up, knowing I can't afford for him to hang up on me.

"Bullshit. You never have cash."

"No, I promise!" I lie again and double down. "Trust me, it's been a good morning." I look down and hold my breath. Simon would forgive me for this, for using his death as leverage. He would understand where I'm coming from. He would do the same.

The voice on the line pauses for a second. "Okay, okay. Northwest Fourth and Flanders. But hurry up, man. I'm almost sold out."

"I'm on my way. Give me fifteen minutes." I slam the phone down and take off running, thanking God he's within reach.

One Hit Away: A Memoir of Recovery by Jordan P. Barnes is the winner of 2020's "Best Book of the Year" Award by IndiesToday.com, a Finalist in both the 15th Annual National Indie Excellence Awards and the 2021 Independent Author Network Book of the Year Awards, as well as the recipient of a B.R.A.G. Medallion. It is available on Amazon, Audible and anywhere else books are sold.

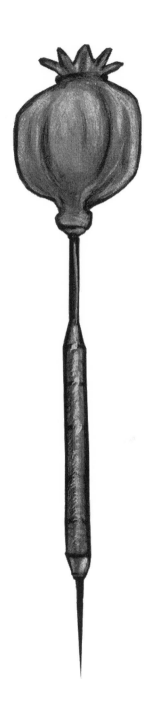

Made in the USA
Las Vegas, NV
11 March 2022